City of Song

City of Song

Music and the Making of Modern Jerusalem

MICHAEL A. FIGUEROA

OXFORD

UNIVERSITY PRESS

OXFORD
UNIVERSITY PRESS

Oxford University Press is a department of the University of Oxford. It furthers
the University's objective of excellence in research, scholarship, and education
by publishing worldwide. Oxford is a registered trade mark of Oxford University
Press in the UK and certain other countries.

Published in the United States of America by Oxford University Press
198 Madison Avenue, New York, NY 10016, United States of America.

Library of Congress Cataloging-in-Publication Data
Names: Figueroa, Michael A., 1984- author.
Title: City of song : music and the making of modern Jerusalem / Michael A. Figueroa.
Description: New York : Oxford University Press, 2022. |
Includes bibliographical references and index.
Identifiers: LCCN 2021033962 (print) | LCCN 2021033963 (ebook) |
ISBN 9780197546437 (paperback) | ISBN 9780197546475 (hardback) |
ISBN 9780197546444 (epub)
Subjects: LCSH: Jews—Music—History and criticism. | Jerusalem—Songs
and music—History and criticism. | Music—Political aspects—Israel.
Classification: LCC ML3776 .F55 2021 (print) | LCC ML3776 (ebook) |
DDC 780.89/9240569442—dc23
LC record available at https://lccn.loc.gov/2021033962
LC ebook record available at https://lccn.loc.gov/2021033963

DOI: 10.1093/oso/9780197546475.001.0001

1 3 5 7 9 8 6 4 2

Paperback printed by Marquis, Canada
Hardback printed by Bridgeport National Bindery, Inc., United States of America

"For Monica, my everything"

CONTENTS

List of Figures

Acknowledgments

The subject of this book occupied most of my scholarly energies over the past decade. During that time, I was graced by relationships with many people who greatly shaped my thinking, professional trajectories, and the creative spirit of this book.

I first thank my collaborators in the field. Many of their voices are represented in the pages of this book, either explicitly through quotation or implicitly through their incalculable influence on my ideas. A number of working musicians, poets, and other individuals gifted their professional and intellectual labor to this project by granting me formal interviews, sometimes allowing me to impose on them on more than one occasion. Their insights form the heart of the book.

Israeli academia provided a welcoming yet challenging atmosphere during my stays in Jerusalem. Special thanks are due to Edwin Seroussi, who mentored me through much of my early research for this project. He kindly arranged for me to affiliate with the Hebrew University of Jerusalem as a Visiting Research Fellow in 2011–2012 and interceded on my behalf for connections with other folks in and around Jerusalem. I am thankful to Nili Belkind, Oded Erez, Yael Reshef, Assaf Shelleg, and Abigail Wood for sharing their feedback on various aspects of this project with me over the years. Gila Flam, Amalia Kedem, Gil Stein, Anat Wax, Matan Wygoda, and Tamar Zigman at the National Library of Israel's Music Department, where I spent many of my days, welcomed me into their family from day one. They were collaborators, allies, and benefactors, wearing whatever hat I needed them to wear each and every time I called on them for help, whether in person or from abroad. Many other folks were instrumental in helping me to secure copyright permissions for the many texts and images included in this book, particularly Yael Harari, Nurit Krausz, and Daniel Taharlev. In the field, on many occasions Marlena Fuerstman and Edwin Seroussi and Amir Fink and Yossi Maurey were gracious dinner hosts who made Jerusalem feel like a home away from home. I look forward to many more meals with them.

Gratitude is also due to colleagues around the world with whom I collaborated and corresponded during the development of this research. Several of them also took the time to read drafts and provide feedback, for which the text is undeniably stronger. Philip V. Bohlman is one of my chief influences and most ardent supporters. Our many conversations whisper in the margins of this book. Rachel Adelstein, Cesar Favila, Luis-Manuel Garcia, Andrew Mall, Michael O'Toole, Shayna Silverstein, Martha Sprigge, and Lillian Wohl remain some of my closest friends from our Chicago days, and I am very lucky indeed to have benefited from their kindness and support during the years leading up to this book's publication. I owe so very much to Rumya Putcha, who has been a constant source of support, wisdom, and encouragement. Her friendship means the world to me.

I also learned a great deal from sharing the stage at organized conferences and symposia with a number of scholars whose critical creativity impact on my research through the relationships we subsequently have formed; this includes Sylvia Alajaji, Alessandra Ciucci, Ruth Davis, Jonathan Glasser, Mark Kligman, Mili Leitner, David McDonald, and many others. I thank especially Ilana Kogen-Webster for challenging me to take risks in my writing, and for always lending a sympathetic ear or a critical eye when I needed it.

Folks at the Oxford University Press deserve all the credit for the polished design and quality of the book. I thank my editor, Norman Hirschy, for the patience and support he has invested in me. Ponneelan Moorthy handled the gargantuan task of managing the production process that brought these words to life, Samantha Zerin and Jamie Conway assisted me with Hebrew-language copyediting, and Erin Maher prepared the index; these are the too-often unsung heroes of the publishing industry for whom I hum a tune of gratitude. Significantly, anonymous reviewers were tremendously helpful in pushing me to whip the manuscript into shape through revision. Perhaps better than anyone else, they demonstrate the fact that "monograph" is a misnomer and that, in truth, books are collaborative endeavors.

I am very grateful for the inspiration of my colleagues at the University of North Carolina at Chapel Hill. I am indebted especially to my friends within the UNC musicology program, including Allen Anderson, Andrea Bohlman, Mark Evan Bonds, Tim Carter, Annegret Fauser, David Garcia, Aaron Harcus, Mark Katz, Stefan Litwin, Anne MacNeil, Jocelyn Neal, and Philip Vandermeer. Andrea Bohlman is a true partner, frequent collaborator, and occasional cycling companion. I cherish our friendship beyond words—even though she always seems to find the words for everything. I am fortunate to have collaborated so closely with Annegret Fauser, whose mentorship was vital to my professional journey during the years in which I wrote this book. Tim Carter helped me to find breakthroughs in drafts of my writing with his keen editorial eye. Mark Katz treated me to many a cocktail over the years, showing me the power of good listening as he allowed me to vent my frustrations and share my successes. Allen Anderson has been an invaluable friend who helped remind me of the value of embracing uncertain outcomes through our shared music making.

I am also beyond privileged to have learned from colleagues at the Carolina Center for Jewish Studies, Center for Middle East and Islamic Studies, and Center for Urban and Regional Studies. Yaakov Ariel, Gabrielle Berlinger, Ruth von Bernuth, Andrea Dara Cooper, Carl Ernst, Emma Harver, Charles Kurzman, Joseph Lam Michele Rivkin-Fish, Yaron Shemer, and Shai Tamari, among others, were sounding boards for my ideas and for general commiseration throughout the process of bringing this book to fruition. So too were our colleagues across town at Duke University, and among them I thank in particular Shai Ginsburg, who was a generous supplier of resources and advice during the late stages of revising the manuscript.

Current and former graduate-student colleagues have inspired me more than they know and even weighed in on earlier drafts of my work. I am grateful for the brilliant students from my 2016 seminar "Music and Historiography in Israel/Palestine"—Amanda Black, Barkley Heuser, A. Kori Hill, Alexander Marsden, H. Megumi Orita, Michele Segretario, and Sarah Tomlinson—and from my 2018 seminar "Urban Ethnomusicology"—Cody Black, Cade Bourne, Tyler Bunzey, Aldwyn H. Hogg Jr., Michael Levine, Stella Li, Sinclair Palmer, Erin Pratt, and Sierriana Terry. My PhD advisees John Caldwell, Melissa Camp, and Tara Jordan have shown me that mentorship is a two-way street, and in many ways the ideas presented in this book reflect our many hours of conversation over the years.

This project would not have been possible without material support from a number of organizations. I thank UNC's College of Arts and Sciences for providing me with research support, including periods of leave during which I prepared much of this manuscript, along with several competitive grants, including a Junior Faculty Development Award and travel grants from the Carolina Center for Jewish Studies, the Institute for the Arts and Humanities, and the Duke-UNC Consortium for Middle East Studies. The richness of the book's ethnographic and archival materials would not have been possible without the University's support. During earlier stages of the project, I received generous funding from the American Musicological Society, Ford Foundation, Fulbright Foundation, Targum Shlishi, University of Chicago, and United States-Israel Education Foundation. As with any long-term research project, the drive toward completing this book involved learning from both successes and failures, and so I also thank the organizations—too numerous to list here—that rejected my funding applications but provided helpful feedback that enabled me to refine the scope and framing of the book.

My life has been graced by many friends inside and outside of academia who supported me emotionally and hosted me in their homes during my research. Thank you, Russ Armstrong and Greta Lee, Andrew Bentley and Elizabeth Bentley, Keven Brown and Samantha Brown, Jonathan Flowers, Daniel Green and Miriam Goodman, Sharina Martin, Eric Metelka and Amber Metelka, and Jonathan Milam and Ama Appenteng-Milam. Local friends—especially Kacy Gordon and Daniel Matute, AJ Melnikas and Aaron Wark, and Rachel Schaevitz and David Schaevitz—gave me plenty of chances to put the book down and make much-needed frivolity. Nearly every day, Daniel Kramer, Neeraj Malhotra, Luke Peacock, and Ameer Saleh provided me with community, escape, and humor (often at my expense!). I truly could not have done this without their love and encouragement.

Finally, I dedicate this book to my spouse, colleague, and best friend, Monica Figueroa. We married just weeks before departing for a year of fieldwork in 2011 and have gone on to explore the world together in the years since. We have been by one another's side through thick and thin, success and failure, privilege and hardship, and watched our relationship grow stronger and more meaningful every single day of the last decade. Monica, our son Bruno, and our extended families are my greatest sources of strength and inspiration. As the great Teyana Taylor sings, "I never could have made it without you."

Michael A. Figueroa
Chapel Hill, NC

Note on Transliteration

As a study of Israeli musical discourse, this book includes substantial discussion of Hebrew-language materials. In transliterating those materials, which include texts, interview transcriptions, and academic writing, I have generally adopted the system proposed by the Academy of the Hebrew Language. The main exceptions here are names of people and places that are widely known and conventionally rendered in Roman characters. For Arabic terms, I have employed the International Journal of Middle East Studies standard, and for Armenian and Greek terms, which appear rarely, I have used American Library Association/Library of Congress standards.

Musical Jerusalem

Listening to the City of Song

Jerusalem, as everyone knows, is a name of a city. But what is this city whose name is Jerusalem? That is a more difficult question. There is an earthly city whose name is Jerusalem, and there is also a heavenly one. There is a Jerusalem of stone and a Jerusalem of paper, a Jerusalem of iron, and a Jerusalem of gold. There is a Christian, a Muslim, and a Jewish Jerusalem. Evidently there is also a Jerusalem as the capital of a Palestinian state, which is but a dream and a symbol of a national struggle, as well as Jerusalem as the capital of the State of Israel, which claims today to encompass all the other cities in one city "united forever."

—Ariella Azoulay (2001: 189)

September 2018, On the Road to Jerusalem (from the West)

To enter Jerusalem from the West is to be confronted with a monumental statement of the city's musicality. Traveling by car, once the rolling hills and valleys fade and the terrain transforms into concrete edifices, overpasses, and tunnels, the tallest structure of Jerusalem's cityscape comes into view. Gesher Ha-Metarim, or the "Chords Bridge" (lit. "The Bridge of Strings"), was conceived by the Spanish architect Santiago Calatrava as a physical embodiment of the second hemistich of Psalm 150:3 from the Hebrew Bible: "Praise Him with psaltery and lyre" (halleluhu be-nevel ve-khinnor). This cantilever-spar cable-stayed bridge enjoys traffic from both pedestrians and light-rail trains, and in the context of this ancient city it represents a "shrine of modern design" (Kaufman 2007).[1] The structure is shaped as a deconstructed lyre, masted by a 390-foot-tall frame unfolding in space, thereby enshrining the biblical verse

---

[1] David Kaufman refers to the bridge as "Jerusalem's *first* shrine of modern design" (emphasis added), but it is actually far from the first built structure in the city to adhere to modernist

City of Song. Michael A. Figueroa, Oxford University Press. © Oxford University Press 2022.
DOI: 10.1093/oso/9780197546475.003.0001

and representing the figure King David (1040–c. 970 BCE), the second king of the United Kingdom of Israel and Judah who conquered the Jebusite city of Jerusalem and established it as an Israelite settlement at the turn of the tenth century BCE. King David was as renowned for his superlative musicianship on the lyre (kinnor) as he was for his mastery of warfare and governance, and he is assumed by legend to be the author of several of the Psalms, including Psalm 150, quoted by the bridge's architecture. The lyre-shaped bridge thus embodies a thorough entwinement of music and conquest from Jerusalem's antiquity and projects it boldly into the city's modernity. In its very materiality, Jerusalem is a city of song.

Controversies surrounding the Chords Bridge's dedication represents one iteration of the complicated relation between music and politics in Jerusalem, a city that lies at the center of Jewish, Christian, and Muslim religious imaginaries but remains under the exclusive sovereignty of the State of Israel. As construction on the bridge concluded in 2008, this addition to Jerusalem's monumental landscape drew protests from a variety of ideological perspectives. Many Israelis criticized the cost of the bridge at NIS 246 million (approx. 73 million USD at the time) along with the grandiosity of its massive opening dedication ceremony, which cost NIS 2 million (approx. 572,000 USD), at a time when much of the city lived (and continues to live) in abject poverty.[2] Such a jubilant occasion, which reportedly involved 20,000 participants (Lis 2008), naturally featured music in the form of live performances and broadcasted musical recordings. A scandal played out, however, when multiple news outlets reported that planners at the municipality forced the female dancers who would accompany the live musical performances to wear hair coverings and floor-length skirts, in a move designed to appease members of the city's ultra-Orthodox Jewish community who threatened to mount a protest disrupting the ceremony if women were to appear in costuming that

---

aesthetics: there are too many to list—whole neighborhoods were built on internationalist, brutalist, and other styles over half a century before Calatrava was awarded the bridge contract.

[2] According to the 2008 edition of the *Statistical Yearbook of Jerusalem*, 66.8% of non-Jewish Jerusalemites (33,011 families) and 23.3% of Jewish Jerusalemites (33,087 families) were living below the poverty line, defined as "state of relative distress that can be assessed in relation to the standard of living that characterizes a society: a family is considered poor if its living conditions are noticeably worse than those typical to the rest of the surrounding society, not if it is unable to purchase a given collection of goods necessary for its existence" (Choshen 2008: 179). According to the most recent 2018 edition, using the most recently available data from 2016, the numbers had risen to 72% of non-Jewish residents (described now as "Arabs") and 26% of Jewish residents living in poverty (Choshen 2018: VI/2).

they deemed to be immodest (Lefkovits 2008; Associated Press 2008). The city government's capitulation to such demands earned the dancers the nickname "Taliban Troupe" (Lefkovits 2008), drawing an analogy to the Sunni Islamist organization in Afghanistan that forced women under its power to wear the burqa (full facial and bodily covering) in public and that was infamous for enacting outright gender violence against them (see Dupree 2001).

For other Israelis, the bridge itself had unintended symbolic resonances. In a column published in the center-left newspaper Haaretz, *political scientist and cultural commentator Meron Benvenisti, who thirty years earlier had served as Deputy Mayor of Jerusalem (1971–1978), called the bridge "a monument to the stupidity of Jerusalem's monstrous expansion" and wondered whether its prominent placement so far away from occupied East Jerusalem represented "an awakening from the illusion of a unified city" (Benvenisti 2008). This illusion of unification—what Palestinians and many Israelis would call "the occupation" (Arab.: al-ihtilal; Hebr.: ha-kibbush)—stems from the State of Israel's unilateral rule since 1967 over a city that is at once its own capital and is also the capital of the would-be State of Palestine; it is a single city with multiple peoples. The illusion of the city's "unification" is not only a visual phenomenon but one that resounds noisily in space and time. As the Chords Bridge controversy illustrates, twenty-first-century Israeli attitudes about rule over Jerusalem are agonistic, and they are expressed through emotionally charged musical symbolism.*

Listening to the Past, Writing the Present

In *City of Song*, I argue that popular song has been an essential discursive site for Israelis' production of spatial knowledge about Jerusalem, the main contested territory within the Israeli-Palestinian crisis. Through studying this musical discourse, I reveal how members of the State of Israel's ruling class had (and, to some extent, continue to have) conflicted orientations toward the city, while showing how the present conflict over Jerusalem is not a timeless problem but rather one that was produced in modernity, as musicians and associated figures grappled with the question of the city's meaning in the context of Jewish and Israeli identity.

There are many approaches that one could take in exploring how musicians produce spatial knowledge within the Israeli-Palestinian crisis. I have chosen to concentrate on Jerusalem, listening to its representations in music, because the city's politicization has been the most significant barrier to peace in the region. But to which "Jerusalem" should one listen, when there are so many, according to the introductory epigraph provided by Ariella Azoulay? Israeli, Palestinian, Jewish, Christian, and Muslim Jerusalems all exist in spite of overlapping cartographic imaginings of space that would make the boundaries between them impossible to draw. And there are yet many other Jerusalems about which one might write: Armenian Jerusalem, Greek Jerusalem, Syrian Jerusalem, Ethiopian Jerusalem, Anglo Jerusalem, and many other versions of the city that accord to national or ethnic identity constructs, to say nothing of religious groupings that sometimes move across such identities or else divide them by sect or denomination. More Jerusalems are present, too, if one listens closely enough.

This book is about mainstream Israeli popular music identified with Zionism. It provides a synthesis of diverse Zionist perspectives on Jerusalem through the poetics of Israeli song, whose representational and poetic patterns resonate with a broader Israeli political discourse about Jerusalem. The people concerned are primarily Israeli Jews, mostly (but not only) from European-descended (Ashkenazi) families, who were associated with various facets of the Labor movement and the political and media establishments that it controlled during the Yishuv era (1880–1948), early statehood period (1948–67), and across the divide of the 1967 War until Labor's demise in the 1977 elections. I chose this group because I wanted to understand the meanings of Jerusalem in the language of the majority.[3]

Over the course of modern Jewish settlement of Palestine and Israel, starting in the late nineteenth century, the question of Jerusalem's meaning and status proved to be not a static ethical question but rather one that served as a subject for debating social values, a way of working out ideas about nation and community, of mediating understandings of self and others through religion and religiosity, and of doing something creative with the rich repository of tropes, signs, and symbols that constitute Jewish thought and culture in the *longue durée*. Music, as I discuss throughout the book's five chapters, was a key site for imagining an Israeli future in Jerusalem.

[3] By the term "majority," I do not refer to demographic distribution but rather to the group that exercises its right to self-determination in a context marked by asymmetries of power. In this case, the majority are the dominant group of Jewish Israelis who enjoy the full benefits of citizenship, unlike marginalized Israeli citizens (including Palestinian Israelis), Palestinian refugees in the Occupied Territories and in exile in neighboring countries, or other minority groups in the region.

Methodologically speaking, this is a historical study driven by the political concerns of the present. Now, in the third decade of the twenty-first century, Jerusalem faces an impasse in grappling with its modernity, which is at once an existential or experiential paradigm that is altogether distinct from pre- (or post-) modernity, a process of modernization via civil engineering and the mechanisms of the capitalist mode of production, and a postcolonial modernity, in which the city and the people who constitute its cultural geography emerged from the ashes of western colonialism. But Jerusalem's modernity was not merely historically produced; it was also geographically produced through music and its mediated multimodality, in the form of poetic lyrics, rich melodies, and associated modes of performance, circulation, and citational practices. When Israelis join their voices together to sing "Jerusalem, Jerusalem, / From your ruins I will rebuild you!," the closing refrain of Avigdor Hameiri's "From the Summit of Mt. Scopus" (1929), surrounded by the very buildings from which the Israeli municipality governs the built-up modern city, they draw on the dual registers of biblical prophecy (the promise of rebuilding, apparently fulfilled) and Zionist nostalgia (the song is a classic of the Yishuv) to produce a jubilant metanarrative of spatial redemption within the material cityspace itself.

Music provides a powerful point of historiographical inquiry into the present—precisely because all performances of past repertory are fundamentally an exercise in historical memory, as in the aforementioned performance of "From the Summit of Mt. Scopus," which I witnessed on Jerusalem Day 2017 (and discuss in further detail in Chapter 1). That performance, like the others I discuss throughout the book, is part of the song's genealogy, which has unfolded through multiple iterations since the mid-nineteenth century. Part of my methodology is to account for those multiple iterations in the lives of the songs under discussion. In her examination of the many versions and political uses of a Catholic hymn in late twentieth-century Poland, Andrea F. Bohlman writes, "[T]his sedimented history's particles are infinite. Another methodological approach . . . is to figure these performances as the residue, or even accumulation, of a longer historical practice of singing 'God Save Poland' that is the crucible of [trade union] Solidarity's musical solidarity" (Bohlman 2020: 260; see 234–80). Likewise, in *City of Song* I examine the residue left by individual songs' multiple instantiations, compositional and performance gestures, citational practices, and agglomerated meanings, in order to chart the emergence of Jerusalem's centrality in Israeli political discourse across the long twentieth century.

I also study how songs participate in a larger genealogy of a musical discourse on Jerusalem involving multiple songs.[4] Martin Stokes, writing about the anthemic status of "Aziz İstanbul" in modern Turkey, has claimed that songs are "experienced as 'text-artifacts' in relation to others" (2010: 7). He suggests that "they are also, simultaneously, articulations of voice . . . [understood] as being complex and collective discursive constructions—Feld, Fox, Porcello, and Samuels's 'timbral socialities'—that take shape over periods of time longer than the life cycle of the specific songs in question" (Stokes 2010: 7; cf. Feld, Fox, Porcello, and Samuels 2004: 341). It follows, then, that the bounded concept of "song" is flexible enough to accommodate a seemingly infinite number of variegated listening experiences, as long as they figure into broader social discourse. In his pioneering aesthetic monograph *Rhythm and Noise* (1996), philosopher Theodore Gracyk attempts to address this issue using the concept of "instantiation"—the process by which multiple hearings of a recording or separate recordings of the same song, even on different media, serve as instances of a singular conception of a work. A song's "work identity" is why a listener can recognize the song "Bab El-Wad," whether it is performed by Yaffa Yarkoni or Shlomo Gronich, or subject to parody or interpolation, as I chronicle in Chapter 3. In general, the first instance of a song forms the basis of a work, and subsequent hearings often accumulate to listeners' concept of that work.

Every song has a genealogy, and that genealogy in turn connects to genealogies of other kinds of knowledge, including spatial knowledge, in the sense that Foucault developed the concept as a "method of writing critical history: a way of using historical materials to bring about a 'revaluing of values' in the present day" (Garland 2014: 372; see, e.g., Foucault 1977). A genealogical approach to music and space creates opportunities to think outside of historical logics that would render the present (i.e., the vista of writing) as inevitable. As David Brackett writes:

> The purpose of using the concept, genealogy, is not to contrast simply a presentist view of history—a role that might be filled by canonical narratives in which a cause-and-effect teleology leads from a point of origin to the present in order to confirm contemporary beliefs about a subject—with a historicist approach that reconstitutes the historical horizon in which

---

[4] "From the Summit of Mt. Scopus" was written and performed in 1929, but its prehistory stretches back to 1847, as I discuss in Chapter 1.

events and texts emerge. Rather, such a genealogical approach seeks both to analyze the conditions that make it possible for an event to occur and, at the same time, to not occlude the current events to which an interest in the past is responding, what Foucault terms a "history of the present." (Brackett 2016: 6)

Through a musical history of the present, the past's forgotten contingencies—its messiness and plurality of possible futures—come more fully into view. The political fate of Jerusalem—the present whose history I write here—emerged out of a past in which musicians helped regulate "facts on the ground" about what Jerusalem meant and to whom it belonged by generating genealogies of meaning through composition and performance (Abu El Haj 2001). A history of the present in Jerusalem is not merely a poetically rendered study of cultural memory but rather a way of writing that places the stakes of contention front-and-center in the analysis. To put it simply, I regard the conflict over Jerusalem as a modern problem and thus examine how historical actors produced the city's modernity in the context of music.

A central premise of this book is that, within the realm of Israeli arts and media culture, popular song emerged as the predominant mode of Israeli place-making. In examining the place-making power of music in other settings, music theorist Adam Krims suggested that scholars attend to "[s]trategies of musical poetics . . . [that] form a complex subjective unity with the spaces that societies build in their continuous self-production" (Krims 2007: xxi). In the context of Zionism, while there are common "strategies of musical poetics" that inform Israeli society's "continuous self-production," there is relatively little to be found in the form of "subjective unity," even within the same ethnoreligious group. In order to capture this intragroup diversity of perspective, I have produced a musical genealogy of Jerusalem through listening to Zionism's musical apparatus—represented by songwriters, poets, performers, media institutions, and other kinds of historical agents—from the origins of Zionism in the late nineteenth and early twentieth centuries through "the end of the golden age of the ideologically-laden folksong" in the late 1960s and early 1970s, which coincided—unsurprisingly—with rampant social and political changes, conceptions of national identity and culture, and the very cultural geography of Jerusalem as a lived city, as I discuss in what follows (Reshef 2012: 170; also Regev and Seroussi 2004: 49–112). The pages of the book therefore are filled with famous names such as Naomi Shemer, Dan Almagor, Nechama Hendel, Yaffa

Yarkoni, Menashe Ravina, Gil Aldema, and other representatives of that musical apparatus, as I trace the development of a symbolic lexicon about Jerusalem in Zionist and Israeli music, which itself is a mixture of inherited symbols and poetic procedures. Critical to the genealogical method I propose in this study, I also examine how more contemporary figures have more recently engaged with the repertory, tropes, and general symbolic economy embodied by those figures through covers, parodies, allusions, and other intertextual strategies. In short, each song is situated at the point of conception but also examined through what came before and after. Close readings of lyrics and close listenings to their musical settings naturally form a central part of the book's exposition.

The repertory that I discuss, largely consisting of canonical popular songs and poems (whether made canonical by their association with historical phenomena such as wars or through explicit canonizing projects, e.g., retrospective television programs and anthologies), along with some lesser-known examples, has never been treated as a thematic repertory as such—largely because music scholars have taken on issues other than the city's processes of territorialization. At the same time, at first listen some of the repertory presented in the book may appear to be only loosely connected, because the songs emanate from a variety of cultural practices. But this kind of eclecticism—a willingness to transgress boundaries of genre, discipline, and cultural domain—is precisely what is demanded by a genealogical approach. Brackett writes:

> Simply because a musical text may not (to paraphrase Jacques Derrida) belong to a genre with any stability does not mean that it does not participate in one, a distinction that emphasizes the temporal, experiential, functional, and fleeting quality of genres while nonetheless retaining the importance of the genre concept for communicating about texts. Put another way, genres are not static groupings of empirically verifiable musical characteristics, but rather associations of texts whose criteria of similarity may vary according to the uses to which the genre labels are put. (Brackett 2016: 3–4)

He compels music scholars, "Rather than focusing on *what* constitutes the contents of a musical category, the emphasis here falls on *how* a particular idea of a category emerges and stabilizes momentarily (if at all) in the course of being accepted across a range of discourses and institutions" (Brackett 2016: 5–6). The question of whether Jerusalem song constitutes a genre, across historical periods and among different constituencies, and that is discrete and separate from other musical genres, is therefore less relevant to the analysis of the place of Jerusalem in Israeli music than is the question of how the songs in question participate in a broader discourse on the city within Israeli national culture.

As it happens, many of the songs I study in this book do connect according to their intertextual or paratextual relations with one another, through shared connections with older repertory (especially the Psalms and other parts of the Hebrew Bible), or through tropes or literary devices strongly associated with Jerusalem in Jewish cultural production writ large. Several of the songs were synthetically connected by historical actors themselves by way of anthologization on compilation albums that explicitly called into being the genre "Jerusalem songs" (*shirey Yerushalayim*), especially after 1967. Analyzing the place of Jerusalem in the canon of Israeli popular music might help scholars operating within and outside of music studies to understand more deeply how Jewish attachment to Jerusalem—to be sure, a powerfully constructed legitimation of Israeli rule over the city—has been much more complex, dynamic, and subject to change within modern history.

Through my research, I focused on the contributions of members of this particular Israeli ethnic group, but my argument provides no moral justification for Israeli rule over Jerusalem, nor does it aid a politically driven process of demonizing Israeli Jews (e.g., antisemitic conspiratorial thinking). Clearly, there are historical traumas at play that many other scholars working within Middle Eastern and Israel Studies have addressed and will continue to address as a matter of course. Instead, I approach this subject from the perspective of wanting to examine the production of spatial knowledge, which people may take for granted as being natural or self-evident, that undergirds the exercises of power that compel many scholars, myself included, to write about them.

In other words, in pursuing this research I wanted to know why (or why not) the place mattered so much to people, how that spatial knowledge became politicized, and how memories of past eras continue to be commemorated or reworked in the present. This is not, therefore, a presentist study searching desperately for historical *causality* that proves the inevitability of the present but rather an investigation—a musicological investigation—of the *emergence* of a particular view, or cluster of views, about Jerusalem among the people who came to dominate the city "out of specific struggles, conflicts, alliances, and exercises of power, many of which are nowadays forgotten"

(Garland 2014: 372). Tracing the genealogy of those views across points of migration and across historical divides (e.g., wars and the formation of the state), while acknowledging the role of imagination in constructing such continuities, is critical to understanding the history—and historicization—of Jerusalem's present.

As in the Chords Bridge controversy of 2008, where even the musical celebration of the completion of an architectural project became a prime opportunity for political critique, so too do moments in the city's past reveal the forgotten "struggles, conflicts, alliances, and exercises of power" that compose the history of Zionism in Palestine and Israel.

Listening to the Present, Writing the Past

As a genealogical study, the book includes mixed musicological methodologies. The primary methodologies are historical and hermeneutic: my analyses are anchored in both archival detail and close listening to songs whose contents, contexts, or associations reveal important insights into the place of Jerusalem in Zionist discourse. In searching for those songs, I scoured the sound archives of the National Library of Israel for every recording I could find that mentioned Jerusalem in one way or another—through song or album titles, lyrics, visually on cover art—and for recordings that I knew to be important through my discussions with Israelis in the field or through secondary literature. Ethnographic writing supplements those approaches in order to accomplish three main aims: (1) to provide testimony from historical subjects (e.g., musicians, poets, or others) who were still living during my research period (2010–2020), or in some cases from their surviving relatives; (2) to situate the reception of past repertory in contemporary performances I attended in the field; and (3) to discuss the city's cultural geography in the ethnographic present as a window into the historical conditions illuminated by musical analysis.

I invoke the "ethnographic present" for this historical study after anthropologist Kirsten Hastrup's attempt to "reinvent" and rescue the term from the depths of postmodern criticism, which held that fixing the ethnographic field research in the present tense ran the risk of denying people a past. She sees the ethnographic present as being instead "a necessary construction of time" that "preserves the reality of *anthropological* knowledge" (Hastrup 1995: 14, emphasis in original). For me, ethnography is a way of relating to history; as Foucault stated, "I set out from a problem expressed in the terms current today and I try to work out its genealogy. Genealogy means that I begin my analysis from a question posed in the present" (quoted in Kritzman 1988: 262; see also Garland 2014: 367). My field notes that are woven into the historical exposition treat the present as an epistemological standpoint that structures, limits, and enables knowledge of the past and the historical materials under discussion. In Hastrup's words, "Evaluating the present is to make claim to potentiality as well as actuality" (1995: 14). By reflecting on the present, in the text I acknowledge the historically contingent nature of spatial knowledge. I do not "authentically" represent Jerusalem but rather produce the city as I write (and you produce it as you read). "My" Jerusalem is different from others' Jerusalems, as Dan Almagor expresses in the musical that provides the analytical centerpiece of the book's final chapter.

Songs and Spatial Representation

What does it mean to write a musical genealogy of Jerusalem in Zionist thought? In both Israeli and Palestinian societies, music is a privileged medium through which the region's social groups have forged national culture and identity from the fires of international conflict, as Nili Belkind (2021), Moslih Kanaaneh (2013), David McDonald (2013), Motti Regev and Edwin Seroussi (2004, 2013), Tanya Sermer (2015), and many others have shown. Musicians have also taken it upon themselves to play across national divides (Brinner 2009); to maintain or transgress ethnic, racial, and gender identities (Bohlman 1989; Hankins 2015; Webster-Kogen 2018); to serve a foreign colonizing mission (Beckles Willson 2013); to participate in transnational circulations of musical style (Horowitz 2010; Shelleg 2014); and to intervene in a host of other social functions ascribed to music. As Edwin Seroussi argues,

> The dialectics underpinning our relation to sound, namely between what we choose to listen to and what we are obliged to hear by the sonic environment surrounding us (even if we do not focus our attention on those sounds) or imposed into us at any given moment, are a basis for discussing how individuals and communities constitute their selves through sound. (Seroussi 2014: 37)

I argue that music not only teaches us about how people constitute their selves but is in fact intensely charged with articulating the very territorial boundaries of Israel/Palestine. In Jerusalem, as Belkind argues in the case of the occupied Palestinian territories, "the Israeli production of space is not only a matter of 'security' but of a gestalt of domination and sense of primordial entitlement to the territory" (Belkind 2021: 126). Musical knowledge and spatial knowledge thus help constitute one another. Music's representational capacity, both as recorded for wide consumption and as performed in public rituals of collectivity, insinuates spatial meaning into the engineering and exercise of power.

It is important to note that while Jerusalem's singers and poets no doubt affect political imaginaries in profound ways, they most often operate outside of official state patronage and even without overt nationalistic motivations. Again, Belkind is helpful here: "as an embodied practice and field of specialization, music provides means for constructing subjectivities, collectivities and modes of resistance that are not overdetermined by the violence that frames the conflict, and hence creates alternative means for re-mapping, or reterritorializing, its confining spatiality" (Belkind 2021: 125). From a historical perspective, then, Jerusalem—despite being the capital of both Israel and the aspirational Palestinian state—is not beholden to its individual nations in the same way that other cities in the region are. Jerusalem is its own kind of space, and one that has endured many political transformations of the slim territory between the Mediterranean Sea and the Jordan River. In every geographical sense except with respect to its physical boundaries, Jerusalem is greater than any national concept that would count the city among its physical territories. This also may be true in a general sense: While nations tend to be socially defined in ways that incline toward homogeneity, cities—by their very nature as sites of migration, pilgrimage, and exchange—often incline toward heterogeneity. Jerusalem's multiplicities overwhelm the city's absolute coordinates within Israel and Palestine. Any attempt to pin down a single, unified, culturally contiguous vision of the city is easily frustrated by just twenty minutes of walking through its central neighborhoods. Difference always rears its head, reminding you to listen for the sounds that helped create the possibility for the current state of affairs.

Representing this "reality," notwithstanding whatever epistemological proscriptions may obscure our knowledge of it, seems like it would be the main task of a book about space and place. But where do musical renderings of space fit into the city's landscape? In their call for an "anthropology of landscape," Christopher Tilley and Kate Cameron-Daum write,

> [Representations of space] are selective and partial, and often highly ideological, ways of seeing and knowing. In fact it is through material experience that we can understand the ideological nature of these representations, the manner in which they quite literally frame the landscape, far better than by undertaking any desk-bound analysis. . . . A materialist approach to landscape is thus a return to the real, and we regard it as a way to reinvigorate and redirect the study of landscape. (Tilley and Cameron-Daum 2017: 4–5)

Required are perspectives that dignify the place-making activities—such as music—that constitute human expressive behavior in order to nuance the materialism of traditional forms of geographical research, particularly those placing themselves within an intellectual legacy of materialist readings of Marxian social theory that discount the critical role of social memory.[5] People sing songs about place for a reason: they reveal, and indeed shape, the "ways of seeing and knowing" inherent to "material experience." To play on the subtitle of Tilley and Cameron-Daum's book, in musical practice one finds the "extraordinary in the ordinary."

The political role of collective memories in Jerusalem's urban processes can be dizzyingly complex, with some processes hidden, some palimpsestic, and some loudly projected in the most public of ways. Ethnomusicologist Catherine Appert builds on anthropologist George Marcus's paradigm of "*non-obvious* applications of multi-sited strategies" (Marcus 1999: 6) by calling for scholarship written in a language that "amplifies the ways in the field site's fracturing or 'multi-sitedness' is a question of not only different *spaces* or *times* in which research happens but of the relationships that cut across, through, between, and around them" (Appert 2017: 447, emphasis in original).[6] Appert's claims for ethnography hold for a genealogical study of music, which cuts across multiple discursive sites, and foregrounds the convergence of music and other spatial practices. As geographer David Harvey

---

[5] It is worth noting that Timothy D. Taylor, in the introduction to a recent book whose title borrows a familiar phrase, "history of the present," explicitly attempts to move beyond what he identifies as "functionalism" within Marxian approaches to the study of music and social relations—in his case those inescapably shaped by the development of capitalism (see Taylor 2016: 1–19).

[6] In her essay, Appert calls for a "regendering of musical ethnography" (2017: 452), by attending to how field relationships and experiences are engendered within and outside of the sites of musical events.

explains, "relational conceptions of space-time bring us to the point where mathematics, poetry, and music converge if not merge. And that, from a scientific (as opposed to aesthetic) viewpoint, is anathema to those of a positivist or crudely materialist bent" (Harvey 2006: 124). He further claims, "there are certain topics, such as the political role of collective memories in urban processes, that can only be approached in this way" (125). After Appert (2017) and others, I move between music per se and music's embeddedness in other forms of cultural expression, especially poetry but also theater, dance, and cinema, in order to account for the "political role of collective memory" in Jerusalem's urban processes in the twentieth century and beyond.

As a book about how musicians produce space, *City of Song* owes a debt to the intellectual genealogy of philosopher Henri Lefebvre and various geographical thinkers working across an immense diversity of fields who have elaborated on and critiqued Lefebvre's influential later works, of which *The Production of Space* ([1974] 1991) is paramount. For example, in his work on globalization and territoriality in Africa, philosopher Achille Mbembe builds on the spatial theories of Lefebvre and Michel de Certeau to argue,

> [A] place is the order according to which elements are distributed in relationships of coexistence . . . [and] is an instantaneous configuration of positions. It implies a stability. As for a territory, it is fundamentally an intersection of moving bodies. It is defined essentially by the set of movements that take place within it. Seen in this way, it is a set of possibilities that historically situated actors constantly resist or realize. (Mbembe 2001: 24)

Place and space, or "territory" as Mbembe calls it, are intimately interrelated according to processes of de-territorialization—a disembedding of place from social relations—and re-territorialization—a reinscribing of space according to the "spatio-temporal order" dictated by particular social groups. In Harvey's words, "What we do as well as what we understand is integrally dependent upon the primary spatio-temporal frame within which we situate ourselves" (Harvey 2006: 128). Space becomes territory via a detour through place. The relationship between space—a site of action—and place—an object of representation—is iterative; both musical performance (in space) and musical representation (of place) actively shape this process of territorialization.

Insofar as national consciousness is territorialized in Israel/Palestine—and a chief premise of this book is that Israeli and Palestinian national consciousness are *indelibly* territorialized—culturally exclusive, narrow, and absolutist conceptions of territory serve to deny political subjectivity to the other and ought to be subject to the rigors of academic critique. Revolutionary voices—even, if not especially, those emanating from within the dominant ethno-national grouping itself—must be amplified. As Amy Horowitz argues, "a close reading of those intra-Jewish Israeli power dynamics can ultimately contribute to a critique of the larger Israel-Palestine struggle and, I hope, contribute to a just resolution" (Horowitz 2005: 204). I share this imperative in *City of Song*.

The Present's Pasts

Jerusalem is not only the subject of local concerns, but, as during its Crusader and Ottoman periods mentioned earlier, its modernity was shaped profoundly by geopolitics. This is evident in the modern city's processes of territorialization. Historian Seraj Assi recently suggested that World War I has never really ended there (Assi 2018). The Sykes-Picot Agreement of 1916 radically redrew the boundaries of the post-Ottoman provinces, with the newly actualized territories eventually accruing to national imaginaries around the region, including Israel's foes in the wars to come, such as Egypt, Syria, Jordan, Lebanon, and Iraq. Indeed, to play on the title of a recent book by Salim Tamari (2017), the Great War "remade" Palestine itself, sparking a renaissance of Palestinian civil society and infrastructure in Jerusalem. The Balfour Declaration of 1917 and the twenty-five-year British occupation of Palestine known as the Mandate (1922–47), however, essentially secured the broader territory known as "Palestine," including Jerusalem, for a future Jewish state. When the British evacuated Palestine in 1947 on the eve of the civil war to come, they left behind a radically altered urban environment in Jerusalem, including its division into confessional quarters—Muslim, Jewish, Armenian, and Christian—and the attendant urban soundscapes that accompanied such divisions as they were traversed by sonic harbingers of modernity such as trains, automobiles, and, especially, radio broadcasting (Stanton 2013).

Developments on the European continent had meanwhile disrupted the world's cultural geographies in previously unimaginable ways. The destruction of European Jewry during World War II, and survivors' difficulty of finding safe haven elsewhere, created a sense of urgency for Jewish self-determination. Palestine was already the site of a burgeoning Jewish society—called the "Yishuv" (Settlement)—and so served as a new home for hundreds of thousands of refugees, who entered at times "illegally" (according to shifting Mandatory policy) before, during, and after World War II until the founding of Israel in 1948, when some 600,000 Holocaust refugees were admitted by the newly formed Jewish state alongside another quarter-million Jews from Arab lands in the early years of statehood (and hundreds of thousands over the ensuing decades).[7] In addition to transformative demographic effects of the waves of migration to Palestine and Israel set off by European antisemitism and the fallout of the First Arab-Israeli War, the threat of extinction at the hands of the outside world colors Jewish views on self-determination at nearly every level. In this sense, Israeli society after 1948 has been linked with global postcolonial struggle. At the same time, however, the resultant state has perpetrated techniques of colonial domination over Palestinians, who make up the majority of the territory's native people and who have their own postcolonial national imaginary and political aspirations. This has given rise to a very modern sense of conflict that departs significantly from the geopolitical tensions that shaped Jerusalem's urban development before the twentieth century.

Since its founding in 1948, the State of Israel's history has been dotted by seven formal wars and the commonplace occurrence of political violence, either against the state or on its behalf. Music has often served to rally support for these efforts or, in a commemorative capacity after the fact, to memorialize the heroic dead and celebrate their sacrifices. During the 1967 Arab-Israeli War, the so-called Six-Day War, Israel defeated the armies of Egypt, Syria, and Jordan and captured the Sinai Peninsula, Gaza Strip, Golan Heights, and, most notably, the eastern half of Jerusalem, home to the most sacred and contested monuments in the city. The redistribution of land following the treaties to end the war radically reoriented the once divided city under Israeli governance, reinstating Jewish access to the Western Wall plaza

---

[7] Approximately 60,000 German Jews immigrated to Israel between 1933 and 1939 under the Haavara Agreement between Germany and Zionist organizations; see Bohlman 1992 for an account of how the migration of German Jews altered the soundscape of Palestine and Israel. After 1939, many Jews who managed to escape landed in European countries that would soon be conquered by the Nazis, and so their refuge was temporary. The United States did take in an estimated 200,000 Jewish refugees during the Holocaust and an additional 140,000 survivors in the decade following (see Dinnerstein 1982; Cohen 2007), but famously turned away others, including 900 aboard the famed S.S. St. Louis in 1939 (see Goldsmith 2014). Figures for Mizrahi migration come from Schindler 2008: 63–64.

and other holy places while scattering much of the Palestinian population to neighboring Jordan, the still-occupied West Bank, and exile abroad. The events of 1967 represented a divinely sanctioned achievement for some and a catastrophe of either diplomatic, moral, or, quite literally, biblical proportions for others. Amid this political unrest, the holy landscape of Jerusalem transitioned from being the remnant of an ancient past to serving in an essential capacity for modern identity politics in the region.

As Gershom Gorenberg writes about the importance of political memory in the Middle East, "history isn't made of rock. It is built from witnesses' uncertain memories. It shimmers and shifts with collective retellings and with scholarly discoveries that sometimes actually convince people to reconsider what they thought was fact" (Gorenberg 2011). In the wake of the 1967 War, both the subject of the war and Jerusalem's monuments drew increased attention from songwriters and poets, fostering great affective potency and collective catharsis for people seeking to reconcile an exilic past with both the violent present and the possibility of a sovereign future. These "Jerusalem songs" survived the events of that year largely through a variety of channels of dissemination—radio, live performances and their televised broadcasts, recorded media, and songbooks. Music is indeed a most penetrating, emotionally fraught experiential mode through which that historical moment has been commemorated, relived, critiqued, and transmitted to new generations of Israelis for whom Jerusalem is a site of intense cultural meaning.

The 1967 War has an outsized presence in this historical retelling, because it ushered in the very state of uneasy "unification" that has been the status quo in the past five decades leading up to the time of writing. It also ushered in a paradigmatic shift in Israeli cultural production, music especially, toward a re-territorialization of Jerusalem as a "unified" city, suturing together "East" and "West" that had been divided by the events of 1948–1949 under the rule of a single state. Israel's conquest of Jerusalem during the 1967 War represents a pivotal moment in the region's history, in the sense that Lefebvre considered "moments" to be "significant times when existing orthodoxies are open to challenge, when things have the potential to be overturned or radically altered, moments of crisis in the original sense of the term" (Lefebvre 2004: x). At the same time, Assaf Shelleg cautions against the overemphasis of political dates in Israeli music historiography: "Regardless of the pedagogical usefulness, such events do not spawn new aesthetic approaches; at best, they accelerate and amplify preceding (and often historiographically sidelined) phenomena rather than punctuate them" (Shelleg 2019: 255). This is a significant observation, and one that I uphold by focusing on periods of relative inactivity in the production of Jerusalem song as a self-conscious genre (e.g., in Chapter 2) through examining how songs and poems referencing Jerusalem or drawing on its symbolic lexicon participated in that genre without necessarily "belonging" to it, per David Brackett's genealogical approach to genre.

This being said, it is difficult to overestimate the effect that 1967 had on the place of Jerusalem within Israeli cultural production specifically because of how people responded directly to this political development. As Ranen Omer-Sherman writes, the occupation of Jerusalem following the war "unleashed an unparalleled wave of highly rhetorical and ideologically inflected verse, much of it undoubtedly triumphal or otherwise awestruck, in response to the culture's access to every quarter of the city" (Omer-Sherman 2006: 222). Naomi Shemer's "Jerusalem of Gold," for example, became the song of the moment, programmed constantly in live performance and over the state radio to celebrate the military victory. Following 1967, musicians and their publics imagined a variety of possible futures for the city, responding in kind to the political and cultural changes Jerusalem underwent as the Israeli state added itself to the long list of conquerors in the city's history.

From 1967 until the beginning of the First Palestinian Intifada (1987–1991), Jerusalem "functioned as a center of urban agglomeration under Jewish dominance" (Keidar 2018). The Intifada mobilized Palestinian masses toward a concerted national movement, realized at times through nonviolent protest, at others through violent political action, and in both cases met with suppression by the Israeli military. Following on the heels of the First Intifada, in 1993 the signing of the Oslo Accords, a set of agreements between Israel and the Palestinian Liberation Organization (PLO), ushered in unprecedented momentum toward a peaceful resolution of the Israeli-Palestinian crisis, only to be disrupted tragically and abruptly with the 1995 assassination of Israeli Prime Minister Yitzhak Rabin, who had negotiated with PLO leader Yasser Arafat toward radical changes to the region's geography that likely would have included the establishment of an independent State of Palestine, comprising most of the territories occupied by Israel since 1967.

The First Intifada represented a clash of national interests and entities, and the issues at its root were much broader than the question of Jerusalem's final status. During the Oslo process, the future status of Jerusalem was always up in the air, as it was among the messiest issues to be negotiated between the parties. But during this era, the city served as a critical battleground for the conflict, precisely because it was, and remains, a tangled crossroad between Israel and Palestine. Three studies—Benjamin Brinner's *Playing Across a Divide: Israeli-Palestinian Musical Encounters* (2009), David McDonald's *My Voice Is My Weapon: Music, Nationalism, and the Poetics of Palestinian Resistance* (2013), and Nili Belkind's *Music in Conflict: Palestine, Israel, and the Politics of Aesthetic Production* (2021)—chronicle the politicized music-making of these periods to great effect, with many of the explicit intercultural music projects, protest concerts, and other musical events set in Jerusalem, the epicenter of the conflict. But as Belkind summarizes, "While the 1990s cultural renaissance reflected the optimism accompanying the peace process, the entry of the new millennium only brought further cycles of violence" (Belkind 2021: 2).

The euphoric mid-1990s were followed by extreme disillusionment on both sides, and a Second Palestinian Intifada (sometimes called the Al-Aqsa Intifada) began in 2000, lasting until 2005. This time, Jerusalem would become ground zero for the unrest, as an already smoldering fire left by the failure of the Camp David Summit, along with Israel's withdrawal from its long-standing occupation of southern Lebanon, would be ignited by a provocation by Prime Minister Ariel Sharon, who visited the Temple Mount/Noble Sanctuary flanked by a massive escort of Israeli riot police. This uprising was bloodier than the First Intifada, with a proliferation of spectacular violence perpetrated by Palestinian suicide bombers and disproportionately large-scale responses by the Israel Defense Forces; the violence resulted in an estimated 4,000 casualties, over twice as many as died in the earlier uprising.[8] The years of the Second Intifada were among the most traumatic for Jerusalemites who lived through devastating personal loss and political uncertainty.

One result of the Intifadas has been increasing securitization of Jerusalem, with the erection of checkpoints, roadblocks, domestic bomb shelters, and the most significant barrier to Palestinian mobility: a massive border wall—called *Geder ha-Hafrada* (Separation Fence) in Hebrew and *Jidār al-Faṣl al-ʿunsuri* (Apartheid Wall) in Arabic.[9] The Israeli government erected this wall, stretching around the majority of the West Bank, including through East

---

[8] For these estimates, I am using figures compiled by the Israeli Information Center for Human Rights in the Occupied Territories (B'Tselem); see https://www.btselem.org/statistics.

[9] See Shapiro and Bird-David 2017 for an anthropological study of Israeli bomb shelters.

Jerusalem, in order to stem the tide of violent attacks on Israeli citizens; however, it also "annexes 9.4 percent of the West Bank, integrates eighty Israeli settlements, and separates about fifty-five thousand Palestinian Jerusalemites from their kin in East Jerusalem" (Larkin 2014: 134). Construction began in 2002, with most of it completed within the next year (although construction would continue well into the next decade), inspiring a plethora of politicized artistic responses and international solidarity movements (see Larkin 2014; Belkind 2021). The effects of all of these events on the urban fabric of Jerusalem are palpable; as sociologist Noga Keidar writes, citing Shlay and Rosen (2010), "The fence not only served security goals, but also created economic and social separation between Israel and the West bank, impoverishing East Jerusalem of its metropolitan character" (Keidar 2018: 1215).

This violent history of partition, unification, occupation, and other attempts to "claw" at Jerusalem's "dust"—as Nechama Hendel sang in "Around Jerusalem"[10]—leads me toward the moment of writing, when 1967 continues to cast its shadows onto the Israeli-Palestinian crisis in the present—not only locally in Jerusalem but also in international interventions into the peace process. During my time researching for this book, several world leaders have appealed to the 1949–1967 spatial paradigm, in which the West Bank and East Jerusalem were under the custodianship of the Jordanian state (then named Transjordan). During US-brokered peace talks in 2011 and 2013–2014, led by the government of President Barack Obama, negotiations over the borders of a prospective Palestinian state took as their starting point the borders that existed prior to the Six-Day War—that is, they made demands for the liberation of Palestinian territories in exchange for land swaps elsewhere between Israel and a future Palestinian state. Obama's calls for a return to pre-1967 borders caused a major rift in his already shaky relationship with Israeli Prime Minister Benjamin Netanyahu, as well as dissent from members of the American Israel Public Affairs Committee (AIPAC), a hawkish supporter of Israeli occupation and state-sponsored violence against the Palestinians (Landler and Myers 2011; Mualem 2011). In 2018, the US regime led by Donald Trump took a definitive stance, endorsing Israeli rule over both halves of Jerusalem by opening a new embassy (previously located in Tel Aviv) in Jerusalem's Arnona neighborhood. The embassy building

---

[10] Here, I am referring to the lyrics of "Around Jerusalem" (*Saviv Le-Yerushalayim*), originally published as a poem by Dalia Rabikovitch in 1959, later set to music and recorded by Hendel in 1997; see Chapter 2 for a fuller discussion of this poem and song.

straddles the very armistice line that Israel crossed in its occupation of East Jerusalem beginning in 1967.

It is clear that the social and political ramifications of the crisis over Jerusalem are still quite alive to all parties involved in the conflict. As Ian Black writes in a recent history of the Israeli-Palestinian conflict, "There is no sign whatsoever that this conflict is about to end, so understanding it matters more than ever" (Black 2017: 10). Simon Goldhill puts it another way: "Perhaps it is just the naïve idealism of a historian to hope that a better understanding of the past could put a small brake on the careering machine of shrill ideology, even in Jerusalem" (Goldhill 2008: 103). The reader will find no such political idealism in *City of Song*, written at a moment when the crisis over Jerusalem and over the fate of Israel and Palestine seems as bleak as ever. It is my hope, however, that a scrupulous and at times creative, genealogical study of music will model for readers how a focus on the meanings produced through past creative practices have impressed on everyday life in the present. Only then will scholars be able to inspire the "revaluing of values," as Garland (2014) phrased it, that are embedded in the political status quo in which early twenty-first-century Jerusalemites and onlookers find themselves.

Overview and Structure of the Book

City of Song is organized into five chapters, each presenting historical episodes, ordered chronologically from the *longue durée* of Jewish cultural production into the Yishuv era (1882–1948), the early statehood period (1948–1967), the narrative climax of 1967, and the postwar period immediately following 1967. Taking the headings from Anabel Wharton's *Selling Jerusalem* (2006) as inspiration, I have given each chapter of the book a parallel main title: Metaphorical Jerusalem, Forgotten Jerusalem, Haunted Jerusalem, Gilded Jerusalem, and Heterotopian Jerusalem. Each term represents a distinct analytical emphasis for the audible histories contained therein.

Although this is a more-or-less chronologically oriented historical study (to be sure, there is overlap between chapters), the timeline will sometimes jump anachronistically as my authorial voice shifts. I explain the rationale for this more fully in Chapter 1, but in essence this treatment of temporality is in keeping with the experience of historical memory in the layered, palimpsestic city. I am rather more deliberate here, however, in that I might shift from the early or mid-twentieth century toward a more contemporary moment, for example, because the latter musical example is a reworking of the repertory and tropes concerned in the historical case study, thus revealing how the past projects into the present through a musician's conscious remaking of that memory. For the same reason, in some cases the timeline will jump to my field experiences, rendered through ethnographic interludes or interview material. I move between these voices throughout the text, transitioning between sections presenting analyses of songs, social histories, and ethnographic narratives.

In the first chapter, I establish Jerusalem song's poetics as a relation between metaphorical and material states. The chapter begins with a meditation on the trope of longing, through an analysis of Avigdor Hameiri's "From the Summit of Mt. Scopus" (1929). Continuing the discourse, I investigate the intertextual resources and literary devices on which modern musicians have drawn, discussing them in the context of Psalm 137 and in Israeli musical settings of medieval Andalusian poetry written by Yehuda Halevi. In Chapter 2, I turn toward the injunction against forgetting Jerusalem in Judaism during the Yishuv era (1882–1948), when Jerusalem appeared to have been all but absent from Jewish cultural production in Palestine. I argue that a conceptual Jerusalem was actually adumbrated in Zionist songs about Tel Aviv and rural Palestine, via liberatory tropes associated with Jerusalem in diasporic history. There, I also address the expression of anti-Jerusalem sentiment in the artistic circles identified with the late Yishuv and the State Generation, revealing how the city is characterized as possessing a female body that is subject to a process of poetic "whoring," driven by biblical imagery, that served as a vehicle for singers and poets to voice their ideological orientations toward Jerusalem.

In Chapter 3, I draw out the relation between commemorative song and commemorative landscape, discussing how music and monuments work in tandem to narrate past violence from the early statehood period (c. 1948–1967). Through my analysis of the career of "War Singer" Yaffa Yarkoni and her and others' performances of memorial repertory, such as Haim Gouri's "Bab El Wad" (1949) and Yoram Taharlev's "Ammunition Hill" (1968), I argue that Zionist political theology thrives on the poetics of bereavement and document its emplacement within Jerusalem. Chapter 4 is organized around the work most directly identified with the genre of Jerusalem song, Naomi Shemer's "Jerusalem of Gold," written and debuted in 1967, on the eve

of the Six-Day War, and commonly referred to as an unofficial national anthem. I chronicle the song's reception over the ensuing five decades, showing
how the representational strategy of the lyrics has become a point of contention within national political discourse.

In the final chapter, I evaluate the political efficacy of song during the
turbulent period from 1967 to 1977, when the Labor Zionist paradigm of
cultural politics reached its end, through a discussion of musical representations of Jerusalem as a heterotopian site of cultural difference. In examining
the chapter's musical centerpiece, Dan Almagor's musical *My Jerusalem*
(1968), which was written in response to the outpouring of Jerusalem song
after "Jerusalem of Gold," I argue in favor of the ethics of heterotopia while
critiquing its conceptual relevance in a space marked by power asymmetries.

The book presents a series of investigations into critical aspects of the
musical production of Jewish, Zionist, and Israeli space, contextualized
within the considerably larger social fabric of the city of Jerusalem. In the
spirit of moving from concept to embodiment, from a city of poetic fantasy
to a space for social life, I begin with the ontology most strongly associated
with Jerusalem in the long history of Jewish exile and in the global imagination that gave rise to the series of geopolitical crises that helped shape the
cityspace itself: metaphorical Jerusalem.

1

Metaphorical Jerusalem

Longing in Zionist Cultural Production

May 2017, Jerusalem City Center

I traveled to Jerusalem in May of 2017 in order to witness celebrations of the fiftieth Jerusalem Day. In observance of the holiday, cultural institutions around the city hosted several kinds of events, from lectures, concerts, and screenings to educational tours and parties. Most stores were closed for the day, and people poured into the streets in throngs as they made their way to commemorative events throughout the day. Transit did not run that day, so people from West Jerusalem walked along the light rail tracks running down Jaffa Street toward the Old City.

On the evening of May 23, I attended an evening concert called "White Night" (Layla Levan), planned by the municipality and featuring the Jerusalem Symphony Orchestra and singers Kobi Aflalo, David Daor, and Miri Mesik, meant to commemorate the fifty years since the State of Israel unified/occupied Jerusalem during the Six-Day War of 1967. Throughout the night, the musicians on stage presented an expansive repertory to mark the auspicious occasion, but the climax of the performance was a grand rendition of the evergreen "From the Summit of Mt. Scopus."

"From the Summit of Mt. Scopus" (*Me'Al Pisgat Har Ha-Tsofim*) was one of the earliest Zionist musical expressions of longing for Jerusalem, and one that has a fascinating intertextual history. The story of its genesis and reception reveals much about the shifting metaphorical attachment to Jerusalem, as expressed in Zionist and Israeli songwriting over the twentieth and early twenty-first centuries. The song's composer, Avigdor Hameiri (1890–1970), was far better known for his satirical prose than he was for verse, but he would eventually become Israel's first poet laureate. He wrote the song in 1929, in the Zionist context of the Yishuv, to which he had migrated only eight years earlier

City of Song. Michael A. Figueroa, Oxford University Press. © Oxford University Press 2022.
DOI: 10.1093/oso/9780197546475.003.0002

from Odessa.[1] The song appeared at a time of intense compositional activity for Hameiri, who had recently founded the Kettle Theater (*Ha-Kumkum*) in 1927, an event that is widely credited as the main catalyst for the birth of satire in Palestine/Israel.[2] Eliyahu Hacohen characterizes this period as one in which "the country had been drained of its composers" (Hacohen 2018: 40).

Strictly speaking, this was not true. During the first half of the twentieth century, including during the 1920s, Jerusalem boasted a robust musical scene centering primarily, but not exclusively, on Palestinian social life. Heather Bursheh summarizes this well, indicating that during the decades leading up to the 1948 War, Palestine "was a vibrant center of musical activity on all levels. From folklore to festivals, household gatherings to major stars performing at large venues, Palestine before the Nakba was clearly on par musically and culturally with its neighbors and perhaps surpassed some of them in terms of its cosmopolitanism" (Jalal, Boulos, and Bursheh 2013: 51–52).[3] This observation is corroborated by the diary entries of musician Wasif Jawhariyyeh (1897–1972), who chronicled his musical activities and political developments within the city in a way that indicated, at times, intercommunal engagement among Jerusalem's multiple communities, Jews included, through the city's musical culture. During the 1920s, and certainly by the next decade, Jerusalem also functioned as an important outpost of the region's multi-urban music economy. Jawhariyyeh describes visits to the city by Egyptian musicians such as Zaki Murad, an Alexandria-based but Aleppo-born Jew with family in the city, in 1921 (Jawhariyyeh 2014: 151–52), and Muhammad Abdul-Wahab, eventual superstar of the Arab world, in 1927 (177–79).

Eliyahu Hacohen's assertion is nevertheless important when considering the concerted effort to build an explicitly Zionist musical culture in Palestine, especially in the early years of the British Mandate, when the political future of the region was not at all clear. From Hameiri's perspective, this effort was endangered by the deaths of his colleagues Hanina Karchevsky (1827–1925)

---

[1] Hameiri grew up in a small village in the Carpathian Ruthenia area of Austro-Hungary and fought in the Hungarian army during World War I before settling in Vienna and then Odessa, where he was "warmly welcomed by the circle of Hebrew writers there, who helped him resume his Hebrew writing career" (Holtzman 2010).

[2] The name of the theater was apt, for as theater scholar David Alexander writes, "the whole system of the new Jewish settlement in Palestine was indeed going to be scalded by the Kettle's steam" (Alexander 1998: 166).

[3] In making this claim, Bursheh is drawing primarily on oral historical testimony. Working from archival materials held in Palestine, Israel, and the United Kingdom, David McDonald shows how this period also witnessed the development of a rich repertory of protest song beyond the confines of Jerusalem—using, too, the word "vibrant" to characterize Palestinian musical life at the time (McDonald 2013: 41).

and Joel Engel (1868–1927) and the departure of several other musicians to the United States and Europe to pursue composition, performance, or research. Hacohen writes that Hameiri "urgently needed tunes. With no choice, he adapted his songs [lyrics] to popular tunes he knew. He did everything with his ten fingers: wrote almost the entire repertory of 'Kettle shows,' including the songs" (Hacohen 2018: 40).[4]

As it turned out, the music for "From the Summit of Mt. Scopus" was the product of far more than ten fingers. Hameiri based his song on an 1886 song by the Polish songwriter Baruch Shafir (1858–1915), who published the original in a bilingual Yiddish-Hebrew edition. The Yiddish title was "Midnight" (*Khtsos*); the Hebrew title came from the fifth verse of Psalm 137: "If I Forget Thee, Jerusalem."[5] Shafir's earlier song told "the story of a Jewish elderly man wearing a white beard sitting in the attic on a frigid winter night dreaming of Jerusalem" (Hacohen 2018: 40). According to Hacohen, Hameiri was inspired when he heard "Midnight," the Yiddish version, performed by a woman named Raizeleh, who was the grandmother of the poet Dahlia Rabikovitch (whom we will meet in the next chapter) and a neighbor of Rabbi Yechiel Michel Pines, an early Jewish immigrant to Palestine (1878) and an important figure in the development of religious Zionist thought. In fact, the version of Shafir's song that Hameiri probably heard had been circulating as an unattributed "Yiddish folksong," both orally and in some cases textually, through its 1913 publication in the German newspaper *Ost und West* and later in the ninth volume (1932) of A. Z. Idelsohn's *Hebräisch-orientalischer Melodienschatz* (Eliram 2008/9: 3).

The melody's genealogy goes even deeper: both Shafir's and Hameiri's songs are simplified contrafacts on the melody of the aria, "Szumią jodły na gór szczycie" (Firs Are Soughing on the Mountaintops), from the Polish composer Stanisław Moniuszko's 1847 opera *Halka* (Eliram 2008/9: 4).[6]

---

[4] In translating Hacohen's insights, I have converted from the present to the past tense for consistency within the body text of my own writing. The essential meaning is unchanged.

[5] For a view of the published version of the bilingual edition, see http://web.nli.org.il/sites/NLI/English/music/daily_song/Pages/old/har_hazofim.aspx.

[6] In the twentieth century, Moniuszko and his music became nationalized within Polish public discourse, being dubbed by at least one figure as "a Polish cultural 'diplomat,' ignoring his significance across the multiethnic landscape of nineteenth-century Eastern Europe" (Bohlman 2020: 56–57)—a significance to which his role in this song's genealogy attests. At the same time, Talila Eliram points out that although most Israeli commentators refer to the Polish origins of the melody, rarely is the original Moniuszko aria mentioned. See Eliram 2008/9 for a fuller study of the melodic aspects of the song's transformations.

As Talila Eliram writes of the melody's gradual metamorphosis (*gilgul*), "Although parts of the original composition remained one way or another in the present-day composition, many changes were made to it, which made it simpler, catchy to the popular ear and easier to remember and perform" (Eliram 2008/9: 15). Owing to its intertextual and intercontextual entanglements, Hacohen characterizes "From the Summit of Mt. Scopus" as an "old-new song" (*shir ḥadash-yashan*).

The genesis of this modern Jerusalem song, as it is with many others, has cosmopolitan resonances that attest to the journey out of exile toward Jerusalem, a *telos* produced within a Zionist framework. It was within this framework that Hameiri reworked the song into the lyrics for "From the Summit of Mt. Scopus." The lyrics of the commonly performed first and fourth verses, excerpted here, are rooted in the poetics of longing for Jerusalem:

> From the summit of Mt. Scopus
> I will bow down to you.
> From the summit of Mt. Scopus
> Peace to you, Jerusalem!
> For a hundred generations I dreamt of you.
> To cry, to see the light of your face.
> Jerusalem, Jerusalem,
> May you welcome me!
> Jerusalem, Jerusalem,
> From your ruins I will rebuild you!
>
> From the summit of Mt. Scopus,
> Peace to you, Jerusalem!
> Thousands of exiles from every corner of the world
> Gaze their eyes upon you
> From a thousand benedictions you were blessed
> A temple of a king, a royal city
> Jerusalem, Jerusalem
> I'm not moving from here!
> Jerusalem, Jerusalem
> Let the messiah come!

מֵעַל פִּסְגַּת הַר הַצּוֹפִים
אֶשְׁתַּחֲוֶה לָךְ אַפַּיִם.
מֵעַל פִּסְגַּת הַר הַצּוֹפִים
שָׁלוֹם לָךְ, יְרוּשָׁלַיִם.
מֵאָה דוֹרוֹת חָלַמְתִּי עָלַיִךְ
לִזְכּוֹת, לִרְאוֹת בְּאוֹר פָּנַיִךְ.
יְרוּשָׁלַיִם, יְרוּשָׁלַיִם,
הָאִירִי פָּנַיִךְ לִבְנֵךְ!
יְרוּשָׁלַיִם, יְרוּשָׁלַיִם
מֵחָרְבוֹתַיִךְ אֶבְנֵךְ!

מֵעַל פִּסְגַּת הַר הַצּוֹפִים
שָׁלוֹם לָךְ, יְרוּשָׁלַיִם
אַלְפֵי גוֹלִים מִקְצוֹת כָּל תֵּבֵל
נוֹשְׂאִים אֵלַיִךְ עֵינַיִם
בְּאַלְפֵי בְּרָכוֹת הֱיִי בְּרוּכָה
מִקְדַּשׁ מֶלֶךְ, עִיר מְלוּכָה
יְרוּשָׁלַיִם, יְרוּשָׁלַיִם
אֲנִי לֹא אָזוּז מִפֹּה!
יְרוּשָׁלַיִם, יְרוּשָׁלַיִם
יָבוֹא הַמָּשִׁיחַ, יָבוֹא!

The lyrics begin with the singer addressing Jerusalem from an exilic position, founded in the dreams of "a hundred generations" (*me'a dorot*) who wished to rebuild the city, and they conclude with a jubilant celebration of the ingathering of exiles in the very place for which their ancestors longed. Notably, the use of apostrophe appears in the second line of every couplet. Aside from the titular line and the name Jerusalem, the lyrics are so filled with phrases such as "to you" (*lakh*), "of you" (*alaykh*), and suffixes indicating Jerusalem's possession of some bodily feature (*-aykh*), such as "your face" (*panaykh*), that the velar fricative *kh* produces a consistent consonance throughout the song, as I remembered when hearing David D'Or sing it in 2017. The lines with the doubled "Jerusalem, Jerusalem" (*Yerushalayim, Yerushalayim*) are a carry-over from Baruch Shafir's "Midnight" and have even served as an alternative title for "From the Summit of Mt. Scopus" throughout its near-century-long history.

To be sure, this is the literature of return, a metanarrative of Jewish history written by a migrant author who had moved within the Zionist circles of east central Europe before securing a pathway for migration to Palestine in the wake of the First World War and the political changes that it wrought on Jerusalem. Whereas Shafir's elderly man from "Midnight" dreamed of Jerusalem from afar, Hameiri's narrator is filtered through the color of exile as he gazes down on the actual Jerusalem from the summit of Mt. Scopus to the city's northeast. This is longing fulfilled by return, and the singer's prostrations testify to the gravity of this realization. The staging of "From the Summit of Mt. Scopus" at Hameiri's theater, the Kettle, emphasized this point:

> On the stage, displayed as a backdrop was a large painting of a pioneer standing on Mt. Scopus by moonlight and looking out to the walls of Jerusalem. When the actors sang the first verse, the stage was half dark, and with each additional verse the light grew stronger. By the end of the fourth verse the entire stage was flooded with light. (Hacohen 2018: 42)

This performance of longing for Jerusalem must be further contextualized within the development of the city around the time of the song's original composition and staging. The establishment of the Hebrew University on Mount Scopus was among the most significant achievements for the Zionist project in Jerusalem during the 1920s.[7] As the architectural historian Diana Dolev argues, this development was run through with Third Temple imagery, "with the Hebrew University being depicted as almost equivalent to the ancient Holy Temple placed in front of it" (Dolev 2016: 16). In fact, Mt. Scopus (Har ha-Tsofim) is so named because of its splendid vista of the Temple Mount/Noble Sanctuary complex in the Old City. Dolev concludes, "Through this symbolism the concept of the future Hebrew University and its location were rooted in the ancient heritage of the Hebrews and the site became a substitute sanctuary in a way" (Dolev 2016: 17). There is thus a sweet and poignant irony to Hameiri's placing of the song's narrator on Mt. Scopus as he longs for Jerusalem below, since for many Jews living in the Yishuv, the actual Mt. Scopus represented a fulfillment of the divine promise of Jerusalem's rebuilding. The same also has been true for later Jerusalemites. As the painter Menashe Kadishman (1932–2015) stated, "When you stand

---

[7] The first cornerstone was laid in 1918, but it was not until Albert Einstein's lecture on the theory of relativity there in 1923 and, finally, the official inauguration on August 1, 1925, that the dream of a Jewish institution of higher learning would be established in Palestine/Erets Israel (see Dolev 2016: 1–24).

on Mount Scopus and look out at Jerusalem on the one side and the Judean desert on the other—you feel that you are floating, you feel part of eternity" (Omer 1999: 214; cited in Omer-Sherman 2006: 223).

All of these expressions of longing are central to the reception and canonical interpretation of "From the Summit of Mt. Scopus." It is likely the main impetus behind the song's programming in the Jerusalem Day 2017 concert. But there is more to the story.

The concert was one of several musical events planned on Jerusalem Day. During the eve of Jerusalem Day (preceding the daytime observance of the holiday, in accordance with the Jewish calendar), some pubs hosted intimate concerts by local musicians performing Jerusalem songs, which ranged from those composed in modern Israel to settings of older poems about Jerusalem written in diaspora, while others simply continued their normal programming of rock, jazz, or other genres, and concerts that were nominally unmarked by Jerusalem Day spilled into the commemorative soundscape. Other events featured music having no direct associations with Jerusalem, and instead music served the purpose of festivity itself, as in a booth set up in the middle of Ben Yehuda Street, one of the main pedestrian thoroughfares in City Center, where DJs blared electronic dance music tracks late into the night for passersby and spontaneous dancers, and buskers competed with the amplified sounds with their acoustic instruments.

Official musical events enjoyed the largest degree of public participation. The "White Night" concert was geared toward projecting the state's largesse loudly and brightly into Jerusalem's night sky—in much the same way as other Jerusalem Day events, such as the famed light show that projected symbols of the Israeli state (the blue and white flag and star of David) onto the nearby Old City walls as fireworks exploded overhead and Naomi Shemer's "Jerusalem of Gold" played through a battalion of loudspeakers.

At the concert, a large video screen depicted a carefully curated image of Jerusalem as a culturally heterogeneous city, with footage of Jews across denominations and a few conspicuous images of hijab-clad Muslim women, in a display of neoliberal multiculturalism that served the ends of government public relations during an event that brought a sizable contingent of international visitors. Naturally, the event included speeches from politicians who echoed this measure, such as city councilperson Ofer Berkovitch, who was in the middle of a meteoric rise in Jerusalemite politics that ended in an unsuccessful mayoral run in 2018. Berkovitch asked the assembled audience to focus not only on Jerusalem's antiquity and past traumas but also on "Jerusalem of the Future" (Yerushalayim shel Atid), as a site of technological advancement and neoliberal expansion. This mixed appeal to the past and present in service of a particular political project, so characteristic of top-down modeling of Jerusalem's cultural geography, would carry through the musical performances themselves.

Much of Hameiri's output during the time when he wrote "From the Summit of Mt. Scopus"—which, again, was originally performed at the Kettle Theater—focused on satirizing every aspect of the Jewish settlement enterprise in Palestine. This was not meant as opposition to the Zionist cause, for even his satires were not "uttered in pessimistic hatred and out of despair, but rather were directed by an optimistic point of view which believed in healing vices" (Alexander 1998: 167). "From the Summit of Mt. Scopus" reflected this balance between Hameiri's satirical bite and his sincere commitment to the Zionist cause. The original version included not only the verses discussed previously but also two middle verses that departed in striking ways from the tone of the first and last verses:

> With a faithful heart, I came here
> to build your wreckage.
> But how will I build your Temple
> if there is no peace between your sons?
> Sephardim, Ashkenazim, Yemenites, Falashas,
> Urfans, Georgians, Haredis, and others.[8]
> Jerusalem, Jerusalem
> I didn't envision this in the dream!
> Jerusalem, Jerusalem,
> between your children I bestow peace!
>
> You became an unwalled city, my Holy,
> each of your bolts became broken.

---

[8] Falashas (from the previous line) are Beta Israel (Ethiopian Jews); Urfans are Jews from the Turkish city of Urfa. For Georgian Jews, Hameiri uses the antiquated term *Gurjim* (*Gruzinim* would be the contemporary usage). Finally, I have translated the word *Ḥafsim* as "others" rather than "free ones," because in context it seems to indicate those who do not belong to the named groups; alternatively, the term might be understood to refer to secular Jews, but this would not be in keeping with the listing of ethnic groups—except, perhaps, as a contrast to *Haredim* just before it, meaning that both Haredis and secular Jews would represent Ashkenazis here.

But one of your gates remained close;
this is the Messiah's gate.
A great many of your sons summoned me to you,
Jerusalem, Jerusalem.
I vowed in the name of the Lord:
Jerusalem, Jerusalem,
may you welcome me.

בְּלֵב בּוֹטֵחַ בָּאתִי הֲלוֹם
הָקִים אֶת הֲרִיסוֹתַיִךְ
אַךְ אֵיךְ אֶבְנֶה אֶת בֵּית מִקְדָּשֵׁךְ
אִם אֵין שָׁלוֹם בֵּין בָּנַיִךְ?
סְפָרַדִּים, אַשְׁכְּנַזִּים, תֵּימָנִים, פָּלְשִׁים
אוּרְפָלִים וְגוּרְגִ'ים וַחֲרֵדִים וְחָפְשִׁים
יְרוּשָׁלַיִם, יְרוּשָׁלַיִם
לֹא זֹאת חָזִיתִי בַּחֲלוֹם!
יְרוּשָׁלַיִם, יְרוּשָׁלַיִם
בֵּין בָּנַיִךְ הַשְׁרִי נָא שָׁלוֹם!

עִיר-פְּרָזוֹת הָיִית עִיר קָדְשִׁי
נִשְׁבַּר בָּךְ כָּל בְּרִיחַ
אַךְ עוֹד נִשְׁאַר בָּךְ שַׁעַר סָגוּר,
זֶה שַׁעַר הַמָּשִׁיחַ.
רִבְבוֹת בָּנַיִךְ שְׁלָחוּנִי אֵלַיִךְ
לִמְסֹר לְיָדִי אֶת מַפְתְּחוֹתַיִךְ.
יְרוּשָׁלַיִם, יְרוּשָׁלַיִם
נִשְׁבַּעְתִּי בְּשֵׁם אֲדֹנָי:
יְרוּשָׁלַיִם, יְרוּשָׁלַיִם
הָאִירִי פָּנַיִךְ אֵלַי

In these lines, Hameiri focused on the "inter-ethnic hostility that prevailed in Jerusalem's neighborhoods" (Eliram 2008/9: 1), calling out various Jewish communities by name and indicating his disappointment to find such discord: "I didn't envision this in the dream [of returning to Jerusalem]!" In the third verse, Hameiri locates these social problems in the city's metaphorical character, suggesting that Jerusalem's messianic value could only be realized once all of God's children achieved peace with one another. This sentiment still resonates in the present, as intra-Jewish and international social discord reign:

Jerusalem Day is a holiday most strongly associated with religious nationalist groups who support rightwing parties such as Likud and the Jewish Home (Ha-Bayit ha-Yehudi). *Large groups, primarily men and young boys who study at* yeshivot *(religious schools) in the occupied West Bank, gathered around the Old City to chant songs attesting to the might and permanence of Jewish rule over the city, then loudly processed through the Old City's Damascus Gate and through the Muslim Quarter, where on any other day of the year it would have been uncommon to see large groups of Jews wearing markers of religious observance such as* kippot *(head coverings, also known as* yarmulkes) *and* tsitsit *(ritual fringes). For the participants these actions represent "a celebration of spatial dominance and control" (Shlay and Rosen 2015: 30). Such processions are often meant to instigate violent clashes with Palestinian residents of the Old City. As an explicit act of aggression occurring at the flashpoint of Israeli-Palestinian relations, Jerusalem Day is controversial among Israeli Jews themselves, many of whom refuse to take part in the festivities because of how religious-nationalist* (dati-le'umi) *groups have co-opted the meaning and intent of the day's observance for the purpose of enacting political violence onto an already-subjugated people.*

Other events marking "Jerusalem Day" were less overtly violent in subjective terms—that is, with clearly identifiable agents perpetrating acts of violence—but they expressed the objective, systemic violence of occupation through the projection of Israel's power in Jerusalem through sound (see Žižek 2008). These events were not intended as expressions of objective violence; they were intended to be opportunities for religious-nationalist Jews to celebrate and reflect on the achievements of the Israeli state. But they were perceived as such by both Israeli and Palestinian critics of the occupation.

It is worth noting that the only other notable popular song explicitly concerning Jerusalem during the 1920s, Emmanuel Harussi's "Grandfather's Gifts" (*Tishrey Saba*)—which, to be sure, did not enjoy nearly the same cultural status as "From the Summit of Mt. Scopus" in subsequent years—takes a similar approach to satirizing social life in Jerusalem.[9] The lyrics for that

---

[9] In addition to lyrical content, discussed in subsequent sentences, "From the Summit of Mt. Scopus" and "Grandfather's Gifts" share some other similar qualities. Both used preexisting "folk" tunes for melodic inspiration ("Grandfather's Gifts" is based on a Hassidic tune), and both were associated with the emergence of satirical theater; Emmanuel Harussi would become the house pianist for the Broom Theater (*Ha-Matate*), which opened two years after the Kettle in 1929).

song focus on the unemployment crisis of the time, during which labor-
ers "settle for two working days per week," according to the song (Hacohen
2018: 43). The refrain invokes a timeworn form of addressing Jerusalem in
the second person, placing the city in a position of agency, before lamenting
the lack of work:

> Jerusalem, Holy City,
> Why, oh why
> This month why didn't you give me
> Two days out of the week?

יְרוּשָׁלַיִם עִיר הַקֹּדֶשׁ
לָמָה וּמַדּוּעַ
לֹא נָתַתְּ לִי בָּזֶה הַחֹדֶשׁ
יוֹמַיִם בַּשָּׁבוּעַ?

All in all, it seems that songwriters paying musical tribute to Jerusalem in the
early decades of the twentieth century were much more interested in cap-
turing the difficulties, and not only the glories, of Zionist settlement than
would be many later performers of their music.

Although the middle verses of "From the Summit of Mt. Scopus" were
part of the song's original performance, they were virtually never performed
in recorded versions of the song, which proliferated primarily during the
early decades of Israeli statehood (late 1940s–1960s). As I note in the next
chapter, Jerusalem song was a fairly dormant musical field in the Yishuv
(1880s–1948) and pre-1967 Israel, with a few notable exceptions. During
the period between the 1948 War, when the state was founded, and the 1967
War, when Israel unified/occupied Jerusalem, there were virtually no newly
composed songs of any cultural significance about the city. There were
songs written about specific sites in and around Jerusalem, particularly sites
of war, as I discuss in Chapter 3, but the trope of longing for Jerusalem—so
characteristic of diaspora poetics—all but vanished from Israeli songcraft
during that period.

At the same time, during the 1950s, 1960s, and early 1970s, "From the
Summit of Mt. Scopus" entered its greatest period of popularity, becoming
a favorite evergreen of Yishuv-era songwriting. It was recorded several times
over by musicians across a range of musical disciplines, such as Yehoram
Gaon, Nechama Hendel, Karel Salmon, Hadassah Sigalov, Moshe Silberman,

and others. Being that the song's original musical arrangement was rooted in a transnational European aria tradition, most of those recordings feature a spare accompaniment by a piano or light orchestration, in order to showcase an operatically inflected voice. Yehoram Gaon (1939–), the singer most strongly associated with the song through his many versions over the past six decades—most especially the one on his 1971 album *I Was Born in Jerusalem* (*Ani Yerushalmi*)—departs from these conventions, using his flat, crooning voice and contemporary stylistic conventions to effectively transform the song into a pop standard, and a culturally significant one at that.

"From the Summit of Mt. Scopus" took on a new valence as the material space of Jerusalem once again became a metaphorical vision—of a dream lost—after the city's division resulting from the 1948 War. Gazing on Jerusalem from such close proximity, rather than from afar, transformed into a painful experience. Of course, during the 1948–1967 period it would have been difficult to actually gaze on the Old City from the vantage point of Mt. Scopus itself, since it was an island of Israeli-controlled territory surrounded by Jordanian East Jerusalem. But Gaon and other musicians would use the opportunity to remake this song as an expression of longing for a vision of the city before it was divided as a result of the 1948 War.

At the point at which "From the Summit of Mt. Scopus" accumulated these associations with the political realities of the divided city, by far the most commonly performed verse was the opening one, which was sometimes followed by the final, fourth verse on a smaller number of recordings. As the song joined the canon of Israel song, therefore, musicians highlighted the poetics of longing, and occasionally "resolved" the crisis of exile through the jubilant final verse. Lost in these renditions was Hameiri's nuanced treatment of Jerusalem's social problems and the difficulties involved in Zionist settlement of the city.

The accrued meanings of "From the Summit of Mt. Scopus" served as the vehicle for the Jerusalem Day 2017 performance by David D'Or and the Jerusalem Symphony Orchestra in Safra Square that I attended:

> *The 2017 arrangement preserved the homophonic texture of the reference recordings that maintained the primacy of the voice, but it also took on the song's soaring melodies within the accompaniment, lending a grandiose, "official" feel to the otherwise intimate song. David D'Or, who like many other Israeli musicians rose to new heights of stardom after his 2004 appearance in the Eurovision Song Contest,[10] gave a polished performance with extensive*

---

[10] D'Or placed fifth in the semifinal with a Hebrew-English bilingual song that he cowrote with the late songwriter Ehud Manor, "To Believe" (*Leha'amin*).

use of a number of vocal gestures meant to enliven the text, such as a judi-
cious use of breathy timbre and rubato; he savored each word and syllable in
order to highlight the poem's layers of exile. The performance included both
the first and final verses, with a brief instrumental interlude between them,
but no middle verses. By the final four lines—"Jerusalem, Jerusalem / I'm not
moving from here! / Jerusalem, Jerusalem / Let the messiah come!"—the ma-
jority of people in the audience were singing along loudly with him, standing
on their feet with arms raised to the sky, to the point where D'Or stopped
singing twice to affirm and encourage their participation, as they declared
in song their resolution to maintain a Jewish presence in Jerusalem until the
end of days.[11]

The Binary Condition of Musical Jerusalem

Within Israeli national culture, modern Jerusalem was forged in an encounter between two cities: one metaphorical and one material. Traditionally,
Jerusalem's duality has been represented in Jewish thought as heavenly
and earthly, rendered in Hebrew by the respective phrases *Yerushalayim*
shel Ma'ala (heavenly/celestial Jerusalem; lit. Jerusalem of above) and
Yerushalayim shel Mata (earthly/terrestrial Jerusalem; lit. Jerusalem of
below). In the diasporic context, heavenly Jerusalem took on many different
metaphorical forms, comprising the sacred visions, dreams, and fantasies
of Jerusalem's onlookers—much like the main character in Baruch Shafir's
"Midnight." This metaphorical city was the object of longing in the long history of exilic Jewish cultural production. Writing about Jerusalem's suspen-
sion between metaphorical and material states, Hebrew literary scholar Sidra
Dekoven Ezrahi argues,

This process is facilitated by a radical and sustained poetic conceit. For
some two thousand years after the second destruction in 70 CE, in the
absence of a temple, a republic, or any form of territorial or political sovereignty and at variable distances from the ruined shrine [Temple of
Jerusalem], Jewish poets managed to preserve Jerusalem in its symbolic
state. (Ezrahi 2007: 223)

[11] A photograph of this moment serves as the book's cover image.

Given this symbolic status, liturgical, musical, and literary renderings of Jerusalem had little need to keep fidelity to the terrestrial city, which continued to function as a home to several communities who were situated in a built environment with unique sounds, sights, and odors and the dynamics of urban life that characterized it as a city of polyrhythmic difference. Ezrahi characterizes the special temporality of this metaphorical space as "the prolonged meantime between destruction and redemption" (2007: 223–24). It is the aestheticization of this "meantime" that I discuss here.

Metaphorical and material Jerusalems often exist in a binary construction—one longed-for from afar and one realized in the actual cityspace—but in reality, the two are much more intertwined. A visual testament to this intertwinement illustrates the point well. At the entrance to Safra Square, one of the main sites of public music-making where I would attend numerous events throughout my research in Jerusalem, stands a curious map of the world, rendered in brightly colored ceramic tiles against a backdrop of pale limestone.[12]

This map, created in 2008 by local Armenian ceramics master Arman Darian, is a reproduction of a famous 1581 woodcut by the Hannover-based artist Heinrich Bünting (1545–1606). The map depicts a relational geography (see Figure 1.1).[13] Shown here as a metaphorical clover, the world springs forth from Jerusalem. The woodcut original, writes Tanya Sermer, "artistically emphasizes Jerusalem's place at the geographical crossroads of the three continents and the central spiritual place that the city holds" (Sermer 2015: 35). The placement of this tile reproduction in modern Jerusalem promotes the city's popular status as the origin of civilization, as the concept around which diasporas form, and as the center of the religious imaginaries and colonial ambitions of multiple polities (Benvenisti 1998; Klein 2001; Goldhill 2008). The municipality's celebratory orientation toward the city's centrality affirms a narrative continuity between a foreign gaze on Jerusalem, which placed the city at the center of the world, and the everyday political machinery of the modern Israeli city, which places centralizing representations of itself at its own center. Various metaphorical Jerusalems are re-centered in the material cityspace of modern Jerusalem.

---

[12] Safra Square is also an important field site for Tanya Sermer's ethnography of music and politics in Jerusalem (see Sermer 2015: 65–68).

[13] For more on the development of Armenian ceramics in Jerusalem, and the artform's importance to the Old City's modern visual culture, see Sato Moughalian's biography of the artist David Ohannessian (Moughalian 2019).

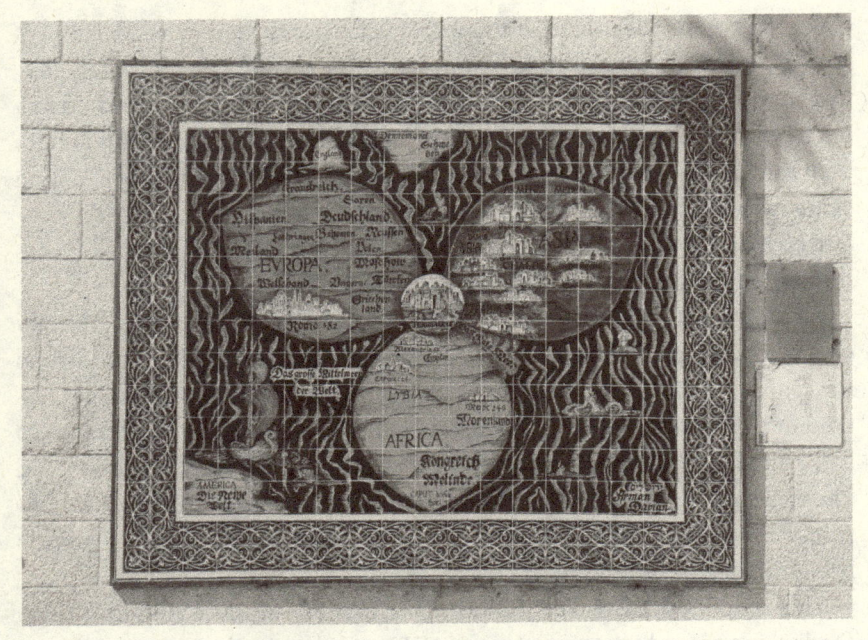

Figure 1.1 Tile reproduction of Heinrich Bünting by Arman Darian, *Die Welt als Kleeblatt*, woodcut (1581). Photograph by author, September 9, 2018.

Examining the city's built environment can help explain not only the relation between the present and its pasts but also the relation between symbolic representation *about* Jerusalem and symbolic representation *in* Jerusalem, as I discussed in the urban development of Mt. Scopus around the time of Avigdor Hameiri's staging of "From the Summit of Mt. Scopus" at the Kettle Theater in 1929. The city is built on a projective geography, developed in accordance with the religious, literary, and musical projections of space that have shaped both indigenous and foreign political imaginaries; at the same time, Jerusalem's geography is projective in the sense that disparate cultural practices, including music, synthesize a geographical project in service of de-territorializing and re-territorializing the city according to the needs of its current ruling power, the State of Israel. In modernity, metaphorical and material Jerusalems are, in effect, coextensive: one cannot be known outside of its relation to the other.

The built environment of the material city flattens millennia, along with opposing religious and national versions of that history, into impossible adjacencies that are nevertheless experienceable in simultaneity—especially through sound, as Abigail Wood has demonstrated (Wood 2013a, 2013b, 2014). At the conclusion of one her essays on "disruptive listening" in Jerusalem, Wood writes, "Sounds serve as a site of agency in shaping and interpreting shared spaces, and in articulating everyday life, both reinforcing and undermining ingrained narratives of conflict and structures of violence and power" (Wood 2013b: 305). There and elsewhere, Wood accomplishes this through listening to the sounds of pilgrimages by Latin and Orthodox Christians, the cyclical soundings of religious time (e.g., the five daily prayer calls for Muslims, church bells heralding the start of Christian services, sirens marking the end of the Jewish high holidays), the internal soundscapes and external soundings of permanent religious spaces (e.g., the Church of the Holy Sepulchre, various other churches, and mosques), Palestinian children's play, Israeli and Palestinian cultural festivals, and other sources. Such disruptive listening reveals how, as she writes in a different essay, "the mixing of sounds emanating from visually and topographically distinct sources textures the experience of time" (Wood 2014: 289). Of particular value is Wood's focused attention on the mundane and its interaction with (or disruption of) the sacred, the political, and other sites of ideological narration.

In attending to the intersection of the celestial and the terrestrial, and the metaphorical and material, I profit greatly from Wood's insights, transferring them to my study not of sound in Jerusalem but rather of Jerusalem in music. I remain mindful of the fact that musical representations of Jerusalem impose an epistemological proscription on the lived city, for the superimposition of metaphorical Jerusalem's symbolic content onto the actual, heterogeneous material space of Jerusalem forecloses the possibility of "authentic" knowledge of the city outside of its modes of representation.[14] The encounter between metaphorical and material Jerusalems is thus made possible by virtue of the poetic strategies that characterize representations of the city within shifting Zionist frameworks, most especially those served by music. Just as architectural historians have shown in studies of city planning and building aesthetics (e.g., Nitzan-Shiftan 2007, 2017), in Israeli musical life people reworked exilic expressions of longing for Jerusalem, projecting the city's pasts into modernity in service to contemporary political projects through composition and performance.

---

[14] See the Introduction for a discussion of how coming to terms with this foreclosure affects the methodology employed in this book.

In the context of modern Hebrew literary culture, Dan Miron articulates the city's poetic status in what he calls "the binary condition of literary Jerusalem" (2010: 359): the various conceptual dualities present in Jerusalem literature "that produce in the reader a feeling of being 'torn'" (361). In engaging with Miron, Shai Ginsburg writes, "the structure that governs the manifold appearances of Jerusalem in Hebrew literature is that of an unresolved conflict, an unending struggle" (Ginsburg 2014: 149). The sheer abundance of literary and musical examples of this phenomenon present a challenge to critical scholarship on the city, for as Ginsburg reminds his readers, "Jerusalem seems to set critics between a rock and a hard place: it forces on them two alternatives that render their discourse trivial and banal" (Ginsburg 2014: 146). What to do? Miron chooses to concentrate on the confrontation of metaphoric, idealistic representations of Jerusalem with metonymic, realistic takes on the city's material spaces, moving from the nineteenth-century Zionist context into the mature Israeli national culture of the 1970s with hermeneutic breadth and precision. As Ginsburg shows, however, Jerusalem's binarisms have long been a structuring principle of investigations into Jerusalem's place within modern Hebrew literature (Ginsburg 2014: 147–48).[15] For his part, he makes a compelling case for *close reading*, arguing that it would "impart the unique contribution literary analysis may have for a multi-disciplinary intellectual project"—referring there to the volume in which the essay appeared—adding:

> For close reading puts into relief the inherent indeterminacy that haunts Jerusalem as a topos—not only as a literary topos, but also as a historical, a political, a religious, and a social topos—an indeterminacy that challenges the endeavors to account for it critically. Whereas this indeterminacy is commonly glossed over or even suppressed for the sake of a clear and decisive presentation . . . close reading explores it and its consequences for our conceptualization of the subject matter. (Ginsburg 2014: 144)

---

[15] He synthesizes a large number of studies that employ binarism to varying degrees (see, among several others, Ben-Porat 1987; Holtzman 1994, 2003; Ezrahi 2007).

My approach in this book takes Ginsburg's methodological remit seriously, while examining the songs subject to close analysis through a genealogy of their intertexts, metaphors, melodies, and versions.

Like the earlier extended analysis of "From the Summit of Mt. Scopus," as this chapter continues I show how Jewish and Israeli musicians inherited, and perpetuated, a diverse symbolic lexicon through which to represent the city, by examining the intertexts that modern Jerusalem songs form with diasporic expressions of exile that have undergone renovation and renewal in the context of Zionist cultural production writ large. A poetics of longing thus serves to articulate a politics of attachment.

The content of this book is therefore not an overview of historical process, "a clear and decisive presentation," but rather an overview of several discursive patterns in the representation of metaphorical Jerusalem in an interconnected set of texts (religious, poetic, and musical). In analyzing the musical intertexts that songs form in this composite discourse, I consider not only the meanings of words but also their musical transformations, in order to understand the lexicon of metaphors, symbols, voices, and gestures on which musicians and poets draw. The structure of the current chapter, as is already evident, reflects the city's projective geography, with discussions of older repertory extending into discussions of their intertextual lives in modernity (and in some cases within the ethnographic present), resulting in some jumps in the chronological presentation of materials. I have already begun with an analysis of the first modern Jerusalem song, Avigdor Hameiri's "From the Summit of Mt. Scopus" (1929), using its genealogy to introduce some of the discursive parameters of the genre more generally. From here, I pick up the discussion through an examination of that song's main inspiration and perhaps the most widely known and cited attestation of Jewish longing for Jerusalem, Psalm 137. I interrogate one of the psalm's central literary devices, apostrophe, and its use in anthropomorphizing the city—an important characteristic of Jerusalem song more generally. In the latter half of the chapter, I turn to another poetic wellspring for the poetics of longing in modern Jerusalem song, the twelfth-century Andalusian poet Yehuda Halevi, through an examination of how Israeli musical settings of Halevi's poetry contributed to, and nuanced, his elevation as a "Zionist" figure in the twentieth century. The conclusion serves as a brief meditation on the meaning of metaphor in the context of material Jerusalem, bringing the city's ontological binarism back into focus.

Psalm 137 and Anthropomorphic Apostrophe

The case of "From the Summit of Mt. Scopus" shows how a genealogical treatment of a song's lyrics, musical aspects, and cultural associations can reveal the complex place of song within the evolving contingencies of historical process—especially as that process plays out in a contested city with long-standing connections to religious and national identity. Avigdor Hameiri's song, and to a lesser extent Emmanuel Harussi's "Grandfather's Gifts," effectively initiated the practice of invoking the poetics of longing for Jerusalem within popular song as it developed in the Zionist society of Palestine. But while such songs served specific functions within that context (e.g., for socialization or for satire), it is critical to understand how songwriters explicitly, and self-consciously, rooted their expressions in an inherited repertory of symbols, phrases (both lyrical and melodic), and citations developed in the context of diaspora—even when those songwriters participated in the negation of diaspora, in keeping with the Hebrewism of the Yishuv and early statehood eras.

Psalmody looms large in the genealogy of "From the Summit of Mt. Scopus" and other Jerusalem songs, with Psalm 137 enjoying greatest pride-of-place in modern citational practices. The text, as literary scholar David Stowe writes, is "poetic catnip, a siren song luring musicians and composers" (Stowe 2016: i):

> By the rivers of Babylon, there we sat down, yea, we wept, when we
>   remembered Zion.
> Upon the willows in the midst thereof we hanged up our harps.
> For there they that led us captive asked of us words of song, and our tor-
>   mentors asked of us mirth: "Sing us one of the songs of Zion."
> How shall we sing the Lord's song in a foreign land?
> If I forget thee, O Jerusalem, let my right hand forget her cunning.
> Let my tongue cleave to the roof of my mouth, if I remember thee not; if
>   I set not Jerusalem above my chiefest joy.
> Remember, O Lord, against the children of Edom the day of Jerusalem;
>   who said: "Rase it, rase it, even to the foundation thereof."
> O daughter of Babylon, that art to be destroyed; happy shall he be, that
>   repayeth thee as thou hast served us.
> Happy shall he be, that taketh and dasheth thy little ones against the
>   rock.[16]

[16] This translation appears in the Jewish Publication Society Hebrew-English *Tanakh*.

עַל נַהֲרוֹת, בָּבֶל—שָׁם יָשַׁבְנוּ, גַּם-בָּכִינוּ:בְּזָכְרֵנוּ, אֶת-צִיּוֹן.
עַל-עֲרָבִים בְּתוֹכָהּ—תָּלִינוּ, כִּנֹּרוֹתֵינוּ.
כִּי שָׁם שְׁאֵלוּנוּ שׁוֹבֵינוּ, דִּבְרֵי-שִׁיר—וְתוֹלָלֵינוּ שִׂמְחָה: שִׁירוּ לָנוּ, מִשִּׁיר צִיּוֹן.
אֵיךְ—נָשִׁיר אֶת-שִׁיר-יְהוָה: עַל, אַדְמַת נֵכָר.
אִם-אֶשְׁכָּחֵךְ יְרוּשָׁלִָם—תִּשְׁכַּח יְמִינִי.
תִּדְבַּק-לְשׁוֹנִי, לְחִכִּי—אִם-לֹא אֶזְכְּרֵכִי: אִם-לֹא אַעֲלֶה, אֶת-יְרוּשָׁלִַם עַל רֹאשׁ שִׂמְחָתִי.
זְכֹר יְהוָה—לִבְנֵי אֱדוֹם אֵת יוֹם יְרוּשָׁלִָם הָאֹמְרִים עָרוּ—עָרוּ עַד הַיְסוֹד בָּהּ:
בַּת-בָּבֶל הַשְּׁדוּדָה אַשְׁרֵי שֶׁיְשַׁלֶּם-לָךְ אֶת-גְּמוּלֵךְ שֶׁגָּמַלְתְּ לָנוּ:
אַשְׁרֵי—שֶׁיֹּאחֵז וְנִפֵּץ אֶת-עֹלָלַיִךְ אֶל-הַסָּלַע:

Psalm 137 has been a popular subject for musical setting, or else for intertextual play, in the history of Jewish cultural production across geographical and historical expanses, including for multiple Zionist expressions during the long twentieth century in Palestine and beyond. Stowe notes that the psalm, like the great majority of the Hebrew Bible, was written in the context of exile (or else shortly thereafter). He associates the first four verses of the psalm with *history*, standing in a tripartite relation with *memory* (verses 5–6) and *forgetting* (verses 7–9), according to the categories set forth in Paul Ricoeur's philosophical magnum opus *Memory, History, Forgetting* (2004).[17] But Stowe also associates them with music, as he notes that those first four verses "have generated by far the most musical settings" on a global scale (xi). As "poetic catnip," the verses not only provide lyrical material for a litany of songwriters, but they also identify Jerusalem song itself as a genre, and one that—like the very text in which it appears—is crystallized in the context of exile.[18]

During the Babylonian captivity (c. sixth century BCE), according to the text, Jews were compelled by their "tormentors" to entertain them with a "Song of Zion" (*Shir Tsiyon*) after having expressed no desire to make music ("hanged up our harps"; *talinu kinnoroteynu*), owing to their exile from Jerusalem. To be sure, forced singing has been a common tactic employed by dominators and enslavers across the globe, but in the context of the next great Jewish exile—the one spanning late antiquity until the project of Jewish modernity that culminated in the founding of the State of Israel in 1948, according to Zionist historical narratives—Jews would

---

[17] I discuss Ricoeur's text in more detail near the end of Chapter 2.
[18] For a thorough synthesis of the historical discourse on the conditions and circumstances of the exile, see Stowe (2016: 1–14).

in fact sing often and of their own accord about Jerusalem, even if in many of the settings in which Jews found themselves the grief of exile left little to inspire song.

References to Psalm 137 will recur throughout this book, but its inclusion here as a fundamental text of Jewish belief and practice is meant to emphasize that nearly every aspect of Jewish ritual life, across traditions, sociocultural settings, and varying degrees of observance, from South Asia to the Americas, and during the whole history of rabbinical Judaism from late antiquity to the time of writing, has involved explicit reference to the destruction of Jerusalem and the promise of its reconstitution, in a consistently performed attachment to Jerusalem as the center of Judaism and as a perceived homeland. Its ubiquitous presence within Jewish social life is perhaps best embodied by its recitation by grooms during the climactic moment of every Jewish wedding (regardless of the families' levels of religiosity) just before the iconic breaking of the glass—itself a commemorative act reminding those present to remember the destruction of the Temple of Jerusalem. The great majority of people who have partaken in these invocations of Jerusalem, whether in prayers, table songs, or in various other forms of liturgical, paraliturgical, and folk practices, had no direct exposure to the actual city of Jerusalem; they sung from afar, with no pretense of bodily return to the land where the ancient Israelites once flourished—and perished—as a more-or-less intact sociopolitical entity.

With the advent of Zionism, the concerted program of immigration to Palestine, and the flourishing of a musical culture there, Jewish songwriters turned to Psalm 137 as an intertextual and symbolic resource. The House of Hebrew Song (*Bayit La-Zemer Ivri*), a digital archive of musical recordings made in Israel and Yishuv-era Palestine, lists twenty-one entries for songs recorded between 1930 and 2017 that quote the psalm's opening words, "By the rivers of Babylon" (*Al Naharot Bavel*), or else use them in the title. Sixteen entries quote the end of the third verse, "Sing us one of the songs of Zion" (*Shiru Lanu mi-Shir Tsiyon*), and sixteen quote the fourth verse, "How shall we sing the Lord's song in a foreign land?" (*Eykh nashir et Shir Adonai al Admat Nekhar*). A whopping twenty-six entries quote the famous fifth verse, "If I forget thee, Jerusalem" (*Im eshkaḥekh Yerushalayim*). There is naturally some overlap in all of these results, since some songs quote the original verses at length, but the point is that quotation of Psalm 137 has been widespread in Hebrew song.

Assaf Shelleg discusses the psalm's interpolation in Israeli art music, in the context of Mordechai Seter's 1966 *Jerusalem* (for eight-part chorus with brass and strings), arguing "Seter's compilation [of texts from the Psalms as well as Lamentations and Isaiah] forged a bold teleological narrative etched in biblocentrism and in accordance with his perception of the Bible as a national myth and a collectivist ethos" (Shelleg 2019: 261). This perception of the Bible characterized its general presence in non-religious music, dating to the early development of compositional procedures for concert music and *Shirey Erets Israel* alike. As linguist Yael Reshef argues, biblical references were thoroughly integrated into Yishuv-era songcraft, "either in verbatim quotations or in paraphrases." She continues, "While a strong biblical influence marked the period's written language in general, its impact on the folksong [*Shirey Erets Israel*] was particularly notable, reflecting the folksong's function as secular liturgy" (Reshef 2012: 163; see also Reshef 2001, 2004).[19] As Shelleg points out, prior to the mid-1960s music had been part of the Hebrewism that "promoted territorial nationalism through a bibliocentric discourse and exotic imagery," channeled into a language of return (Shelleg 2019: 255).

The city rendered through such music was metaphorical Jerusalem— a symbol of redemption after the traumatic loss of the Temple in 70 CE. Metaphorical Jerusalem always has been associated with exile and the endlessly deferred restoration of the Temple, and it also has been a rich site of intertextual play that gives rise to new meanings as Jews' religious and political lives became more and more diverse. In the east central European Jewish context, even long before the advent of Zionism after *Haskalah* (the Jewish Enlightenment), Philip V. Bohlman argues,

> The symbolic connections of Jewish ritual and the performance of metaphors of return to Jerusalem invested the journey across the Mediterranean with an everyday presence, while the great difficulty of return intensified the sense of its timelessness. . . . The journey across the Mediterranean takes place only in ritual time, with historical time being deferred to the future. (Bohlman 2008: 40)

---

[19] Here, Reshef is synthesizing the insights of her much longer 2004 study, in which she systematically analyzed the texts of 450 Hebrew songs.

Momentarily putting aside the specific meanings of the Mediterranean in this context, it is important to examine the value of metaphorical Jerusalem within modern Jerusalem, where the "performance of metaphors of return" take place *in* historical time, after the point of actual return to the material city, as in the genesis and reception of "From the Summit of Mt. Scopus." In a manner of speaking, this is to suggest that the city's exilic state is a quality created by the *commemoration* of metaphors of return, beginning with Psalm 137. Such commemoration is rendered through musical (and nonmusical) expressions of longing for metaphorical Jerusalem that play on the symbols of the exilic imagination within Zionist cultural production.

An important poetic technique for commemorating these metaphors of return is through characterizations of Jerusalem as embodying human traits. Recall the opening verse of "From the Summit of Mt. Scopus":

From the summit of Mt. Scopus
I will bow down **to you**
From the summit of Mt. Scopus
Peace **to you**, Jerusalem!
For a hundred generations I dreamt **of you**
To cry, to see the light of **your face**.
Jerusalem, Jerusalem,
May **you** welcome me!
Jerusalem, Jerusalem,
From your ruins I will **rebuild you**!

מֵעַל פִּסְגַּת הַר הַצּוֹפִים
אֶשְׁתַּחֲוֶה לָךְ אַפַּיִם.
מֵעַל פִּסְגַּת הַר הַצּוֹפִים
שָׁלוֹם לָךְ, יְרוּשָׁלַיִם.
מֵאָה דוֹרוֹת חָלַמְתִּי עָלַיִךְ
לִזְכּוֹת, לִרְאוֹת בְּאוֹר פָּנַיִךְ.
יְרוּשָׁלַיִם, יְרוּשָׁלַיִם,
הָאִירִי פָּנַיִךְ לִבְנֵךְ!
יְרוּשָׁלַיִם, יְרוּשָׁלַיִם,
מֵחָרְבוֹתַיִךְ אֶבְנֵךְ!

In these lyrics, moments of apostrophe and anthropomorphism appear in bold. One might understand such poetic maneuvers as an incarnated form of the metaphor/material binary described earlier. Musicians and poets have depicted Jerusalem in human, quasi-human, and super-human (godlike) forms since the earliest writings paying tribute to the city. Anthropomorphism is endemic to monotheistic religion; Jews, Muslims, and Christians imbue the deity with human characteristics as a matter of course. But the poetic incarnation of Jerusalem within Jewish cultural production contradicts paradigmatic understandings of anthropomorphism in psychology and anthropology, which typically recognize such gestures as a "cognitive mechanism of elicited agent knowledge," meaning that anthropomorphism is a method for making sense of the inanimate world by animating it—rendering it metaphori-cally human—possibly for the sake of interacting with it (Epley, Waytz, and Cacioppo 2007: 866). I would argue that the anthropomorphism of *space*, being an inanimate object only in a strictly material sense, works somewhat differently (Gregory 1997; Harvey 2006: 117–48; Lefebvre 1991, 2004). The interactions described in such anthropomorphiza-tions are usually metaphorical, serving as an immaterial domain of spa-tial knowledge similar to what David Harvey describes as a "space of representation": "the lived space of sensations, the imagination, emo-tions, and meanings incorporated into how we live everyday" (Harvey 2006: 130).

Although Jerusalem is anthropomorphized via several kinds of poetic devices, by far the most common technique has been *apostrophe*, a speech act that imbues the city, via poetic address in the grammar of the second person, with the agency of listenership. The city bears witness to the in-vocation. Every other line of "From the Summit of Mt. Scopus" uses this device, via the repeated appearance of the second-person possessive. Formulas such as "O, Jerusalem," "for thee, Jerusalem," and other forms of calling out to the listening city are ubiquitous in the *longue durée* of Jewish cultural production. In such expressions, the city is not treated as an *object* but rather as a *subject*. Apostrophe, furthermore, is always a sonic phenom-enon, as the poet uses their voice to beckon the inanimate object into an intersubjective space.

The most iconic example of apostrophic anthropomorphism occurs in the fifth and sixth verses of Psalm 137. The verses mark a moment in the psalm when Jerusalem transitions from the third person to the second person, and therefore from an object to a subject. The first verse of Psalm 137 casts the city as an *object* of remembrance:

By the rivers of Babylon,
  There we sat down, yea, we wept,
    When we remembered Zion.

עַל נַהֲרוֹת, בָּבֶל—שָׁם יָשַׁבְנוּ, גַּם-בָּכִינוּ: בְּזָכְרֵנוּ, אֶת-צִיּוֹן.

In verses five and six, Jerusalem is a *subject* of address:

If I forget thee, O Jerusalem,
  Let my right hand forget her cunning.
  Let my tongue cleave to the roof of my mouth,
    If I remember thee not;
    If I set not Jerusalem
    Above my chiefest joy. (emphasis added)

אִם- אֶשְׁכָּחֵךְ יְרוּשָׁלָ͏ם—תִּשְׁכַּח יְמִינִי.
תִּדְבַּק-לְשׁוֹנִי, לְחִכִּי—אִם-לֹא אֶזְכְּרֵכִי: אִם-לֹא אַעֲלֶה, אֶת-יְרוּשָׁלַ͏ם עַל רֹאשׁ
שִׂמְחָתִי.

The verse is written in the second person in order to give grammatical form to the emotional connection between the singer and the city for which they long.

  Composers of modern Jerusalem song would take up this trope in order to express their own emotional connections to the city, while placing themselves in line with earlier singers and poets who established the genre's canon of representational strategies and intertexts. This thorough integration of anthropomorphic apostrophe in Israeli song persisted long after Avigdor Hameiri's compositional activities, although "From the Summit of Mt. Scopus" would continue to be associated with other songs using this device. A later song, whose very title indicates this gesture, provides but one example of how this device took hold over twentieth-century Jerusalem song: "For You, Jerusalem" (*Lakh Yerushalayim*), written by Amos Ettinger (lyrics) and Eli Rubinstein (music) and recorded by Ron Eliran in 1973.

For you, Jerusalem
Between the city walls—
For you, Jerusalem
A new light will shine

[Refrain:]
In our hearts, in our hearts,
Only one song exists:
For you, Jerusalem
From the Jordan to the sea.

For you, Jerusalem
An ancient, splendorous view—
For you, Jerusalem
Mysteries and a secret.

[Refrain]

To you, Jerusalem
A song always carries
For you, Jerusalem
City of David's Tower.

[Refrain]

לָךְ, יְרוּשָׁלַיִם
בֵּין חוֹמוֹת הָעִיר—
לָךְ, יְרוּשָׁלַיִם
אוֹר חָדָשׁ יָאִיר

[פִּזְמוֹן:]
בְּלִבֵּנוּ, בְּלִבֵּנוּ,
רַק שִׁיר אֶחָד קַיָּם:
לָךְ, יְרוּשָׁלַיִם,
בֵּין יַרְדֵּן וָיָם.

לָךְ, יְרוּשָׁלַיִם,
נוֹף קְדוּמִים וְהוֹד—
לָךְ, יְרוּשָׁלַיִם,
לָךְ רָזִים וְסוֹד.

[פִּזְמוֹן]

לָךְ, יְרוּשָׁלַיִם,
שִׁיר נִשָּׂא תָּמִיד—
לָךְ, יְרוּשָׁלַיִם,
עִיר מִגְדַּל דָּוִד.

[פזמון]

The verses use parallelism within and between them to emphasize the apostrophe to Jerusalem: the first and third lines of each verse repeat the phrase, "For you, Jerusalem" (*Lakh Yerushalayim*). The melody reinforces this: that repeated phrase, save for its appearance in the refrain, never deviates from the simple 1-5-5-5-4-1-4 (D-A-A-A-G-D-G) melody before it is answered by a cadence (usually but not always an imperfect cadence recentering the D-minor tonic). This quasi-antiphonal mode of delivery is reflected at a more microscopic level, as the up-tempo "oom-pah" feel involves a synced alternation of kick and snare drums, on the one hand, and of bass and piano, on the other hand (the kick and bass sound as a pair, as do the snare and piano, all in alternation). Attesting to the quickness of the tempo, even though the singer runs through the whole poem and sings the refrain twice at each occurrence, the whole track clocks in at a tight two minutes. Stylistically, the song is different from the more lyrical recordings of "From the Summit of Mt. Scopus" discussed in this chapter but is very much in keeping with the aesthetics of late 1960s and early 1970s popular song. To put a finer point on the matter, the widespread use of apostrophe as a technique for anthropomorphizing Jerusalem as a human listener that bears witness to its own songful invocation spans across musical styles and periods of Israeli music history.

Songs employing apostrophe, such as "From the Summit of Mt. Scopus," "For You, Jerusalem," and any number of renditions of Psalm 137, facilitate the imagining of an intersubjective relation between singer and Jerusalem as a quasi-carnal entity that has the capacity to receive the messages ensounded in song, demonstrating how this move is a long-standing trope in Jerusalem song before and after the advent of Zionism.

Echoes of Yehuda Halevi

The bibliocentrism of Zionism, musical and unmusical, is an important strain of its genealogy. It is important to keep in mind, however, that this is not a direct line between the ancient text and modern practice but rather a complex history mediated by traditions of interpretation, in the realms of both theology and poetry. One important mediator of tradition who brought the theological and poetic together in his prolific output of *Jerusalem poems* was medieval Andalusian Hebrew poet Yehuda Halevi (c. 1075–1141), who has loomed large in Israel as a symbol of devotion to Jerusalem. Emerging as an icon for the cultural flourishing of Andalusian Jewish life, within the Haskalah and the development of modern Zionism since the late nineteenth century, Halevi's memory has often represented the archetypal Mediterranean journey to Jerusalem—the traditional object of Jewish diasporic longing. It is not surprising, therefore, that his poems have provided powerful lyrical and symbolic material for a number of Israeli musicians. Halevi's canonization and lionization in modernity reveals how, as Tanya Sermer reminds us, "Zionism is not a monolithic ideology, but a field of contestation" (Sermer 2015: 212). The Zionist context of the Yishuv (and later), when Jews actually settled their ancestral homeland, created a complicated reception path for Halevi's poetry. The differing uses and interpretations of Halevi's legacy reveal important ideological diversity, particularly among the streams of Labor, religious, and political Zionisms. Halevi's poems and philosophical writings resonate across Jewish-Israeli musical practice, and, as I show here, across the "field of contestation" his modern echoes obtain a distinctly Mediterranean inflection, locating Jerusalem song itself in the context of exile: in al-Andalus, which represents an exilic chronotope and attendant poetics of longing within Zionist musical discourse.

Israeli musical settings of Halevi's poetry betray the easy elision of the poet's exilic attachment to the Holy Land and Jerusalem with the specific ideological needs of several strands of Zionism that lay territorial claim to it. Musicians have done this by ensounding exile through Mediterranean musical gestures that locate Halevi's words within their original Andalusian context, called *Sefarad* in Hebrew. The popular song "Yefe Nof" ("O, Beautiful") is particularly illustrative of this phenomenon. The song's text is brief but intimate and saturated with biblical imagery:

> O beautiful, joy of the world, city of the great king.
> My soul longed for you from the edge of the West!
> If only I could be endowed with your stones and be restored
> and taste your clods, to my mouth it would be sweet as honey!

יְפֵה נוֹף מְשׂוֹשׂ תֵּבֵל קִרְיָה לְמֶלֶךְ רָב
לָךְ נִכְסְפָה נַפְשִׁי מִפַּאֲתֵי מַעְרָב
הֲלֹא אֶת אֲבָנַיִךְ אֲחוֹנֵן וְאֶשְׁקֵם
וְטַעַם רְגָבַיִךְ לְפִי מִדְּבַשׁ יֶעְרָב

The phrase *yefe nof*, which literally translates to "beautiful view" (or land-scape or vista) but is translated earlier as "O beautiful" and later as "Fair in situation," is also a traditional nickname for the city of Jerusalem in the Hebrew Bible, specifically in the third line of Psalm 48:

> Fair in situation, the joy of the whole earth;
> Even mount Zion, the uttermost parts of the north,
> The city of the great King.[20]

יְפֵה נוֹף מְשׂוֹשׂ כָּל־הָאָרֶץ הַר־צִיּוֹן יַרְכְּתֵי צָפוֹן קִרְיַת מֶלֶךְ רָב

Nechama Hendel (1936–1998) originally performed Halevi's "Yefe Nof" at the 1965 Israel Song Festival, held at Jerusalem's Binyanei Ha-Uma convention center, and recorded it to be included on multiple albums appearing in the aftermath of the Six-Day War of 1967, when Israel conquered and occupied several territories, including the Old City of Jerusalem. Between 1967 and 1968, her recording was released on her own album, *And Maybe . . .* (*Ve-Ulay . . .*, 1967) is and on at least two Jerusalem-song compilation albums: *Songs of Jerusalem* (1968) and the similarly titled *Songs of Yerushalayim* (1968). The latter of these albums, which was "produced in cooperation with the World Zionist Organization Department of Education and Culture in the Diaspora," includes trilingual (English, Hebrew, and Spanish) declarations about Jerusalem's eternal place in the hearts of Jews everywhere:

> This record contains twelve songs of Jerusalem—some that were sung in the early days of its history and others created in our great and tempestuous days.
>
> Jerusalem—crowned with hymns and prayers, songs of yearning and songs of battle on its walls.
>
> Its people sang when they dwelt in the city before it was laid waste; they sang in exile, never forgetting it, bearing it always in their hearts; pilgrims

---

[20] Translation from *JPS Tanakh* (1917).

sang when they visited it, in joy and trembling and tears, kissing its sun-scorched stones; Jews sang when they returned to stay, standing on the peak of Scopus after centuries of dreaming.

And a new song of our time has been added to the age-old songs of Jerusalem: "Jerusalem the Golden"—which was sung at the Temple Wall by battle-weary paratroopers on the day when Jerusalem became one city, "a city that is compact together."

This record, which is issued in Jerusalem, Capital of Israel, is designed to be a musical emissary from the Land of Israel at the Diaspora, so that these songs may be heard by Jews wherever they may be.

We hope that those who hear it will join in and sing together with the singers—and go on singing the songs of Jerusalem by themselves: in the family circle, in the schools, in the youth movements, and on the road to Jerusalem. (*Songs of Yerushalayim* 1968)

Hendel's arrangement of the song, produced in collaboration with composer Yanon Ne'eman, corroborates this emotional language. It includes a sparse texture, moments of rubato, and a timbral interplay between the singer's voice and its accompaniment. Hendel's voice intones Halevi's words unaccompanied for the first line, at the end of which (on the word "rav" [great]) a lone guitar enters, creating a moment of drama at the song's outset. Her effective use of rubato to emphasize specific moments of profound poetic meaning in the text was typical of her performance style during the mid-1960s and beyond. On guitar, Hendel plucks a *habanera* rhythm in counterpoint between the thumb and fingers, with repeated Phrygian cadences that are stereotypical of Spanish musical folklore and flamenco presented on the world stage (Labajo 2003; Hess 2001).[21] By drawing on a musical lexicon signifying Spain—a musical lexicon and political formation that both, to be sure, postdate Halevi's lifetime by centuries—Hendel's vocal and instrumental gestures underscore Halevi's exilic condition using the contemporary exoticism and multicultural nostalgia that, in Israel, was associated with his homeland, al-Andalus.

---

[21] Although habanera emanates originally from Cuban music and is associated with *tango* (see Manuel 2009), it has been absorbed into Spanish musical folklore to such a degree that it has become emblematic of Spain in external musical representations in art and popular music alike (see Hess 2001: 25; Llano 2011; cf. Neustadt 2002). Furthermore, Hendel does not use a typical right-hand flamenco *toque* (e.g., *rasgueo*) but rather produces flamenco mimicry through dynamics, melodic gestures in the left hand, and the aforementioned modality.

The musical framing of Halevi as an icon of exile here and in several other songs serves to suggest the idea that the poet-philosopher himself aligned with and presaged Zionist conceptions of exile and homeland, for the musical setting casts his longing for Zion as a historicized longing, projected into a past and at a distance that ultimately will be overcome by Jewish return. It is a commemoration of longing; the song is a way of examining exile at close range while celebrating its distance from the current state of affairs, in which Jews occupy their ancestral homeland. In order to understand the genealogy of this idea, it will be important to examine the historical process of Halevi's rediscovery in modernity and his subsequent metamorphosis into a proto-Zionist figure.

Many historians (e.g., Menocal 2002) have understood medieval Iberia to have hosted a "Golden Age" of cultural production that flourished under Islamic political formations that governed Muslim, Jewish, and in some cases Christian communities in southern Iberia, while others (e.g., Cohen 1995) have taken issue with the mythologization of these relations. The "Golden Age" view is to some extent a product of proto-Zionist thought. As Ruth Davis observes, "Enlightenment Jewish historians viewed al-Andalus as a paradigm of religious tolerance, equality, and secular cross-cultural interaction. Crucially, they used it as a model and precedent for contemporary European Jewish emancipation" (Davis 2015: xv). In other words, European Jewish thinkers created a historical narrative that served the ends of urgent contemporary politics, in line with a broader pattern of shaping the memory of al-Andalus according to what Dwight Reynolds has called "protonationalist agendas" (Reynolds 2015: 2). In the context of Zionist cultural production later in the nineteenth century and extending through the twentieth and twenty-first centuries, in many ways the mythologization of al-Andalus worked hand-in-hand with the mythologization of ancient Israelite society as a narrative authenticating modern Jewish settlement of the territory: both bolstered modern claims of Jewish attachment to the land, using deeply rooted expressions of exile layered with pathos and religiosity stemming from their ritual function, both in diaspora and in Palestine/Israel. The revival of Andalusian music and poetry, especially poetry written by Yehuda Halevi, played a critical role in this process.[22]

---

[22] The phenomenon of "performing al-Andalus," to borrow Jonathan Shannon's phrasing, is remarkably common around the whole Mediterranean, within and beyond Jewish cultural contexts, as many ethnomusicologists have demonstrated in recent years (see especially Shannon 2015, Glasser 2016, and the various contributions in Davis 2015).

Halevi was born around the year 1075 in northern Iberia, probably in Tudela, and spent the majority of his life active in the southern, Muslim-ruled part of the peninsula in the cities of Córdoba and Granada and, famously, in Christian-ruled Toledo. Although scholars have turned up few details about Halevi's upbringing, his poetic and philosophical writings demonstrate a thorough grounding in Jewish learning and a strong grasp over biblical, Talmudic, and rabbinic literature. He achieved literary fame early in his career by catching the ear of the renowned poet Moshe Ibn Ezra through a poem in which he responded to one of Ibn Ezra's *muwashshahāt* (girdle poems; sing. *muwashshah*) with deft allusions to the Hebrew Bible and sophisticated wordplay within the strophic poetic form. Halevi was prolific, having written at least 800 poems (that we know of) on a range of subjects, from the sacred and semisacred to love and friendship to wine, as was in keeping with the Andalusian culture in which he was raised.

Although evidence of Halevi's personal life is scarce, his poetry demonstrates a thorough Andalusian enculturation, drawing as his poems do from poetics, tropes, and subjects that transcended the more-or-less discrete boundaries of Jewish and Muslim communities. He mastered various Arabic-derived forms, including innovative use of Arabic meter and its adaptation for Hebrew poetics, as in the case of the fateful muwashshah. As little as we know about Halevi's personal life, we know even less about the circumstances of his death. He spent his last few years in pilgrimage to Jerusalem, the city whose virtues he spent a career extolling, but it is unclear if he ever made it. Some accounts hold that he eventually did reach Jerusalem, only to be killed shortly upon his arrival, but there is much debate about the veracity of this story and the circumstances of the poet's final days in Egypt and Palestine (see Malkiel 2010; cf. Goitein 1954/55, 1959, 1977; Yahalom 1995; Fleischer 1996; Scheindlin 2008). As David J. Malkiel writes, "this incident is one of a small group of historical tales from late Antiquity and the Middle Ages that assumed tremendous importance to latter-day historians because it spoke to their own metahistorical concerns, which is also why it aroused passionate debate" (Malkiel 2010: 2). These metahistorical concerns are driven by the deployment of Halevi's memory—as with that of other Andalusian figures—for the support, negation, or nuancing of Zionist historiography.

Halevi's renown as a poet is a relatively recent phenomenon. During the seven centuries between his mid-twelfth-century death and the Haskalah, Halevi was known primarily for his philosophical magnum opus, the *Kuzari*, a creative and methodical defense of Judaism based on an apocryphal tale of the conversion of the Kazarite kingdom to Judaism. His poetry was more-or-less lost to the written record until 1840, when Samuel David Luzzatto edited and published sixty-six poems from a *diwan* (poetry collection) of Halevi's poetry recently discovered in Tunis. This was a small portion of the literary trove, and the complete diwan was published in 1864 by Mekize Nirdamim, a small, newly established society in East Prussia that was dedicated to the publication of medieval Hebrew literature (Yahalom 1995: 24). It was not until 1894, when Heinrich Brody published a version of the diwan in Berlin, that Halevi's poetry began to circulate in earnest beyond the Mediterranean networks of learning connecting medieval, Muslim-ruled cities like Córdoba and Cairo.

By the turn of the twentieth century, European Jews read and listened to Halevi's poems with great interest, reciting sacred and secular texts alike. "Zion Won't You Ask" (*Tsiyon Halo Tishali Lishlom Asirayikh*), for example, was recited as a consolatory text during services on Tisha B'Av to commemorate the destruction of the Temple of Jerusalem, thus recontextualizing Halevi's diasporic longing as a narrative of the destruction of an intact Jewish society into hope for its reconstitution in Palestine. Solomon Schechter's discovery of the Cairo Geniza in 1896 turned up new evidence of Halevi's journey east and renewed European Jewish interest in appropriating Halevi to serve as a figure of national liberation and attachment to Zion (see Hoffman and Cole 2011: 167–91). Furthermore, Franz Rosenzweig's translations, published in 1924 and 1927, were among the first to create a presence for Yehuda Halevi's poetry in the secular, east central European Jewish wellspring of political Zionism, a branch of the movement with which Rosenzweig actually often found himself at odds (Benjamin 2007).

It is in this light that later thinkers across the spectrum of Zionism would understand Halevi's poetry as being essentially "proto-Zionist." As Halevi's biographer Hillel Halkin writes, "Secular Zionism's keenness to claim Halevi as a precursor fit into its overall project of 'Zionizing' Jewish history, regarded by it as the long march of a people back to their land" (Halkin 2010: 266). This was part of a broader project of historicizing Judaism itself by reading the Bible and other older texts as ancestral history. Halkin gives some weight to this point by demonstrating that Halevi was the first major Jewish figure to call for literal return to Zion without deferment to a messiah, claiming that he initiated a shift in Jewish cultural production that focused on Erets Israel—that is, he is credited with interpreting the age-old Judaic injunction against forgetting Jerusalem, as articulated in Psalm 137 and the Babylonian exile to which it attests, as a mission for Jews to find themselves once more in terrestrial Zion rather than to wait for a heavenly Zion to which they would "return" at the end of days.

There is no denying the aesthetic power of Halevi's Zion poems within the disparate contexts of medieval al-Andalus, nineteenth-century Europe, and twentieth-century Israel; however, the poet's framing as a proto-Zionist is ultimately a historiographical construction that fails to capture the poet's rootedness in al-Andalus, as evidenced by the aesthetics of the very works being deployed in service of that framing. As Christopher McDonald argues, "Within the perceived discontinuity between ha-Levi's [sic] socio-literary and prosodic theories, there lies both a touting of artistic and religious Zionism and a simultaneous celebration of Arabized prosody. The poet-philosopher in no way argues for a wholly Jewish nation or art" (McDonald 1996: 347). McDonald claims that Halevi's cosmopolitanism, characteristic of his thoroughly Andalusian enculturation, complicates the facile treatment of his memory under early Zionism.

Halevi's poetic resurrection from the mid-nineteenth to early twentieth centuries was extremely fortuitous, for it helped to propel the distinctly post-Enlightenment, east central European, Romantic nationalism that served as the ideological basis for modern Zionism as a national liberation movement. At the same time, it empowered musicians coming from a spectrum of ethnic identities and political orientations to speak to the larger issues raised by the national culture that flourished as a result of Zionism's success, Halevi's associations with Mediterranean al-Andalus also providing a platform for negotiation and critique.

Although in many ways Israeli national culture privileged its east central European elements during its formative decades, the country's musical practice is indelibly marked by the Mediterranean Sea. This is first and foremost because of Israel's large population of people who immigrated via complex Mediterranean routes, along with the preexisting populations of Jews and non-Jews alike who were indigenous to Ottoman Palestine and established traditions there over many generations. Those who migrated from Mediterranean locales brought with them long-standing liturgical and secular traditions that employed the aesthetics and modal and rhythmic structures common to the broader societies in which they developed (Seroussi 2006, 2013).

In addition to the several individual musicians discussed here, ensembles such as the Israeli Andalusian Orchestra, founded by Casablanca-born composer Avi Eilam-Amzallag, have brokered the Andalusian musical heritage to national and international audiences. These projects often have taken on a political valence; for example, the Israeli Andalusian Orchestra, who in their marketing materials articulate their mission to spread "the musical heritage which was created during the Golden Age of Jewish culture in Spain" and who have produced many musical settings of Halevi's poems (including "Yefe Nof"), are known for their publicized attempts to include Palestinian musicians in their activities. The intercultural politics of the linked memories of al-Andalus, as chronotope, and Yehuda Halevi, as an embodiment of Zionist longing, will come into fuller view later in the chapter.

The geographical location of Israel/Palestine at the edge of the eastern Mediterranean further orients Israeli musical tastes toward the broader Mediterranean region. In the early decades of statehood, for example, the seaside city of Jaffa was a predominantly Palestinian city and home to clubs that famously hired visiting musicians from Mediterranean Europe during the 1950s, 1960s, and 1970s. Venues such as Café Arianna served as Israelis' musical links to the region and served as incubating spaces for the emergent *Musiqa Mizrahit* (Mizrahi music) and *Musiqa Yam Tihonit* (Mediterranean music) genres (Erez 2016: 75–128; Horowitz 2010: 59–84; Regev and Seroussi 2004: 191–212).[23] These genres themselves involve unapologetic panethnic musical mixture. As Amy Horowitz has shown, "the creators of Mediterranean Israeli music freely employed Greek, Italian, San Remo, and *ha-Shir ha-Erets Yisre'eli* [the Song of the Land of Israel], Turkish, Judeo-Arabic, and Arabic musical style" (Horowitz 2010: 32). Spanish musical folklore, too, figures prominently within those circles, most especially in the recordings of Moroccan-Israeli musicians Jo Amar and Zohar Argov. Their recordings, and those of many other Israelis of North African descent,

> drew on both Spanish popular music of the 1950s (for example, the *paso doble*) and urban Moroccan Jewish music traditions [in arrangements that incorporated] Arabic instruments (such as the qanun and the ʿud), improvised passages in free rhythm (usually in a pseudoflamenco style), and the mizrahi pronunciation of the singer that differs greatly from the sanctioned Israeli pronunciation of modern Hebrew. (Regev and Seroussi 2004: 199; also Horowitz 2010: 85–104)

---

[23] Arguably the most significant influence in the proliferation of those institutions and genres was Greek popular music, which has been since the 1950s and 1960s one of the most popular "imported" musics in Israel (Erez 2016).

Many of the songs from Spain, Greece, Italy, and elsewhere around the region became contrafacts with new Hebrew lyrics (Horowitz 2010: 61). Mediterranean currents furthermore intermixed with the broader establishment of "global Israeliness" via the popular music industry headquartered in Tel Aviv (Regev and Seroussi 2004, *sic passim*). A prime example of this was the inflow of musical currents from Latin America, sometimes via Spain and Portugal, stemming from the rapid globalization of *tango, bossa nova, tropicália*, and other genres during the 1970s and beyond.[24]

Since the 1990s, a veritable "craze" around the incorporation of *piyyutim* (medieval liturgical poems) into popular music has effectively mainstreamed longstanding Sephardic traditions for audiences across intra-Jewish ethnic orientations in Israel (Dardashti 2007; Raz 2015). Carmel Raz summarizes it nicely:

> [I]n response to a complex interplay of social and cultural phenomena ranging from the new identity movements associated with second- and third-generation Mizrahi Israelis to post-Zionism and a renewed interest in various spiritual aspects of Judaism, *piyyutim* have recently emerged as a living tradition in new contexts outside the synagogue. (Raz 2015: 165–66)

In short, the mainstream of Israeli popular music has had an increasing appetite for Mediterranean and other world styles, whether associated with Jewish cultural production or not, since the founding of the state in 1948, as musicians—including Nechama Hendel, as discussed earlier—were eager to claim these currents for the nascent national musical culture.

In the twenty-first century, walking through central Jerusalem or Tel Aviv, one inevitably hears a range of Mediterranean musics, from those imported from Greece and Turkey to the local top-40 *Musiqa Mizrahit* to many other ensoundments of Israeli Mediterraneanism. Concerts and festivals held around the country commemorate this Mediterranean past by sonically mapping direct migratory links between home and host lands, a strategy which, in a reversal of classic diasporic formulations, characterizes

[24] For prime examples of this phenomenon, see the early recordings of Matti Caspi and Shlomo Gronich, who blended Latin genres with the stylings of Anglo-American progressive rock and the poetics of postsymbolist Hebrew poetry.

the local setting as the inevitable home and the old country as the erstwhile host—a phenomenon that historian Christin Hess and others have called "reverse diaspora," in which "formal return to the homeland does not necessarily 'unmake' diasporas" (Hess 2008: 288). To put a finer point on this, although in some cases it may be possible to interpret musical settings of Halevi's poetry in an "exilic" style—using musical elements that signify the lyrics' Hispanic and/or Arabic associations within the Israeli cultural imagination, as in the Hendel example previously discussed—it may also be possible to view them as expressing a seemingly dissonant longing for the exilic setting itself. Being that Israeli musical Mediterraneanism evinces a cosmopolitan ethic, it only stands to reason that Halevi's poetry would yield stylistically diverse modern settings.

A striking "Hispanicization" of Yehuda Halevi is evident in a full album of settings of his poetry released in 2009 by Mizrahi singer Etti Ankri. Her version of "Yefe Nof," like Nechama Hendel's four-decade-old version, draws on stereotypically Spanish musical gestures. While Hendel came from an Ashkenazi background (east central European) and musically was associated with that cultural formation through her performance and recording of Yiddish folk songs, Ankri comes from a Tunisian Jewish family, and thus Sefarad would seem to be a more intimate point of reference. In some of her recordings, for example, she sings in the Arabic dialect of her parents and ancestors (Saada-Ophir 2006: 219).

Although there is no trace of flamenco or habanera patterning like Hendel's version, Ankri's setting draws on a Spanish musical lexicon to perform similar ideological work. The entire song follows a iv-i-V-i harmonic pattern characteristic of Spanish stereotyping, and this proves to be the backbone of the rest of the arrangement, as it supports a vocal melody featuring a tidy descending 4-3-2-1 motive and sequences derived from it. The overall arrangement and expressive gestures of accompanying instruments highlight the emotive quality of the text without resorting to the dramatization of poetic meaning in Hendel's version: an arpeggiated nylon-stringed guitar is present as a sonic signifier of Spanishness and a constant driver of the repetitive harmonic motion, while a lilting tremolo in the swelled accordion and clarinet punctuate the verses with a plaintive quality, as they witness within the lyrics an exilic deferment of historical time, as in the poem's second line: "My soul longed for you from the edge of the West!" Similar to Hendel's musical setting of the poem, here the listener is meant to identify with Halevi's exilic position from a place of return, and this is made possible by transforming the poem through songful Mediterraneanism. Ankri emphasized this point during a 2011 concert at Beit Avi Chai in Jerusalem. She introduced the song in a long preamble discussing Halevi's *Kuzari* and his journey to Erets Israel and Jerusalem, ending with a personal anecdote about ruminating on Halevi's longing for Jerusalem during a banal moment of driving to Jerusalem in her car.[25]

Whereas many Israeli musical settings of Halevi's poetry locate the poet in exilic al-Andalus via musical images of Spain (Christian Spain, to be sure) that are intelligible to a globalized popular music audience, including Israeli listeners, other examples abound that do so by explicitly framing Halevi as part of a "Golden Age" of Andalusian cultural production that included contributions from Jewish, Muslim, and Christian creators. The "convivencia" (Spanish: coexistence) myth has endured since the mid-twentieth century as "inspiration for contemporary forms of multiculturalism" around the whole of the Mediterranean region, as Jonathan Shannon has shown in his *Performing al-Andalus* (2015: 312). What most of those disconnected, or sometimes loosely connected, musical projects around the region honoring shared elements of Andalusian culture have in common is that they are implicitly framed by contemporary local and/or global political circumstances. In the context of modern Israel/Palestine, the idea of a shared Jewish and Muslim Arabic poetic and musical heritage—located within the poetics and performative modes themselves of Arab Andalusia—presents for many musicians and audiences the chance to explore the possibilities of coexisting in the present, as I discuss in what follows.[26]

The most frequently performed musical setting of Halevi's poetry in its modern canonized form is "My Heart Is in the East" *(Libi Be-Mizraḥ)*. Its popularity is hardly surprising, considering the fact that the poem has served— since the rediscovery of Halevi's poetry in the mid-nineteenth through early twentieth centuries—as a classic expression of what Barbara Mann calls "the problem of Jewish geography" (Mann 2012: 47). This is, according to Mann, "the spiritual shock experienced by rabbinic Judaism living in the wake of the

---

[25] Video of this performance is available on Beit Avi Chai's YouTube channel: https://youtu.be/v11AuXN33U0.

[26] Beyond the Andalusian framework, Benjamin Brinner discusses Israeli-Palestinian musical projects exploring shared heritage in his *Playing Across a Divide* (2009). (For examples of such practices in literature, see, among others, Alcalay 1993; Hever 2002: 175–204; Levy 2014.)

Temple's destruction, distant from Jerusalem" (Mann 2012: 47). The text of Halevi's poem appears here:

> My heart is in the East, and I am in the West,
> as far in the West as west can be!
> How can I enjoy my food?
> What flavor can it have for me?
> How can I fulfill my vows
> or do the things I've sworn to do,
> while Zion is in Christian hands
> and I am trapped in Arab lands?
> Easily I could leave behind
> this Spain and all her luxuries!—
> As easy to leave as dear the sight
> of the Temple's rubble would be to me.[27]

לִבִּי בְמִזְרָח וְאָנֹכִי בְּסוֹף מַעֲרָב—אֵיךְ אֶטְעֲמָה אֶת אֲשֶׁר אֹכַל וְאֵיךְ יֶעֱרָב?
אֵיכָה אֲשַׁלֵּם נְדָרַי וֶאֱסָרַי, בְּעוֹד—צִיּוֹן בְּחֶבֶל אֱדוֹם וַאֲנִי בְּכֶבֶל עֲרָב?
יֵקַל בְּעֵינַי עֲזֹב כָּל-טוּב סְפָרַד, כְּמוֹ—יֵקַר בְּעֵינַי רְאוֹת עַפְרוֹת דְּבִיר נֶחֱרָב!

The meaning of the distance expressed in this poem is commonly missed in the text's intertextual and musical careers (e.g., its appearance in subsequent texts, often via musical settings). As Raymond Scheindlin points out, "There is no forward motion in this poem, for all its pairs are in equipoise: East and West, Zion and Christians, al-Andalus and Arabs, the wealth of al-Andalus and the ruins of the Temple" (Scheindlin 2008: 170). Accordingly, he argues that the poem's "balancing" through adherence to the poetic form (i.e., the balancing of hemistichs) and of the pairs of oppositions just enumerated "suggests a stasis that is at odds with the calculation [in favor of abandoning al-Andalus for Palestine]" (Scheindlin 2008: 170). It is primarily a statement of the exilic condition in which Halevi found himself. In her analysis, Mann concurs with these observations but adds an important insight: "The distance in question . . . is not necessarily geographic in nature . . . [and] should be understood in messianic terms: the city that remains at the center of the poet's theological world (his 'heart') will also remain in physical ruins until some future time" (Mann 2012: 48). In other words, to play on Mann's prose,

---

[27] Translation by Raymond P. Scheindlin (Scheindlin 2008: 168–69).

Halevi's poem expresses the emotional problem of distance, not a solution by means of migration, for the Jerusalem of his time was not the Jerusalem of his religious imagination, as the text makes clear. But in the end, migration was the solution that Halevi himself chose when he set voyage for Palestine near the end of his life.

Musical settings of "My Heart Is in the East" often locate the poem and its sentiment in al-Andalus according to a diversity of interpretations of the Andalusian soundscape. Nechama Hendel's rendition of "My Heart Is in the East," for example, would conform to some extent with the stylistic elements of her "Yefe Nof," discussed earlier, locating Spain predominately in the harmonic motives and instrumental timbres. Ruchama Raz, an Iranian-Israeli singer from Jerusalem, recorded her version of "My Heart Is in the East" for a 1993 compilation album called *Golden Poets: Spanish Romances and the Poetry of Sephardic Jewry* (*Meshorerei Zahav: Romansot Sfardiot u-me-Shirat Yehudat Sfarad*). In addition to Raz, the album includes performances by Suzi Uziel, Ron Shoval, Lior Yeini, Efrat Carmon, Geula Nini, and Kutnot Pasim Band—quite a diverse group of musicians, with their own stylistic and genre associations running the gamut of Israeli popular music in vogue at the time.[28] The poem was written in medieval Hebrew, the literary and liturgical language of Andalusian Jewry, and within an Arabic form, as was customary practice for Halevi and his contemporaries, some of whose poems are also featured on the album.[29] This and other Hebrew song settings on the album appear alongside folk songs in Ladino, a transnational Judeo-Spanish language spread across the Sephardic Mediterranean (Iberia, Greece, Turkey, and Palestine). The album thus demonstrates a range of musical and linguistic possibilities for the memory culture surrounding Andalusian Jewry during the medieval period.

Raz's version of "My Heart Is in the East" shows off instrumentation contemporary to early 1990s popular music production while emphasizing the Hispanicized elements of the song: digital string pads underlie much of the song texture while steel- and nylon-stringed guitars pluck stereotypical melodic flourishes associated with flamenco (but not the characteristic *toques*),

---

[28] The CD includes an English title that is very different from the Hebrew, which I have given in more-or-less literal translation earlier. Printed prominently on the cover is "Jewish Ladino Songs from the Golden Century," a title that draws on the mythic *convivencia* historiography described earlier that views al-Andalus, particularly in the eleventh and twelfth centuries, as an incubator for cultural and scientific advancement, forged in the crucible of friendly intercommunal relations.

[29] In addition to Halevi, there are musical settings of poems by Samuel ibn Naghrillah, Abraham ibn Ezra, Moses ibn Ezra, and Solomon ibn Gabirol.

while flutes, castanets, and synthesized Latin hand drums reinforce those flourishes, sometimes through punctuation, as in the striking castanets. The harmonic framework is built on Phrygian cadences, as is the case in many Halevi settings. Formal changes from the poem to the song are interesting here. The poem's first and most iconic hemistich, "My heart is in the East, and I am in the West," serves as a refrain for the song. At each appearance of the refrain, the rhythmic ostinato abruptly ceases, giving way to a much slower tempo in order to dramatize the line, which is sung twice for emphasis. The song's first verse includes the second hemistich of the first line of poetry and both hemistichs of the second line, while the second includes the second hemistich of the first line, as before, but this time followed by both hemistichs of the poem's third line. Raz repeats the final phrases of each hemistich, in order to sync the Hebrew poem's Arabic meter with the duple musical meter and popular song form, with each repeated phrase aligning with a musical cadence. The whole thing is capped off with a ritardando repetition of the first hemistich, solidifying the line's iconicity within Jewish cultural production: "My heart is in the East, and I am in the West." These formal changes, and the stylistic procedures through which Raz realizes them, all serve to underscore the "problem of Jewish geography" described by Mann by highlighting the dislocating effects of Jewish exile from Erets Israel.

Many of these musical characteristics place Raz's "My Heart Is in the East" in line with the styles set forth by Hendel's performances of Halevi's poems, particularly the Ne'eman arrangement of "Yefe Nof." Raz's song, as with others described earlier, makes heavy use of instrumental signifiers and gestures, modal figures, and rhythmic contrast in order to create a musical image of al-Andalus that simultaneously celebrates and exoticizes Sephardic Jewry via the relationship to Zion expressed lyrically.

Settings of the poem by Mizrahi-identified musicians sometimes differ from these gestures, using Arabic musical signifiers to express a longing for "home" that is torn between Israel and the places from which they or their immediate family migrated. Since piyyutim began to mainstream in popular music during the 1990s and 2000s in Israel, and religious entertainment mixed with secular song, so too have vocalists, including Mizrahi-identified vocalists, achieved celebrity for their ability to reproduce this liturgical poetry in an Eastern style, drawing on their training in Sephardic liturgy or in classical Arabic music. These performances often take place on prestigious stages such as the Israel Festival and the Piyyut Festival, or else on televised music programs of various kinds. At the same time, over the past few decades there has been a rise in the prominence of observant forms of Judaism, particularly forms of religious orthodoxy, in the national consciousness, media culture, and political landscape. In twenty-first-century Israel, therefore, singing rabbis—whether from Sephardi or Ashkenazi traditions—can achieve musical fame through similar channels to those used by pop stars.

One such performer is Rabbi David Menachem, a prominent rabbi and paytan of Iraqi descent who is a regular fixture in the programming just described and on the international festival circuit, particularly the cluster of festivals held each summer in Morocco, such as the Festival de Fès de Musiques Sacrées du Monde and the Festival des Andalousies Atlantiques d'Essaouira. In addition to being a public figure in his capacity as a rabbi, Menachem is a musician who specializes in performance on Arab and Turkish musical instruments, primarily ʿud and nay. He rose to prominence during the 2010s for his mission to leverage both his religious authority and musical skill as a platform for interfaith dialogue. He regularly collaborates with Palestinian Muslim musicians, such as at the 2014 Sacred Music Festival in Jerusalem, where he and Sheikh Ghassan Manasra, a leader of the Qadiri Sufi order in Jerusalem, led a workshop comparing and contrasting cantorial practice and calls-to-prayer for the festival audience.

A key to Menachem's peace-building strategy is his attempt to depoliticize religion itself in order to allow for examination of theological or ritual common ground between Jews and Muslims that are not overtly colored by the political crisis that serves as the context and impetus for such dialogue. Liturgical music is the chief site for this exploration, as he remarked in an interview with the Jerusalem Post daily newspaper: "Listening to a piyyut is sometimes more important than listening to a sermon. You will always take the music with you—it will keep your heart open and ready to listen to the other" (Cidor 2014). For Menachem, a deeper appreciation of Sephardic religious tradition presents the opportunity to engage seriously with Arab culture, and, in fact, the Iraqi Jewish rabbi-musician is seen in Israel as a broker of both.

This strategy is borne out in his musical practice, including in his work with Yehuda Halevi's poems, such as "My Heart is in the East." At a March 2015 performance during the BeSod Kolot Rabim Piyyut Festival hosted by the National Library of Israel to celebrate the proliferation of piyyutim in Israeli popular culture, Menachem, on ʿud, and his performance partner Shlomi Shaban, on piano, negotiated the cultural distance between Western and Eastern hybridized musical modalities based on maqam Lami, an Iraqi mode. Melodically, the whole performance, across piano, ʿud, and voice, enforced a strong sense of modal center that place it within an Arab musical logic. In moments of intensity, Shaban used his stiffened, elongated fingers to press octave-separated keys in loud, rapid succession, in order to imitate the tremolo of the Arabic qanun, in clear signification of the Eastern Mediterranean style the musicians desired to produce. At the end of the song, the musicians transitioned directly into "Yefe Nof," marking the distinction not only textually but with the entrance of strict meter (iqaʿat maqsum) and a slight modulation to maqam Nahawand (again, hybridized through harmonization, including even a dominant V chord).

To be sure, such negotiations of musical structure are characteristic of Iraqi Jewish musicians throughout the twentieth century—figures of cosmopolitanism who served as arbiters of the modern sharqi (Eastern) style in Baghdad and, in turn, introduced such hybridizations to Palestine, beginning with Ezra Aharon in the 1930s. In light of these gestures, and in the context of Menachem's well-publicized work on interfaith dialogue, the lyrics take on a less politicized meaning than in musical settings that employ a more superficial exoticization of exile. Instead, this musical transformation of the lyrics does no less than suggest a solution to the "problem of Jewish geography" (Mann 2012: 47), in the sense that it takes delight in the poem's "lack of motion" (Scheindlin 2008: 170) by locating the musicians' hearts in cosmopolitan Jerusalem, the space of its performance. The performers are not, as Halevi writes in the original, "trapped in Arab lands" but rather trapped *outside* them, linking themselves to a memory of another "home," now reachable only through imagination in musical performance.

Israeli musical Mediterraneanism acts as a heteroglossic sonic signifier whose multiple meanings resonate in different ways depending on the context in which it functions. In musical settings of Yehuda Halevi's poetry, this Mediterraneanism often functions as a signifier of temporary exile, retroactively casting Halevi's poems as prophecy to be fulfilled by Jewish settlement of Palestine in the twentieth century. This we have seen in the Hispanicized settings performed by Nechama Hendel and Ruchama Raz, where a range of Spanish musical gestures helped to frame Halevi's place in al-Andalus as an exilic condition. In other contexts, such as in settings by David Menachem and other artists showcasing Mizrahi- or Sephardi-identified musical traits, Mediterraneanism functions as an expressive attachment to multiple homes, in keeping with the poet's complex relation to space, East and West. Of course, there is plenty of aesthetic and ideological overlap between these different versions of Halevi, in which the poet is spatialized in terms of his distance from Jerusalem in al-Andalus, across the Mediterranean Sea.

Sonically recasting Halevi into exile paradoxically affirms the bond between Jews and the territory of Erets Israel and the bond between Jews and the lands where they found themselves in exile, such as al-Andalus and other Arab lands. These performances locate exile in the chronotope of medieval al-Andalus and transport their audiences then and there in a manner that frames Halevi's poetry as a powerful attestation to a diasporic longing that could have only resulted in the eventual return of Jews to their ancestral land. In Jewish and Israeli modernity, Halevi's words echo through the corners of the very territory for which he longed in song.

* * *

In a book about the musical production of space, it only makes sense to take metaphors seriously, for some of the most influential work on metaphors in linguistic anthropology employs a spatial metaphor to describe its object: "conceptual metaphors are mappings across conceptual domains that structure our reasoning, our experience, and our everyday language" (Lakoff and Johnson 1999: 47; also Lakoff and Johnson 1980). If metaphors are mappings, then it bears investigating into whether mappings—musical mappings—are themselves metaphors and, if so, what those metaphors might tell us about the material space being mapped. In her work on Israeli poetry and Tel Aviv, Barbara Mann employs Robert B. Riley's concept of "vicarious" landscapes, in which "the real observed landscape leads to an internally experienced landscape that is far richer and more personal than the 'real'" (Riley 1997: 207). Mann claims that this kind of engagement, founded in historical knowledge and imagination, is "a crucial component of modern Hebrew literary production" (Mann 2001: 351).

I discuss the role of Tel Aviv in this discourse in the next chapter, but I have argued in the preceding analysis that the engagement that Mann describes also has been a crucial organizing principle for deeply felt claims to Jerusalem expressed through music, achieved in modernity through the synthesis of metaphorical and material understandings of the city. Individual songs and the musical discourse that they comprise are torn between metaphorical and material Jerusalems, and the tension produced through this binary can be a site of play for songwriters and performers. Musical Jerusalem, with its metaphors, is indeed a site that has been discursively produced in the context of such play.

2

Forgotten Jerusalem

Zionism without Zion?

In the previous chapter, I highlighted how metaphorical conceptions of Jerusalem have been central to the genealogy of Zionist political imaginaries, through analyses of biblical, literary, and musical renderings of the city and its diverse symbolic content. In the current chapter, I turn to a seeming *absence* of Jerusalem within the musical production of space in the Jewish community of Yishuv-era Palestine and in early Israeli national culture. The two chapters do not contradict one another but rather support one another's specific arguments. Throughout this chapter, I discuss the political, philosophical, and aesthetic stakes of Jerusalem's seemingly forgotten status in Zionist cultural production, establishing this patterning in the Yishuv beginning in the 1880s, moving into the 1920s and 1930s, and across the historical divide of Israel's founding in 1948 into the early statehood period (1948–1967). I show how Jerusalem's "urban ethos" (Krims 2007) during this period was actually an ethos of absence and that, in spite of Jerusalem's seeming marginality in Zionist cultural production, the Yishuv period was marked by a poetics of Jewish liberation that was rooted in the exilic attachment to metaphorical Jerusalem—even though it was not marked by a renewed attachment to terrestrial Jerusalem itself.

I argue that a conceptual Jerusalem was adumbrated in Zionist songs about *elsewhere* in territorial Palestine, via transpositions of liberatory tropes associated with Jerusalem in diasporic history. Yishuv-era songwriters and poets did not forget about Jerusalem; most of them located its metaphorical liberatory potential in the terrestrial spaces of Tel Aviv and rural Palestine. As context for this analysis, I also investigate musical discourses implicated in the popular belief that Jerusalem and Tel Aviv represent distinct ways of being Israeli. Rather than highlighting the differences between the two

City of Song. Michael A. Figueroa, Oxford University Press. © Oxford University Press 2022.
DOI: 10.1093/oso/9780197546475.003.0003

cities, I argue for their similarities: both are spatial imaginings of historical redemption.

In Jewish musical thought, redemption—from slavery, persecution, or exile—has been strongly associated with Jerusalem, and this is borne out in the city's representation in music and other cultural forms, be they biblical, liturgical, poetic, novelistic, or otherwise. I begin this chapter by showing how ideological attachment to Tel Aviv as the capital of modern Jewish culture and society has relied on a similar historical narrative, built on a foundation of Zionist thought and literature, and that in some cases using Jerusalem as a negative foil has been critical to its definition. I then provide an overview of the spatial ethos of Zionist song, discussing the nature of Jerusalem's place therein. Near the end of the chapter, I discuss how the spatial ethos established during the Yishuv and early statehood periods projects out into twenty-first-century musical discourse, as a site for working out long-standing agonisms over the place of space in Israeli identity. In an extended conclusion, I bring together the parallel phenomena of forgetting and adumbration, both of which emerge out of the preceding analysis of songs, to discuss the limits and possibilities of—as one of my field consultants put it—"Zionism without Zion."

Mahane Yehuda, Jerusalem, May 2017

> *Walking from City Center toward Shouk Mahane Yehuda, the city's main Jewish open-air market, I encounter a striking piece of graffiti. It reads, "Im Eshkaḥekh Yerushalayim Ze Biglal Tel Aviv"—"If I forget thee, Jerusalem, it's because of Tel Aviv" (see* Figure 2.1). *This provocative graffiti, which remixes an archaic biblical phrase into a modern register of Hebrew, has started to appear around Jerusalem and elsewhere in Israel, including in Tel Aviv and Haifa, where "Tel Aviv" and "Haifa" complete the prepositional phrase in each respective city. For most pedestrians who find themselves standing to read the graffiti, the source of this phrase's play on words hardly requires citation, as it is a clear and obvious reference for all Israeli Jews—such is the widespread power and high citationality of verses five and six of Psalm 137.*

The admonition against forgetting Jerusalem was, and continues to be, a central tenet of diasporic Judaism since at least the sixth-century BCE

Figure 2.1   Psalm 137 graffiti. Photograph by author, May 22, 2017.

Babylonian exile, which is the very subject of Psalm 137. Later during the phase of rabbinical Judaism that rose from the ashes of the Second Temple after its destruction by the Roman Empire in 70 CE and then in the medieval period, and particularly in al-Andalus, the admonition against forgetting colored the way that *paytanim* (poets who wrote Hebrew liturgical poems called *piyyutim*) wrote about Jerusalem in its metaphorical form. As I mentioned in the last chapter, this admonition appeared ubiquitously and banally within Jewish ritual life worldwide, particularly in Jewish weddings, where it was, and still is, recited at the ceremony's climax. Even the early Zionist movement, developing out of nineteenth-century European Jewish thought, named itself in tribute to the powerful centripetal force of "Zion," one of the popular names of Jerusalem[1]—although, as will soon become clear, Zionist thinkers of various stripes did not always (or even mostly) fixate their territorial ambitions on terrestrial Jerusalem itself.

[1] According to Jewish tradition following the Midrash, Jerusalem has seventy names; see Mack and Balint (2019: 36, n. 37), who point to the following textual sources: Numbers Rabbah, 14:12; Midrash Tadsha (Baraita Phinehas ben Jair) 10; Midrash Zuta, Song of Songs 3:1; Midrash ha-Gadol, Genesis 46:8.

Bearing all of this in mind, it might be surprising, then, to encounter such seeming irreverence in the graffiti I found in Jerusalem's streets during the spring of 2017. But this is precisely the graffitist's point: the phrase, "If I forget thee, Jerusalem, it's because of Tel Aviv," is meant to supplant an exilic fixation on Jerusalem, as an endlessly deferred space of liberation, with a political vision centered on a city developed in accordance with Zionist modernity. More than a location issue, such a territorial orientation is rooted in a belief in alternative political values signified by those distinct spaces. As architectural historian Alona Nitzan-Shiftan writes, "The Right summons the symbolic possessions of Jerusalem, located at the heart of the Israeli-Palestinian conflict, to incite nationalist sentiments, while the Left's aversion to the occupation finds comfort in Tel Aviv as a symbol of an agnostic European past, not contaminated by the conflict" (Nitzan-Shiftan 2007: 94).[2]

This formulation—of spatializing the character and ideals of Israeli political identity in terms of different cities—complicates scholars' ability to characterize Israeli national culture in overarching terms. The "modularity" of the global spread of nationalism, as described by historian Benedict Anderson ([1983] 2006), has been critiqued by Manu Goswami, who suggests that an "alternative conceptualization" of nationalism could "specify key processes that conditioned the constitution of a modular nation form within a specific historical conjecture and transnational field" (Goswami 2002: 772). In the context of Israel/Palestine, examining cultural production as a site for those "key processes" will prove critical, for as Nitzan-Shiftan writes:

> it reveals how cultural politics mobilize cultural symbols through a complex net of national and postnational, local and global forces that act simultaneously. Such examination requires a retrospective analysis, so the politics of the dichotomy between the two cities must be historicized, not simply described, asking what forces are at work in this process, by whom are they mobilized, and how do they impact the cities under consideration. (Nitzan-Shiftan 2007: 103)

---

[2] This seemingly symbolic discourse has real political-economic ramifications. As Noga Keidar shows, youth flight from Jerusalem to Tel Aviv has been "caused by the burden of the national conflicts that are concentrated at the city level, inter alia, violent confrontations between Israelis and Palestinians, religious tension between Ultra-Orthodox and Zionist Jews, and high levels of unemployment and poverty resulting from the high percentage of Ultra-Orthodox and Palestinians in the urban population" (Keidar 2018: 1210). As she demonstrates, during the 2010s Jerusalem policymakers adopted an urban development model designed to "make Jerusalem 'cooler'" (1210) in an "attempt to maintain the city's Zionist demographic core and Zionist social and cultural character" (1213).

In a sense, this chapter takes up this very charge, by examining the genealogy of the coextensive musical urbanisms of Tel Aviv and Jerusalem as Zionism historically has mediated its urges toward multiple ideological comportments. The apparent centering of Tel Aviv in Zionist geographies provides important context for the deep divide in contemporary Israeli society between post-Zionist and neo-Zionist orientations to space, which Nitzan-Shiftan and others (e.g., Ram 2005) see as being mapped onto Tel Aviv and Jerusalem respectively: "one stretches modernity to its most radical ends [i.e., post-Zionism], the other [i.e., neo-Zionism] retreats into a reactionary fundamentalism that halts life with irreducible essentialist truths" (Nitzan-Shiftan 2007: 94).

A disconnect between social and political visions of Zionism is precisely the issue into which the Psalm 137 graffitists intercede:

As a testament to Psalm 137's endurance, and to the changing symbolic landscape of modern Jerusalem, when I returned to Jerusalem in September 2018, the graffiti I had previously encountered had been blacked out, the inscription now a barely legible palimpsest of the original pun (Figure 2.2). During the intervening sixteen months, someone had tried to erase this metaphorical statement of long-standing agonisms between the two cities from Jerusalem's

Figure 2.2 Psalm 137 graffiti. Photograph by author, September 7, 2018.

material landscape. I did see more instances of the graffiti in other parts of the same neighborhood, however, so the original messaging lives on.

All in all, these projections of imagined geographies onto the Jerusalem cityspace via artistic intervention connect Jerusalem to *other spaces* of Erets Israel/Palestine. The graffitists' spatialized dual vision of Israeli society has a long musical history, and this is the primary focus of the current chapter. In the Yishuv, musicians actually seem to have "forgotten" about Jerusalem, and the Jewish antiquity that it represented, in order to build up the poetic resonance of other spaces that would serve as sites for the institutionalization of the Zionist project. It is not that there were *no* songs about Jerusalem but rather that—in spite of the proliferation within Zionism's European enclaves of "Love of Zion" (*Ḥibat Tsiyon*) poetry, in which "Jerusalem was endlessly rhapsodized" (Miron 2010: 343)—the songs written and performed by musicians in Palestine itself were far more concerned with other configurations of Jewish liberatory spaces, especially Tel Aviv and rural Palestine. When flipping through Zionist songbooks from the late nineteenth through mid-twentieth centuries, one encounters few mentions of Jerusalem, save for the major exception of Avigdor Hameiri's "From the Summit of Mt. Scopus," discussed in the previous chapter, and a few others best documented by Eliyahu Hacohen (2018).

On first glance, Jerusalem indeed appears to have been minimally important to the "urban ethos" of Jewish cultural production in Palestine during the Yishuv. But it would be disingenuous to conclude that this represented a paradigm shift in the Jewish territorial imagination from a Jerusalem-centered vision generated in the context exile to a Tel Aviv-centered vision upon return. A deeper look into that urban ethos or, as I will shortly indicate, the period's *spatial* ethos, is critical for understanding why this was the case.

Music theorist Adam Krims developed the concept of urban ethos to serve as "a determinative and interpretive tool for a symptomatic reading of expressive culture" (Krims 2007: 27) in terms of that expressive culture's patterns of representing urbanity—whether in music's content or in how music and its multimedia forms exhibit the urban ethos from an analytical perspective. This ethos, as he defined it, is "a regime of representation [that] always seems to ricochet back and forth among parameters of cultural production, in ways that are sometimes unpredictable but that as an aggregate can form some interesting and revealing patterns" (2007: 8). Krims's formulation is sufficiently broad as to leave room for moving across media forms, including such fields as music, literature, television, and film, and he builds his claims about context, primarily martialed toward a critique of post-Fordist capitalist production, upon analyses of multiple cultural artifacts, songs included. His approach is instructive for its "gluttonous" (Nettl 2005: 25–26) consumption of examples pertaining to cities' patterns of musical representation—the better that music analysts might understand the broader cultural patterns within musical production and the place of musical production within broader cultural patterns.

In the context of the current chapter, I would suggest that Krim's *urban* ethos be understood instead as a *spatial* ethos in the broadest possible terms. It may seem out of the ordinary to promote this idea in a book that is situated within urban music studies and that proposes the idea that there is something inherently special about cities, such as Jerusalem, that might be of more general value to the study of music, social life, and politics. My reasoning is that such an approach might be more inclusive of the urban-rural and urban-urban continua that link cities with their surroundings via musical representations, on the one hand, and via the flow of people and their paraphernalia (e.g., repertories, instruments, other capital, knowledge regimes) between cities, on the other hand. Such a hypergluttonous view of urban music would allow for a view of the spatial ethos of Israeli cultural production that links divergent political visions of the nation together. Conceptualizing cities as being more than mere metropoles within a unified system of global capitalism would then allow for perspectives on locality that escape a logic holding that the postcolonial spatiality accorded by global flows of music, culture, and people is in any way inevitable (see, e.g., Lysloff 2016).

In other words, it may be possible to read Krims's urban ethos against the grain in order to apply a "spatial ethos" rubric to a smaller geographical scale, in this case to Jerusalem and the surrounding rural areas of Israel/Palestine, as well as to Jerusalem and Tel Aviv, which are situated less than 60 km apart but conceptually are very distinct. Whether or not Tel Aviv could actually make one *forget* Jerusalem, as the graffitists claimed, it can be stated with confidence that Jerusalem was rarely the focus of Jewish musical activities in Yishuv-era Palestine. Although this fact might appear to suggest an absence of ethos, I argue that precisely the inverse was true: Jerusalem exhibited, as it did in exile, an ethos of absence. The important shift that Zionist songwriters initiated during the Yishuv was that this ethos of absence persisted through *adumbration* rather than through rendering the city's absence conspicuous, as in the expressions of longing discussed in the previous chapter.

So, how should one write about an ethos of absence? In the previous chapter, I documented "regimes of representation" (Krims 2007: 8) that articulated exile through a longing for Jerusalem and a further conceptual splitting of metaphorical and material Jerusalems within Jewish cultural production—the former of which might have been accessed from a place of exile, far away from the terrestrial city itself. Once in Palestine, many songwriters negated exile by applying Jerusalem's poetics to spaces that were contiguous with, and substitutive for, the ancient terrestrial city, which for many Zionist thinkers stood in as the antithesis of Jewish modernity. The urban ethos of Zionism thus transformed a premodern admonition against forgetting Jerusalem, as represented by Psalm 137 and its continuous invocation in Jewish ritual, into a modern sanctioning of forgetting Jerusalem in favor of other Jewish spaces. But—and this is a critical point—this worked by drawing on an ethos of spatialized liberation that musicians and poets had in previous generations used to describe Jerusalem as they sung for deliverance from their conditions of exile.

Zionism without Zion?

In the Yishuv context, a strong but nebulous connection between nation, language, and music vexed thinkers who used competing appellations to identify a burgeoning, largely cohesive body of song. The terms *Shirey Halutsim* (pioneer songs), *Ha-Zemer Ha-Ivri* (Hebrew song), and *Ha-Shir Ha-Israeli* (Israeli song) were used quite interchangeably, but as Regev and Seroussi have observed, "these apparent synonyms denote distinctive ways of perceiving the same musical repertory" (2004: 52). As adjectives, both the terms *Ivri* (Hebrew) and *Israeli* (Israeli) are loaded with temporal meanings that respectively signify the past (Hebrew roots) and the future (routes to statehood) with differing levels of ethnonational emphasis. The distinction between the two terms for "song," *shir* and *zemer*, is an interesting one: *shir* is at once general and demonstrative of the music's connection to poetry (*shira*), while *zemer*, with its commonplace usage in traditional Hebrew literature, evokes the register of antiquity and an accordingly deep connection to the land and culture of ancient Israelite society.

Beyond terminology, the songs to which the above phrases refer exhibit a spatial ethos that is at once rich with landscape imagery and yet mostly missing Jerusalem. For immigrant composers, the ancestral desert and its potential for new life—both sovereign and agricultural—became the new symbol of Jewish utopia. Many composers belonged to organizations founded by the *halutsim* (pioneers), including the agricultural communes called *kibbutsim* and *moshavim*, the labor federation Histadrut, and various youth movements. What all of these organizations had in common, besides personnel—the youth groups often fed into the kibbutsim, for example—was a commitment to the socialist political economy of Labor Zionism and a pronounced importance placed on highly participatory, communal singing. This practice, cleverly named *shira be-tsibbur* (singing in public), was a secular manifestation of the religious concept of *tefilla be-tsibbur* (prayer in public). For the secular majority of Jewish migrants to Palestine, Hebrew song therefore served the purpose once served by Jewish liturgy: performing unity through musical participation. Within this context, participants sang songs that helped spread the modern Hebrew language, articulated the political project of Zionism, and re-territorialized Arab-majority Ottoman Palestine—called *Erets Israel* in Hebrew—as a frontier ripe for Jewish settlement.

Many of the songs they sang moved beyond the cultural *milieux* of Palestine and circulated among diaspora Jews through the postcard project of the Keren Kayemeth, an organization founded in 1901 that still continues today as the Jewish National Fund, set up to encourage diaspora Jews to immigrate and settle the land in Palestine/Israel. The circulation of folksong through musical postcards was a prime tactic for the organization's immigration strategy, as musicologist Hans Nathan (1910–1989) showed through his collection and curation of these postcards, which resulted in a published edition of facsimiles, along with sheet music from art-song settings by a transnational cohort of composers such as Darius Milhaud, Stefan Wolpe, Kurt Weill, Paul Dessau, and others (see Nathan 1994). The songs and the individual compositional voices "formed the context of a new history, from which the modern nation-state state of Israel would emerge" (Bohlman 1994a: 40). Philip V. Bohlman provides an overview of the distribution of artistic labor within this transnational practice, contextualizing it within a broader movement beginning in the late nineteenth century to "endow utopia with a powerful new language" (Bohlman 2008: 133) through the invention of "Jewish music," forging the concept in the overlapping foundries of post-Enlightenment nationalism, post-Romantic aesthetics, and the emergent academic discipline of comparative musicology. Keren

Kayemeth collected "folk songs" from the agricultural settlements, circulated them on postcards that included the text and basic melody, and solicited—via Hans Nathan himself—art-song arrangements by European Jewish composers (Bohlman 2008: 132–37). As Bohlman points out, the "folk songs" were not actually orally composed or transmitted in the traditional sense but "composed folk songs" by some of the Yishuv's most illustrious poets and musicians (Bohlman 2008: 133).

Although the Jewish National Fund postcard project was far from being the only institutionalized music emanating from the Yishuv, the songs included in these circulations engender the habitus and aspirations of the people who wrote, sang, and sent them into the world. The three songs discussed in this section are taken from Nathan's published postcard collection. They are framed there in terms of how compositions inspired by the postcard project served the ends of nation-building, in keeping with the historiography of Israeli music (e.g., Gradenwitz 1996; Hirshberg 1996; cf. Shelleg 2014: 217–32), but here I subject the songs to analysis in more specific terms—namely in terms of how they reflect, and indeed helped to shape, the spatial ethos of Yishuv cultural production.[3]

Pastoral landscape representation was a critical part of the Yishuv's spatial ethos. As Nitzan-Shiftan writes, "Labor Zionists who saw themselves as the founding fathers of the young Israeli state negated the idea of a city wholeheartedly, preferring the promise presented by agricultural settlements . . . a utopia, a new beginning, a departure from the diaspora's bourgeois lifestyle" (Nitzan-Shiftan 2007: 95). Composers of pastoral songs participated in this utopianism by locating the national project in the soil itself. "In the Galilee" (*Ba-Galil*), alternatively titled by its opening line "Atop a Hill in Galilee" (*Aley Giv'a, Sham Ba-Galil*), remains one of the better known Yishuv-era songs extolling the virtues of rural Palestine, of which the verdant Galilee region of northern Palestine was a popular subject for many poets and composers. The text was written by poet Abraham Broides (1907–1979) with a melody by composer Menashe Ravina (1899–1968). Both had migrated to Palestine during the 1920s and contributed to the Yishuv cultural establishment through their artistic labor. Like many songs written during the pre-state period, the lyrics are marked by an easy comingling of pastoralism with the revolutionary message of Zionism that it was designed to impart.

---

[3] A great number of these songs were collected by the German Jewish musicologist Hans Nathan and published posthumously in Nathan (1994). The three songs analyzed in what follows are based on Nathan's translations.

Atop a hill, there in the Galilee,
a watchman sits, a flute in his mouth.
He plays a shepherd's song
to the lamb, the goat, and the wondering sheep.

To every naughty chaser of butterflies,
to the traveler who comes from city and village,
he plays on his flute, saying: "Hello!
Come hither to me, to me!"

There are melodies in the mouth of the flute.
There are legends here in the Galilee.
Once upon a time, there was an ancient hero
who smashed rocks and moved boulders

In the path of the ruins, inside the caves,
he roared with his voice and ignited lights.
With a song of life, he marched into battle
against the great and mighty hordes.

"It is good to die on the guard
for the sake of our country!" so he said.
Once upon a time, there was a mysterious hero
who only had one arm.

עֲלֵי גִבְעָה שָׁם בַּגָּלִיל
יוֹשֵׁב שׁוֹמֵר וּבְפִיו חָלִיל.
הוּא מְחַלֵּל שִׁירַת רוֹעֶה
לְשֶׂה, לִגְדִי, לְשִׂיחַ תּוֹעֶה.

לְכָל שׁוֹבָב רוֹדֵף פַּרְפַּר,
לְהֵלֶךְ בָּא מֵעִיר וּכְפָר.
הוּא מְחַלֵּל, קוֹרֵא: שָׁלוֹם!
אֵלַי, אֵלַי, גְּשׁוּ הֲלוֹם!

יֵשׁ מַנְגִּינוֹת בְּפִי חָלִיל,
יֵשׁ אַגָּדוֹת פֹּה בַּגָּלִיל.
הָיֹה הָיָה גִּבּוֹר עַתִּיק
צוּרִים בָּקַע, סְלָעִים הֶעְתִּיק.

בִּנְתִיב חָרְבָּן תּוֹךְ מְעָרוֹת

רָעַם קוֹלוֹ, הִדְלִיק אוֹרוֹת.
בְּשִׁיר חַיִּים יָצָא לַקְּרָב
מוּל אֲסַפְסוּף גָּדוֹל וָרָב.

'טוֹב לָמוּת עַל הַמִּשְׁמָר
בְּעַד אַרְצֵנוּ!' כֹּה אָמַר.
הָיֹה הָיָה גִּבּוֹר חִידָה,
לוֹ זְרוֹעַ יְחִידָה.

As with other songs appearing in Zionist songbooks, the lyrics themselves make reference to music. In this case, the guardsman protagonist plays a flute, which was as associated with shepherds in the local Palestinian culture (*nay*) as it was in the European imagination. And through his musical prowess the shepherd-flutist disciplines the landscape, here represented by its fauna, in accordance with the Zionist aim of cultivating an uncultivated land—what in other songs and slogans was referred to as "making the desert bloom."[4]

The song's narrative resonance with the story of the biblical King David, master of both lyre and war, as chronicled in the Books of Samuel, must have significantly colored listeners' interpretations. Notwithstanding the gentleness with which the shepherd is characterized in the opening stanzas, the man turns out to be a mighty warrior, empowered by his moral superiority ("song of life") over the "hordes" of Arab enemies. By the final lines, it becomes clear that the man in question is Joseph Trumpeldor, the Russian-born commander who died in 1920 defending Tel Hai, a Jewish settlement in the Upper Galilee, against a Shi'a militia from southern Lebanon. The listener makes the connection to the real-life Battle of Tel Hai through the lyrical setting of Trumpeldor's apocryphal, oft repeated dying words: "It is good to die for our country" (*Tov lamut be'ad artsenu*).[5]

Nathan entrusted the arrangement of this song to Paul Dessau (1894–1979), who seems to have favored pastoral themes for his settings of such songs. Nathan's original collection, *Folk Songs of the New Palastine* (*sic*; 1938) lists six Dessau arrangements, whose titles reveal this preference (or else the assignment as dictated by Nathan): "Lo, I Play upon My Flute" (*Hinne Achal'la Bachalili*), "On a Hill in Galilee" (listed as "*Alei Giva*," or "Upon a Hill"), "Maybe" (*ve-Ulay*), "Ascend My Well" (*Ali B'er*), "On the Banks of the Kinneret" (*Al S'fat Yam Kinneret*), and "O Camel, My Camel" (*Gamal, Gamali*).[6] Dessau's contributions to the Keren Kayemeth project coincided with "a distinctly

---

[4] The Zionist rendering of Palestine as an empty and desolate land waiting to be populated and cultivated has long been criticized by scholars working in a number of fields; see, e.g., George (1979).

[5] See Chapter 3 for a fuller discussion of musical memorialism, including of Trumpeldor.

[6] Here and in what follows, I retain Nathan's original transliterations, some of which do not conform with the standard used in the rest of the book.

religious phase in the composer's activities" (Sprigge 2021: 59) and illuminate ways in which "the techniques he used to do so evoked a long-standing tradition of using communal singing as a frame for a potentially utopian experience" (Sprigge 2013: 76). Martha Sprigge argues that this was the case in the broader context of Dessau's career, particularly in postwar Berlin:

> [C]onfrontations with topics like death and martyrdom, that might induce a great amount of fear, were addressed in a communal setting. From a psychological standpoint, such expressions serve a therapeutic purpose. They allowed Jews to express their fears, or identify with the fears of others who shared their situation. But this can have therapeutic value outside the moment as well: by providing a specific setting in which these expressions are viable, communal singing can serve to structure emotional experiences in more manageable ways. (Sprigge 2013: 77)

In the context of the postcards project of the 1920s and 1930s, memories of the Battle of Tel Hai and Trumpeldor's martyrdom were fresh. As sociologist Yael Zerubavel demonstrates, "From the end of the 1920s until the foundation of the State of Israel, Tel Hai continued to function as the most prominent national myth of the growing Yishuv," even though by the end of that period a split between socialist and revisionist streams of Zionism would attempt "to align the myth with its own political stance," often in bitter opposition to one another (Zerubavel 1995: 148). Zerubavel refers to this opposition as "the plow versus the gun," highlighting Trumpeldor's agricultural and military dimensions, which aligned with the political aims of socialism and revisionism, respectively (Zerubavel 1995: 148–57).

In "He Isn't Dead" (*Hu Lo Met*), a 1941 poem commemorating Tel Hai also written by Abraham Broides (the lyricist for "In the Galilee"), Trumpeldor's dying words are squarely associated with "the task of working the land" (i.e., with the plow; Zerubavel 1995: 155). But in the earlier context of the Keren Kayemeth postcard project, Broides's "In the Galilee," and its various musical iterations—from the kibbuts dining hall to mass-mediated form to piano/ voice art-song arrangement—seem to straddle this divide, drawing on the Davidic archetype of the warrior-shepherd, the shepherd dimension indicated by Trumpeldor's musical prowess on the flute. The Tel Hai myth and its career through different periods within the Yishuv era (and beyond) clearly reveal the ideological diversity of Zionist thought. But the common thread running through it all is most significant for my purpose here: in the narrativized landscape—which is decidedly not Jerusalem, distant in its spatial arrangement and temporal associations—the Jewish martyr's blood fertilizes the soil, his sacrifice serving the ends of planting a new society in the land of his ancestors. I will investigate this nationalized memorialism within Jerusalem in the next chapter.

Two songs with very different spatial imagery share the same melody: "To the Desert" (*La-Midbar*) and "Tel Aviv." Both songs more closely resemble the "folk song" pretense on which the Keren Kayemeth project was premised, in the sense that they both had unattributed authorship, although this will be cleared up in due course. "To the Desert" draws on similar imagery to the previous "In the Galilee," in the spite of the fact that the two songs represent opposite extremes in the Palestinian landscape and climate: the arid deserts of the Negev and Judea versus the lush verdure of the Galilee.

> O take us to the desert
> On camels' backs aloft.
> Upon their necks will tinkle
> The bells in cadence soft.
>
> O take us, O take us
> O take us to the desert.
> Don't play upon your flute, for
> The shepherds are asleep
> While on the paths, the winking
> Bright stars their vigil keep.[7]

לַמִּדְבָּר שָׂאֻנוּ
עַל דַּבְּשׁוֹת גְּמַלִּים,
עַל צַוָּארֵיהֶם יְצַלְצְלוּ
פַּעֲמוֹנִים גְּדוֹלִים.
שָׂאֻנוּ, שָׂאֻנוּ—לַמִּדְבָּר שָׂאֻנוּ,

לַמִּדְבָּר שָׂאֻנוּ...

חָלִילָה לָכֶם תְּחַלְּלוּ—
הָרוֹעִים נָמִים.
וּבַלֵּילוֹת עַל הַשְּׁבִילִים
הַכּוֹכָבִים רוֹמְזִים.

---

[7] Translation by Harry H. Fein, appearing in Nathan (1994: xix). Here and in his other lyric translations cited in this chapter, Fein uses some poetic license in order to allow the text to scan well in English, whereas my own translations elsewhere in this book are more literal.

In the lyrics to this song, a setting of late-1920s poem by Alexander Pen called "Carry Us to the Desert" (*La-Midbar Sa'enu*),[8] the listener hears mention of shepherds and a flute—lyrically emphasizing the communal function of music in the Yishuv—and the human-inhabited natural environs are rendered in their multisensory splendor: bells tinkle and bright stars wink. Animals indigenous to Palestine also make an important appearance, although the bovines of the Galilee are substituted here for desert camels, which represent an iconic exoticizing image of the region used to entice Western interest in exploring the adventures it may offer—operating as what literary scholar Uri Cohen calls "Zionist animals," which Yael Zerubavel points out in her analysis of the song (Zerubavel 2019: 52; U. Cohen 2003). The song forms part of the canon of what Zerubavel considers to be "desert lore." In her words, "The lyrics express deep longing for the desert and a wish to return to it on camelback and experience the profound tranquility and serenity of the desert in the stillness of the night" (2019: 52). She also points to the musical setting as a factor in the song's Zionist mission: "The melody, inspired by a Bedouin folksong, introduces the camels' slow and rhythmic movement, and the repeated trilling adds to the Orientalist depiction of the symbolic desert" (Zerubavel 2019: 52).[9] This analysis tracks with later commercial recordings of the song by Bracha Zefira (c. 1950s), Rakhel Hadass (1966), and others over the decades since the song appeared in print: nearly all of them use similar andante tempi and pleasantly bouncy accompaniments, even when the instrumentation changes significantly from recording to recording.[10]

As in Krims's study of turn-of-the-twenty-first-century Curaçao (Krims 2007: 27–60), the spatial imagery in the above two songs moved across sonic and visual domains of representation. In 1936, the Tourist Development Association of Palestine commissioned the graphic designer Franz Krausz (1905–1998) to create the now-iconic "Visit Palestine" posters to encourage Jewish immigration and tourism to the region, in order to bolster the Yishuv project, both demographically and economically. In two of the most well-known iterations, the boldly featured "Visit Palestine" type in the foreground has the Palestinian landscape as a backdrop (see Figure 2.3). In the "Jerusalem"

---

[8] The poem is not dated with more precision than this. NB: Pen was also the author of the infamous "Jerusalem the Prostitute" poem, discussed later.

[9] Zerubavel associates the melody with a Bedouin folksong, while Eisenstein Baker refers to the source as a Yemenite folksong (Eisenstein Baker 2019: 20). Zemereshet, the main repository of Hebrew song, seems to concur with Zerubavel on this point. https://www.zemereshet.co.il/song.asp?id=629.

[10] I am not able to date Bracha Zefira's recording of the song with precision, as there is no date attested on the record sleeve or in any written records I have found. The recording archived at the National Sound Archive of Israel comes from Kol Israel Broadcasting and is from the early 1950s, but Gila Flam, Head of Music and Sound Archives, has suggested the possibility that this is a duplication of an earlier commercial recording from the late 1940s (personal communication, May 20, 2020).

Figure 2.3 "Visit Palestine" posters by Franz Krausz, c. 1936.

Figure 2.3 Continued

version, the viewer looks out from the Mount of Olives onto the Temple Mount/Noble Sanctuary and the Dome of the Rock, with the cityscape at its back. Nature bookends the whole perspective, with a tree dominating the foreground frame and the hills to the city's west providing the back horizon.

The other poster uses an almost identical structure but exchanges each of its components for northern elements: the singular, mature olive tree is now a set of young palms; desert Jerusalem becomes the lakeside Tiberius on the Galilee; and the arid hills of western Jerusalem are now the peaks of Mount Hermon, covered in snow. Given the positioning of urban and rural elements in both posters, the viewer—who peeks from behind the foregrounded trees—assumes the paradoxical position of voyeuristically gazing on an open, public space.

The packaged imagery of these posters has operated since the turn of the twenty-first century as a polysemic sign that at once testifies to the ethos of Zionist cultural production and to the creative ingenuity of Palestinians living under Israeli occupation. In 1995, Jewish Israeli artist David Tartakover oversaw the mass reproduction of the poster "as a gesture of hope in the post-Oslo environment," in which there briefly appeared momentum toward a just solution to the Israeli-Palestinian crisis (Davis and Walsh 2015: 47).[11] These reproductions are some of the most popular and ubiquitous souvenirs sold in the markets of Jerusalem and Tel Aviv—so ubiquitous, in fact, that the posters' representations of space, particularly the ones depicting Jerusalem itself, have come to shape the material space itself. During the third decade of the twenty-first century it is impossible to walk more than 100 meters in Jerusalem's Old City without passing a row of "Visit Palestine" posters prominently displayed outside a storefront. With this proliferation of revived Yishuv imagery came mis- and reinterpretations of the poster by Palestinian artists, who either interpreted the poster as a testament to Palestinian indigeneity before Israeli statehood or else as an opportunity to play with the signs of Israeli territorialism for provocative political art serving the Palestinian national cause. Rochelle Davis and Dan Walsh (2015) characterize this practice through a musical metaphor—as "remixes" of the original poster, in which, for example, the original images are disrupted by the Israeli border wall that separates

---

[11] Benjamin Brinner (2009) and Nili Belkind (2021) have written extensive studies of musical life in the so-called post-Oslo period.

Israelis and Palestinians, such as in a 2009 silkscreen by Palestinian artist Amer Shomali (see Davis and Walsh 2015: 50).

The posters and their slogan, "Visit Palestine," also inspired musical projects, such as an eponymous one created in 2011 by al-Kamandjāti conservatory in Ramallah, which used an altered version of the Krausz poster to recast "Jerusalem as a Palestinian domain for Palestinians now living on the other side of the separation wall and barred from the city" (Belkind 2021: xiii). As Nili Belkind writes in the Preface to her book, which uses the image on its cover,

> The convoluted history of the poster and the ways it has been appropriated and recreated over the years speak to the important role of cultural products in meaning-making for communities and individuals, the complex processes of remembrance and forgetting involved in the making of identities across time and perennial violence, and the narrative and emotive power of a visual image. (Belkind 2021: xiv)

In both the sonic and visual domains, in the Yishuv and the conflicted context of the contemporary alike, artists working across several media have drawn on the spatial ethos of Palestine in order to re-territorialize the space in service of their (sometimes divergent) political projects. Whereas in the sonic domain of Yishuv-era cultural production, the importance of Jerusalem is lessened if not ignored entirely, in the visual domain Jerusalem occupies the conflicted position of being both centered and de-centered in all of these projects, serving as a symbol of frustrated liberation. What unifies them is a commitment to a spatial ethos that places cities within a natural context that is itself iconic of Palestine-as-frontier.

While many musicians, poets, and designers focused on the arcadian Galilee to the north and the arid Negev and Judean Deserts to the south and east, a great proportion of the musical output of the Yishuv focused on the flourishing cultural life found in the newly established city of Tel Aviv on the Mediterranean coast. Founded in 1909 by a group of Jewish migrant families gathered on sand dunes just north of the port city of Jaffa, Tel Aviv was conceived from the beginning as a modern city set against the backdrop of Jaffa's ancient stepped cliffs and, symbolically, against Jerusalem's preoccupations with prophecy and piety. It was conceptualized as the first modern Jewish city, a secular, modern place for the proliferation of Hebrew culture as the Jewish people live as a normalized nation set in their ancestral home (Helman 2010). This is the space rendered musically in the song "Tel Aviv," also included in the Keren Kayemeth project:

Tel Aviv is a Jewish city.
None but Jews there dwell;
Rich men, poor men, intermingle;
Working men as well.
It's good to live in Tel Aviv
And there to find a home;
To live and patiently to wait
Till the redeemer come.
Then let your voice with praise resound
For Tel Aviv wherein abound
Delight and pleasure all around![12]

תֵּל־אָבִיב הִיא עִיר יְהוּדִית
שֶׁכֻּלָּהּ יִשְׂרָאֵל;
יִהְיוּ בָהּ גַּם הֶעָשִׁיר
וְגַם הַפּוֹעֵל.
טוֹב לִחְיוֹת בְּתֵל־אָבִיב
בְּאֶרֶץ־יִשְׂרָאֵל;
טוֹב לִחְיוֹת וּלְחַכּוֹת
לְבִיאַת הַגּוֹאֵל.
שִׁבְחִי וְהוֹדִי לְתֵל־אָבִיב
הַחֲבִיבָה לָנוּ מִכָּל חָבִיב;
אֲשֶׁר וְעֹנֶג מִסָּבִיב.

This is one of many songs in which Tel Aviv is depicted as a Jewish utopia. In the context of the 1920s and 1930s, the idea of a Jewish city, in which "none but Jews" dwelled (*she-khulah yisrael*), was a fantastical one in a diasporic context, where for the most part Jews lived as minorities among Christian- and Muslim-dominated societies. Curiously, the lyrics reinforce class difference among Tel Avivian Jews by affirming interclass relations. Typically, songs from this era did not explicitly refer to the rich and the poor, or in this case more literally the "worker" (*po'el*), as such but instead presented the idea of a classless "new Jew" in keeping with the socialist political economy of the Jewish society in Palestine.[13] The song's message, furthermore, serves its

---

[12] Translation by Harry H. Fein, appearing in Nathan (1994: xix).
[13] As it happens, the visionary for the "new Jew" image was not a socialist but the founder of Revisionist Zionism, Ze'ev Jabotinsky, who saw the martyr Trumpeldor as an exemplar of this image; see Naor (2011). Notwithstanding the animosity between socialists and revisionists during this time, my claim still holds that popular constructions of social identity were generally framed in terms of the communalism resulting from the Yishuv political economy.

intended use for the "dissemination of the symbolic vocabulary of nation-hood" (Bohlman 1994a: 42) and for the recruitment of diaspora Jews to join the Yishuv and populate the land in preparation for a Jewish state.

In many ways, the song typifies the pioneer-song genre (*Shirey Halutsim*). But what is remarkable about its lyrics is the association of Tel Aviv with the messianism typically associated with Jerusalem. Consider the lines "To live and patiently to wait / Till the redeemer come" (*Tov lihiyut ve-lehakot / Levi'at ha-Go'el*). Although the eschatological tradition is richly diverse, a common thread in several of Judaism's apocalyptic visionaries is the idea that Jews' eternal souls will be returned to their bodies by God after the coming of the messiah. Most strikingly, the final lines, here translated by Harry Fein as "Then let your voice with praise resound / For Tel Aviv wherein abound / Delight and pleasure all around!," are a poetically translated riff on Psalm 147, which is quoted in the antepenultimate line of the original Hebrew lyrics (*Shabhi ve-hodi le-Tel-Aviv*). Verse 12 of Psalm 147 states, "Glorify the Lord, O Jerusalem; praise thy God, O Zion" (*Shabhi Yerushalayim et-YHWH; haleli Elohaykh Tsiyyon*). The Hebrew term *shabhi* (glorify/praise) that opens the line of the song "Tel Aviv" keys the biblical reference and adumbrates Jerusalem into this song about Tel Aviv. As a whole, the psalm compels believers to praise God with music, urging them to use song (variations on *zemer*) and instruments (e.g., *kinnor*, or lyre), as the first line exemplifies: "Hallelujah; for it is good to sing praises unto our God; for it is pleasant, and praise is comely" (*Halelu-yah ki-tov, zamera Eloheynu—ki-na'im nava tehilla*). The psalm's seventh line drives home the point: "Sing unto the Lord with thanksgiving, sing praises upon the harp unto our God" (*Enu ladonay be-toda; zameru leloheynu be-khinnor*). In the context of this modern song, then, Tel Aviv becomes a potential site of redemption for all Jews, who will gather together in song. Indeed, Tel Aviv was a historical wellspring of Jewish cultural life and thus occupies, at a fundamental level, a place of prominence within the Zionist spatial ethos.

Symbolic Gender Violence and Anti-Jerusalem Sentiment

Tel Aviv has also been the capital city for Jerusalem's detractors. The anti-Jerusalem sentiment practiced by Tel Aviv's poets is as much a time-honored tradition as the obsequious genuflection practiced by lovers of Jerusalem.

A popular technique for expressing such sentiment has been to weaponize the anthropomorphic tendencies of Jerusalem song, as discussed in the previous chapter. Insofar as Jerusalem attains human attributes in its metaphorical representation, the city's spatial poetics are overwhelmingly gendered in feminine terms. As with all nominal entities rendered in the Hebrew language, no Israeli cities could escape their associations with gender. On one level, one might consider this to be a banal insight, since in Semitic languages, including Hebrew and Arabic, the names of cities are gendered as feminine. In Hebrew, the head word for "city," *ir*, is feminine. Even though the name *Yerushalayim* (Jerusalem) itself is not inherently feminine, it is actually a beheaded version of the expression *Ir Yerushalayim* (City of Jerusalem), which is a feminine construction, owing to the gendered nature of *ir* (city). *Yerushalayim*, therefore, is always-already feminine in grammatical terms, and so all of its attributes, described lyrically with adjectives and verbs, naturally will conjugate in the feminine.[14] But the gendering of the city extends beyond grammar into cultural practice.

Across its long history of textual depiction, Jerusalem is rendered through several feminine archetypes, such as mother, daughter, lover, bride, and prostitute. The city's anthropomorphization as female appears in its earliest textual representations. Traditionally, Jews refer to the divine presence in feminine terms, welcoming the *Shekhina* as the Sabbath bride (*Shabbat Kallah*) each week during Friday evening prayers. In her extensive study of female Zion in the Hebrew Bible, theologian Christl Maier contextualizes these texts in terms of "how the biblical authors used concepts of sacred space in order to address the political situation of their own time and the religious significance they attribute to Jerusalem" (Maier 2008: 4)—that is, she reads them as products of the society in which they first circulated. After Maier, I examine "the female body as a construct of the symbolic world" (7); however, I analyze the texts not in the context of antiquity but rather in terms of how *modern* singers and poets have used "concepts of sacred space in order to address the political situation of their own time and the religious significance they attribute to Jerusalem" (Maier 2008: 4)—in keeping with the genealogical methods of this book.

---

[14] The same is generally true of other place names; see Waltke and O'Connor (1990: 103–104). It bears mentioning that not all Israeli cities are characterized as feminine spaces even though they are grammatically feminine: Tel Aviv, for example, is overwhelmingly masculinized in Hebrew music and literature.

Drawing on the city's feminine associations in biblical texts, some Israeli poets and musicians have characterized feminine Jerusalem in terms of its danger, transgression, and eroticism. In the early days of statehood, Yehuda Amichai depicts Jerusalem as a difficult, jaded lover. Haim Gouri sees in Jerusalem—as in the Palestinian city of Jaffa—the allure of an exotic, Oriental temptress. For some, this eroticism translates into a temporary, violent sexual possession of Jerusalem's female body, followed by an attempt to shame it and cast it out of the Israeli imaginary. As Sidra Dekoven Ezrahi argues, "The feminization of Jerusalem can give birth . . . to an ecstatic and deadly form of erotic possession, as the poetics of memory through metaphor can give rise to a vengeful form of total recall" (2007: 225). This results in a device that Maier refers to as "whoring Jerusalem" in her analysis of the prophetic texts (Maier 2008: 94–140). As with the other antique projections into modernity described earlier, so too would this practice of metaphorical whoring project into modernity through poetic appropriation.

Alexander Pen's poem, "Jerusalem the Prostitute" (*Yerushalayim Ha-Kdesha*, 1933), rather infamously illustrates this point in its mission to capture the poet's, and his ilk's, anti-Jerusalem sentiment. Pen (1906–1972), who was part of the inner circle of the Tel Aviv–based symbolist poets, was not the first to compare the city to a degraded female body, but his connection of sexual violence to notions of the city's holiness set him apart from his Tel Aviv-based literary peers who questioned the artistic and ideological grounding of Jerusalem song. Unlike most of the examples discussed in this chapter, this was not a poem set to music but rather a poem employing music as a device for articulating a position on Jerusalem. The text leaves little question about the poet's disparagement of the city and its place within Zionist territorial imaginaries:

Every paytan prophesizes,
penetrating you with his poem.
Every prophet waxing lyrical courts you on the organ.
In the spilling of mucous
all "musical instruments" honked
embellishments of his moaning
for your closed charms.

כָּל פַּיְטָן מִתְנַבֵּא
חָרוּזוֹ בָּךְ שִׁקֵּעַ.
כָּל חוֹזֶה-מִתְפַּיֵּט הִתְעַגֵּב עַל עוּגָב.
בְּתִשְׁפֹּכֶת רִירִית

כָּל "כְּלֵי זֶמֶר" גָּעְגַּע
סִלְסוּלֵי אַנְחוֹתָיו
אֶל קִסְמֵךְ הַמּוּגָף.

The high literary register of this poem mixes biblical Hebrew with explicit sexual imagery. The *paytan* courts Jerusalem in song, penetrates her, and ejaculates. The final word in line three, *ogev/ogav*, is a double entendre, referring simultaneously in an archaic register to a suitor or lover and in its modern usage to the pipe organ, itself an image of phalluses and fumbling hands. The vehicle for these meanings is a woman's body, which has been ravaged by a male poet. The poem is an indictment of Jerusalem song itself. Other poets' and musicians' longings for a return to some conceptual Jerusalem, a longing often cloaked in seemingly neutral/natural metaphors and mild messianic language, is recast here as a regressive attachment to a dangerous dream.

The poem's connection to antiquity extends beyond the question of linguistic register and to a deeply enculturated pattern of comparing Jerusalem to a prostitute or otherwise sexually transgressive woman in Hebrew literature. In the Hebrew Bible, there are particularly pronounced moments in Isaiah, Jeremiah, and Ezekiel where the prophets use the term *zona*—"whore" or "harlot"—and its derivations to describe Jerusalem. Isaiah 1:21 begins,

> How has the faithful city / Become a harlot?

אֵיכָה הָיְתָה לְזוֹנָה קִרְיָה נֶאֱמָנָה מְלֵאֲתִי מִשְׁפָּט צֶדֶק יָלִין בָּהּ וְעַתָּה מְרַצְּחִים:

Jeremiah 2:20 combines apostrophe and denigration:

> For of old time I have broken thy yoke,
> And burst thy bands,
> And thou saidst: "I will not transgress";
> Upon every high hill
> And under every leafy tree
> Thou didst recline, playing the harlot.

כִּי מֵעוֹלָם שָׁבַרְתִּי עֻלֵּךְ נִתַּקְתִּי מוֹסְרֹתַיִךְ וַתֹּאמְרִי לֹא [אֶעֱבֹד כ] (אֶעֱבוֹר ק) כִּי עַל־כָּל־גִּבְעָה גְּבֹהָה וְתַחַת כָּל־עֵץ רַעֲנָן אַתְּ צֹעָה זֹנָה.

The term *zona* appears *sic passim* in Jeremiah 3 and 13, and most pronouncedly in Ezekiel 16 and 23. Ezekiel is particularly damning, as Jerusalem is not only described as a *zona* but as an unfaithful spouse. Through apostrophic address, the narrator describes all of the ways in which he cared for his beloved Jerusalem—he washed, clothed, bejeweled, fed, and treated her to the finest treasures—only to be met with a litany of sexual transgressions, which are enumerated ad nauseum from verses 15 through 62.

All of these biblical characterizations of Jerusalem as a *zona* are scornful, bitter expressions of male disappointment in what Jerusalem *has become* due to some kind of development; the passages always imply some change in her character (the unfaithful wife was presumably faithful in the past). Maier traces the Jerusalem-as-whore trope more generally to ancient Israelite concepts of marriage, arguing that such characterizations are rooted in a "prophetic marriage metaphor" first used by Hosea to describe a "collective body" (Maier 2008: 94). She demonstrates that recognizing the hierarchical nature of marriage in the ancient Near East and in the Israelite kingdom in particular is critical to interpreting the *zona* metaphor.[15] Thus, Jerusalem belonged in her husband's possession until she transgressed the covenant binding her to his mastery, and so she is subject—through a process of poetic "whoring"—to degradation in explicitly feminized terms.

As Maier points out, "For a modern reader, prostitution and marriage are quite different topics than they were for the ancient Israelites" (2008: 95). Pen's "Jerusalem the Prostitute" trades in the language of antiquity, but interestingly he chooses not to use the biblical "zona"—which, incidentally, is also a common insult in modern Hebrew—but instead uses the term *kdesha* to characterize Jerusalem as a prostitute. *Kdesha* is a pun on *kodesh/kadosh*, meaning "holy"; *Ir ha-Kodesh*, one of Jerusalem's Hebrew names, translates to "the Holy City." By contrast, *kdesha* is an archaic word that refers to a prostitute who was sacrificed in prebiblical pagan rituals—a filthy, abject woman who must be cast off in order to purify the community. Pen's choice to cleave to the pun on "holy" suggests that the true object of his ire is not, in fact, a metaphorical marriage covenant with Jerusalem per se but rather how the religious fixation on Jerusalem stands in the present as a regressive, or perhaps exilic, cultural attachment that does not fit into his own vision for a modern Jewish future in the Land of Israel and Palestine—a vision he

---

[15] For a fuller exegesis of the biblical "whorings" of Jerusalem, see Maier (2008: 94–140).

shared with the majority of secular Labor Zionists in the Yishuv. The fact that his poetic whoring of Jerusalem exchanges the timeworn *zona* for a pun on a term associated with Jerusalem's religiosity makes this clear. Even though Pen was generally considered a popular lyrical source for songs, as in "Carry Us to the Desert" discussed earlier, "Jerusalem the Prostitute" has not been set to music to my knowledge—a fact that I attribute, at least in part, to the text's explicit indictment of musicians in the unholy business of "moaning / for [Jerusalem's] closed charms."[16] By contrast, Pen and his contemporaries would have no problem "waxing lyrical" about Tel Aviv, the new Hebrew city to the west, or areas of rural Palestine such as the desert.

The symbolist poetics and programmatic subjects favored by the dominant writers of the 1930s and 1940s, including Alexander Pen and especially Avraham Shlonsky and his pupils Nathan Alterman and Leah Goldberg, would eventually be rejected by the State Generation (Dor Ha-Medina), a poetry movement of the late 1940s and 1950s (see Tsamir 2008: 85–86). One of the most powerful female figures bridging the pre- and poststatehood poetic divide was poet Dalia Rabikovitch (1936–2005), whose first poetry collection *Love of the Orange* (*Ahavat Tapu'ah ha-Zahav*, 1959) won her favor with members of both schools. For the title, Rabikovitch's choice to use the phrase *tapu'ah zahav* (literally, "golden apple") rather than its contraction *tapuz* for "orange" draws attention to the sexual overtones of her work. Literary scholar Yair Mazor points out that the title is likely a reference to the forbidden fruit described in the Book of Genesis—an archetypal story of feminine betrayal—and also reminds his readers that the act of eating is a traditional metaphor for sex. In his words, Rabikovitch's poetry in this volume "radiates eroticism" and is "saturated with a sense of tempestuous sexuality" that laid the groundwork for sexually liberated figures who came later, such as rock 'n' roll poet Yona Wallach and singer Nurit Galron (Mazor 1996: 264; also Calderon 2009).

Rabikovitch's poem "Around Jerusalem" from this collection became one of the few literary works that took Jerusalem as its subject during the period between the founding of the state in 1948 and the Six-Day War of 1967. The poet uses a train, as well as other mobile objects and beings, to create a sense of ominous, lustful encroachment on the city's feminized landscape:

[16] Some other well-known Alexander Pen songs include such "Cymbals and Drums" (*Be-Metsiltayim u-ve-Tupim*) and "Learn to Read the Name of the Light" (*Limdu Liqro' et Shem ha-Or*).

There is a train that goes round
And around Jerusalem
At night.

Birds there circle far above her,
Beat their wings, and with a clamor
In the dark they shed a feather
On the Jebus threshing-floor.

Black trees stand beside the track,
The tunnel calls the burrow black.
There's a sheen of polished rock
In the wadi at her back.

At night there's a train
That goes round
And around Jerusalem.

Mountains circle round about her,
Winds make moan from ruins inside her.
Birds are screeching in the calm air
And when night falls, owl eyes glimmer.

Mountains hang upon her breast
Like a crown, a regal vest.

A golem's clawing at her dust,
Growling like a hunted beast.

A clatter in the heart of dark,
In the gloomy hell-pit. Hark:
The golem growling Hallelujah.[17]

יֵשׁ רַכֶּבֶת שֶׁסּוֹבֶבֶת וְנוֹסַעַת, סָבִיב לִירוּשָׁלַיִם בַּלֵּילוֹת.

עוֹפוֹת חַגִּים מִמַּעַל לָהּ, טוֹפְחִים כָּנָף בַּהֲמֻלָּה
וּמַשִּׁירִים בָּאֲפֵלָה, נוֹצָה עַל גֹּרֶן הַיְבוּסִי.

---

[17] This translation by Chana Bloch and Chana Kronfeld appears in Rabikovitch (2008).

עֵצִים שְׁחֹרִים עַל הַמְּסִלָּה, נִקְבָּה קוֹרֵאת אֶל מְחִילָה
עָרוּץ חָרֵב לָהּ לְרַגְלָהּ, וְחַלּוּקֵי סְלָעִים זוֹרְחִים.

יֵשׁ רַכֶּבֶת שֶׁסּוֹבֶבֶת וְנוֹסַעַת, סָבִיב לִירוּשָׁלַיִם בַּלֵּילוֹת.

הָרִים חַגִּים לָהּ מִסְּבִיבָהּ, רוּחוֹת הוֹמִים בָּהּ מֵחָרְבָּה
עוֹפוֹת צוֹרְחִים מִן הַשַּׁלְוָה, עֵינֵי יַנְשׁוּף מִתְנוֹצְצוֹת.

הָרִים תְּלוּיִּים בְּצַוָּארָהּ, כְּמוֹ רָבִיד וַעֲטָרָה
וְגוּשׁ דּוֹרֵס אֶת עָפָרָהּ, וּמְנַחֵם כִּכְפִיר נִרְדָּף.

שֶׁיִּקְשׁוּק בְּתוֹךְ הַחֹשֶׁךְ, כּוּר שֶׁל מַאְפֵּלְיָה, וְגוּשׁ מְנַחֵם הַלְלוּיָהּ.

Interestingly, Rabikovitch's "Around Jerusalem" was not set to music—at least on any extant recording—for almost four decades, until singer Nechama Hendel, who had been incredibly active in the Israeli popular music industry during the 1960s, recorded it for her 1997 album *Outside the Storm*. This album was intended to relaunch Hendel's musical career after a lengthy hiatus (she had not released any recordings since 1979), but it would be the final release before her death the following year.[18]

The song's backing track arrangement is mimetic of train sounds, with Latin auxiliary percussion (shakers) playing a repeated eighth-note figure and accenting the downbeat coupled with the restless strumming momentum of the acoustic guitar. The lack of rests in the arrangement creates a sense of perpetual motion, highlighting the ceaseless efforts of biblical monsters clawing and growling at Jerusalem's body. Hendel repeats the final word, "Hallelujah," as if to hint at the allegory that Jerusalem's body is consumed by fervent religious devotion, whose ugly side, like the sound of trains, is a defining feature of everyday life in the modern city.

This song expresses a temporal distance between the "prolonged meantime" (Ezrahi 2007: 223) of Jerusalem song and the perpetuity of objective and subjective violence that stems from the deep-seated attachments to Jerusalem to which this repertory attests, particularly in this instantiation, which came during a period of political malaise following the failure of Oslo

---

[18] Hendel lived abroad for many of the intervening years, which aided in the dwindling of her popularity. One of my field consultants told me that his parents discarded all of their LPs of her music when Hendel married a German man, changed her first name to Helena, and moved away from Israel. As broadcaster Yisrael Daliot points out, "to her bitter surprise, the public and media took no interest in [*Outside the Storm*]. This response was a tragic blow because she had much faith in this recorded collection" (Daliot 2009).

and the assassination of Rabin in 1995. Unfortunately, neither the song nor Hendel's album gained much traction at the time, but it stands as a compelling musical interpretation of an important example of the poetic feminization of Jerusalem within Israeli cultural production.

As Maier remarks, "Since personification is a special case of metaphor, the personified female city offers a portrait of Zion in which spatial and gendered elements are intertwined. In other words, the personification allows one to think of Zion as a space and as a woman that represents the inhabitants of this space" (Maier 2008: 2). In all of these examples of Jerusalem's feminine representation, sound (most often musical sound) and religion (via its iconic and indexical signs) are used as vehicles for critiquing some facet of the city with which the poet or singer finds fault: its religiosity, its potential abjection from the Zionist imaginary, its alignment with illiberal politics, and otherwise. Jerusalem is represented as a feminized participant in such externally generated acts, with varying degrees of consent, complicity, or victimhood. The intensity with which the sentiments are expressed is in keeping with the biblical intertexts themselves, as the city's poetic gendering indicates a betrayal of a marriage covenant that granted the speaker/singer ownership over the personified city-wife.

The best-known critic of Jerusalem poetry was a poet who actively avoided treating the city as a literary subject: Nathan Alterman (1910–1970). Most of the time, Alterman chose to ignore Jerusalem entirely. In his 1957 collection *City of the Dove* (*Ir Ha-Yona*), which is broadly considered a classic statement of the Statehood Generation's Zionist platform and patriotism for the newly formed state, the name of Jerusalem is omitted entirely. At the same time, however, Tel Aviv appears as a figure of redemption and the locus for an "Era of Regeneration" (see Laor 1999). Alterman's indictment of Jerusalem song as aesthetically and morally bankrupt occurs most potently in a small octavo called *Tunes and Songs* (*Pizmonim ve-Shirey Zemer*, published posthumously in 1976), in which he "deliberately catalogues empty Zionist phraseology and dead rhyme" (Miron 2010: 349), in particular the convenient use of words employing the dual suffix *-ayim*, such as the words *mayim* (water), *shamayim* (sky), *sfatayim* (lips), *arbayim* (twilight), and of course *Yerushalayim* (Jerusalem), or else producing a slant rhyme with it, such as *yayin* (wine).[19] Alterman and the postsymbolist school of Hebrew poetry,

---

[19] Semitic languages account for grammatical number not only in single and plural forms but also in the dual form. In biblical Hebrew, any noun referring to two of something would end with the *'ayim* suffix, and any adjective or verb agreeing with that noun would also need to agree in the dual number. In such cases, end rhymes are completely unavoidable, hence the artlessness that Alterman ascribes to

along with their intellectual forebears, saw in their adopted home city of Tel Aviv a more intellectually and aesthetically viable subject.

Tel Aviv, New Jerusalem

The geographer Maoz Azaryahu describes Tel Aviv as a "mythic city." In his words, this phrase "denotes an ideational construct that is constituted and shared in the sphere of public discourse and cultural signification, where the meanings of the city are pronounced and challenged, produced and reproduced, negotiated and debated" (Azaryahu 2007: 6). The meanings of Tel Aviv *as a place*, in other words, engender specific political, theological, or cultural values that set it off against the rest of the nation in popular constructions, such as in the nickname *Medinat Tel Aviv* (State of Tel Aviv). Tel Aviv is the capital of Jewish modernity, both in the sense that it is ruled by capitalist development and in the sense that Tel Aviv's inhabitants and institutions gave rise to overlapping musical, literary, cinematic, and artistic movements that were founded in aesthetic modernism. This modernism depicts Tel Aviv as a paradoxical site. It is at once a familiar hometown and a place in which to get lost. Poems about the city are full of mimetic images based on the urban topography and toponymy; the naming of streets and specific places, such as Dizengoff, Rothschild, and the Carmel and Livinsky markets, often index and evoke poignant social memories. Unlike Jerusalem, the veneer of youth and possibility covers the mythical streets of Tel Aviv, while Jerusalem's old soul rots in the desert. As Barbara Mann argues,

> A text seeking to describe the city may draw on depictions of these sites as part of a larger reservoir of images that seem mythic in their ability to encapsulate the city's essence. The repeated evocation of such a site, whether in literature, fine arts, or even touristic depictions of the city, furthers the site's monumental character, often without any relation to the site's actual history or its contemporary significance within the city. (Mann 2006: 73)

In an inversion to how representations of metaphorical Jerusalem overlay spaces within the terrestrial city, in Tel Aviv the built environment itself

their use in poetry. Although this grammatical feature has been retained in Modern Standard Arabic (using the suffix -*ān*), in modern Hebrew it is largely absent, save for its vestigial use for terms related to time (e.g., hours, days, weeks, and years), as well as for body parts that appear in pairs (e.g., eyes, hands, and feet) and objects that are associated with them (e.g., sunglasses, gloves, and bicycles).

inspires poetic fantasies of spatial redemption that drive much of the "ideological self-fashioning" of Israeli society.[20]

In the ethnographic present, these images of Tel Aviv as the "first Hebrew city"—an appellation of not only chronology but also of primacy—persist through both commemorative musical activity and the cosmopolitan orientations of the city's music scenes. As a material space providing a site for social life, Tel Aviv is artistically, economically, and symbolically interconnected with other bourgeois urban playgrounds that grew out of the developments of Western modernity and global capitalism. As Mann argues, "Tel Aviv, for its development as a cultural center and the representation of this evolution in society at large, remains a synecdoche for the nation, and for Israel's complex and changing relation to both the local landscape and to the past" (Mann 2001: 352). Tel Aviv is still popularly constructed as Israel's cultural center, standing in juxtaposition to Jerusalem's religious and political extremism. Although the State of Israel considers Jerusalem to be its capital, most other state governments do not officially recognize it as such due to ongoing disputes over Jerusalem's sovereignty. Most embassies, foreign missions, and their staffs are located in Tel Aviv, making it also the diplomatic center of Israel.[21]

The city of Tel Aviv serves as Israel's symbolic link to the rest of the world in other ways, too. It is home to many of the country's major theater, film, fashion, art, and music institutions, which draw international audiences—especially from North America, Europe, and the United Kingdom—at festivals and other major events. As Ilana Webster-Kogen (2018) and Sarah Hankins (2015) have shown, in the twenty-first century south Tel Aviv has become a critical point on the global musical map for Ethiopian-Israeli, Eritrean, and Sudanese music making—a veritable "horn mediascape," as Webster-Kogen calls it (2018: 162). More axes of music's globalization run through the city, too, from North Africa to Russia and the post-Soviet states to Iraq to the Philippines.

Since the 1990s, the city has been major urban participant in the global proliferation of rave scenes, with all-night parties often held in mega-clubs on the beach. Although many of the major rave clubs prominent at the beginning of this trend have since closed, there remains a large electronic

---

[20] Here, I use a phrasing employed by Nadia Abu El-Haj (2001) to describe the uses of archeological artifacts in Israeli society. As I wrote in the Introduction, songs function much like such artifacts—not always as proof of indigeneity or continuity (although in some cases, songs are folklorized for this exact purpose; see McDonald 2013: 34–77)—but as "ground-truthing" (Fischer 2018: 4) performances in the vein of historical or ethnographic writing itself, wherein the meaningfulness of melodies and lyrics is the very substance of national sentiment.

[21] The United States relocated its embassy to Jerusalem in May 2018.

dance music scene concentrated in newer clubs throughout the city. These, combined with Tel Aviv's many rock clubs, restaurants, pubs, cafés, and open outdoor parks, provide numerous spaces of music-making where people can socialize during the day and night. Although Jerusalem boasts the largest population concentration among Israel's cities, as a whole, the Tel Aviv metropolitan area (Gush Dan) is home to almost half of the country's total citizenry (c. 3.5 million out of a total 7 million). As a critical hub for the global tech industry, Tel Aviv is one of the Mediterranean region's major economic centers, with the consequent wealth stratification and bourgeois orientation of similar cities around the world, such as Bangkok, Mexico City, Mumbai, and São Paulo. Tel Aviv, in other words, is self-fashioned as a cultural, political, economic, technocratic cosmopolis standing in opposition to Jerusalem's provincial, conflicted state.

In his work on Asian regionalism, Leo Ching argues that the cosmopolitan imagination is "spatialized in its transnational deterritorialization and yet reterritorialized in a specific configuration bounded by historically invented geography" (Ching 2000: 284). As a "mythic" ideational construct, Tel Aviv's cosmopolitan values, and its musical dislocations, serve as important sites for studying local crises where the effects of globalization and political domination are manifest. In spite of Tel Aviv's largesse on both the national and international stages, popular depictions of the city often promote nostalgia for the city's modest beginnings. As Edwin Seroussi writes, "nostalgia has persisted tenaciously in Israeli cultural spaces from its very beginnings" (2014: 36), and Tel Aviv was no exception.

Nostalgia plays an important role in songs and poems attempting to iconize Tel Aviv as the heart of Hebrew culture, such as in the classic songs of Mordechai Zeira (1905–1968) and in Haim Hefer and Dan Ben Amotz's 1958 cabaret *Little Tel Aviv* (*Tel Aviv Ha-Ktana*), in which Tel Aviv was "shrouded in innocence and impregnated with a sense of unfolding history that was apparent not in heroic gestures, but in scenes of everyday life" (Azaryahu 2007: 99).

Beit Avi Chai, Jerusalem, January 2012

I attended a performance called "One More Song: Rediscovering Mordechai Zeira" at Beit Avi Chai, a prominent musical venue not in Tel Aviv but in Jerusalem. As a prolific composer associated with the powerful group of Tel Aviv poets in the 1940s, Mordechai Zeira hardly required rediscovery, as suggested by the title. Just weeks before this concert, for example, I heard the popular singer Rona Kenan sing a cover version of Zeira's "Layla, Layla," a lullaby set to Nathan Alterman's poem of the same title, to a full crowd of twenty-something concertgoers who sung along and applauded with enthusiasm. An advertisement for the Zeira tribute concert in Jerusalem read,

"Zeira was an activist, a regular in the coffee houses of 'Little Tel Aviv,' a soldier in the Jewish Brigade, and above all—an extremely talented composer. He left us with 'Those Were the Nights' [Hayu Laylot], 'On the Hills of Sheikh Avrek' [Al Geva'ot Sheikh Avrek], and even 'Little Elephant' [Pil Pilon]. An evening full of music for those who love Mordechai Zeira's immortal songs."

Musical director Niv Kaufman adapted the songs in collaboration with composer Rafi Kadishson, and the two of them performed in a lineup that included vocalists Keren Hadar, Dror Keren, and Eyal Haviv.

The event was framed as a celebration of Zeira and the memory of "Little Tel Aviv"—as if the composer and his city were inseparable. There was a short film incorporated into the concert showing nostalgic images of pre-1948 Tel Aviv and nearby Jaffa. The musicians' remarks, combined with this multimedia presentation, invited audience members to remember Tel Aviv as a tiny garden suburb to the north of Jaffa's Old City—an intimate community building a new country that would itself spring forth from the new Hebrew city.

This conceptual smallness is as integral to Tel Aviv's contemporary image as it was to the burgeoning city memorialized in the pioneer songs, such as "Tel Aviv" and many other popular representations of the city that persist into the twenty-first century. As Nitzan-Shiftan argues, "Shining under the Mediterranean light and energized by waves of immigrants, Tel Aviv was reputed for its ethnic 'purity'—a Jewish city under a European mandate, a pacifying alternative to the competing mixed cities that the British chose to develop: Jerusalem and Haifa" (Nitzan-Shiftan 2007: 96). The multimedia performance of *Little Tel Aviv*, done in the heart of modern Jerusalem, promoted Tel Aviv as a monocultural utopia for Jews via patterns of Zionist nostalgia that played with the tensions between ancient and modern urbanism for which Jerusalem previously was representative but now has been supplanted by its neighbor Tel Aviv. This is one of several facets of what Webster-Kogen describes as Tel Aviv's "binary cityscape," demonstrating how the city is a microcosm of "the hierarchies and power imbalances propelled by the political dynamics of the State of Israel" (Webster-Kogen 2018: 166). In effect, the narrative of this event, which typifies other treatments of Tel Aviv in contemporary memory work, suggested that the metaphorical Jerusalem of their ancestors' dreams was built on the vacant dunes of the Mediterranean Sea, just north of Jaffa.

The concept of finding Jerusalem elsewhere has precedence in Jewish cultural history prior to the popularization of Zionist thought and the founding of Tel Aviv. Philip V. Bohlman argues that diaspora and urbanization are co-constitutive concepts in Judaism, reminding us,

> In the Jewish diaspora, the urban symbolism of Jerusalem was displaced, ultimately and temporarily replaced by the synagogue, which supported a completely different type of worship, ritual, and prayer. The diaspora synagogue replaced the temple in Jerusalem, but only temporarily, assuming what functions it could until the return from diaspora. (Bohlman 2018: 161)

The idea of return from diaspora to Jerusalem was central to the ritual texts that enabled Jews living outside of Erets Israel to perform community at regular intervals on the Jewish calendar. The preeminence of Jerusalem imbued the space within which many of those musical rituals took place, as evidenced by the orientation of all synagogues toward Jerusalem (facing eastward from Europe, Africa, and the Americas and westward from the Middle East and Asia).[22] This was a constant reminder—that is, a negation of forgetting—of Jews' exilic conditions outside of Jerusalem. And yet the desire for physical return to the actual city of Jerusalem was not necessarily the point of these Jerusalem-centric practices. As Hebrew literature scholar Irene Zwiep writes:

> Worldly towns like Speyer, Toledo, Amsterdam, and Vilna fulfilled but temporary, worldly needs. As its virtual capital, the-nation-without-a-state needed a town that was thoroughly otherworldly, a site to which they could attribute a transcendent purpose rather than a well-defined authority: and this they constructed Jerusalem, the city of truth (Zechariah 8:3), the city of blood, as the prophet Ezekiel called her (22:2, 24:6, 9), the city of the Lord (Psalm 101:8). (Zwiep 1998: 55)

Although many Jews longed for actual return to Jerusalem—for example, Yehuda Halevi not only wrote panegyric lyrics to Jerusalem but actually traveled to Jerusalem with the intention of dying there—many found "new" Jerusalems elsewhere.

---

[22] This Jewish practice is emulated in Islam by the *miḥrāb*, the prayer niche within mosques that faces the *qibla* (direction of prayer), Mecca (although it was originally Jerusalem).

For some readers, this phrase will have explicitly Christian resonance owing to the phrasing in English translations of the Book of Revelation (3:12, 21:12), but the concept of New Jerusalem actually has roots in the Hebrew Bible, particularly in the messianic text of Ezekiel (40–48), who, like the author of Psalm 137, wrote in the context of the Babylonian exile (sixth century BCE). But the Jerusalem described by Ezekiel and later commentators (e.g., Zechariah and, much later, John of Patmos) scarcely resembled the terrestrial city. In fact, the imagery of New Jerusalem—Ezekiel is rather tedious in his description of what the Third Temple's measurements would be—was premised on a commitment to the idea of heavenly, and not necessarily terrestrial, Jerusalem being the destination of return for diasporic Jews upon death or upon the arrival of the apocalypse.

The prospect of return had to be formed in the context of exile; the concept is, in fact, tautological, because one cannot return to where one currently is. Yet the conceptual schism between celestial and terrestrial Jerusalem produced ideological tension between the former's generative role for Jewish polities in exile and the latter's continued existence as a territory ruled by non-Jewish regimes (in order: Romans, Byzantines, Ayyubids, Crusaders, Mamluks, Ottomans, and British), a destination for pilgrimage, and home to a small community of remaining Jews. By the end of the nineteenth century, the thoroughly Middle Eastern customs and sounds of Jerusalem were foreign to the European Jews who developed the Zionist project that sought to realize Jewish liberation in the historical Jewish homeland.

An infamous instance of attempting to realize "Zion" elsewhere was the so-called Uganda Proposal, in which the founding father of Zionism, Theodor Herzl, sent a memorandum to the British Foreign Office that "called for the establishment of a largely autonomous Jewish protectorate in British East Africa" in 1903 (Penslar 2020: 190). A century later, much misinformation circulates on the ground about this incident. Often trotted out by twenty-first-century Israeli tour guides and other culture brokers as a forgotten moment in Zionist history in which Jews almost found a homeland in Africa, the act of forgetting is actually on the part of "citizen historians" themselves (Ricoeur 2004). The Uganda Proposal came on the heels of a failed plan—squashed by the British—to secure a Jewish territory in the Sinai Peninsula, combined with the pressing need to save Jewish lives with the increasing occurrence of pogroms in imperial Russia, especially the recent Kishinev pogrom, during which forty-nine Jews were murdered in April of 1903 (see Zipperstein 2018). Herzl and other Zionist officials consistently had indicated a strong preference for a Zionist settlement "in or near Palestine," but with the Uganda Proposal, Herzl sought the British Empire's assistance in moving Russian Jews temporarily to the East African colony, with the eventual goal of setting up a Jewish political home in Palestine.[23]

When the proposal was discussed at the Sixth Zionist Congress in 1903, outrage ensued. The idea of having a Jewish territory outside of Palestine was so dissonant for most members of the Zionist Organization that the group experienced a near-revolt of its membership. During his closing address on the final day of the Congress, in order to calm the organization's constituents and to affirm his own commitment to maintaining the place of terrestrial "Zion" within "Zionism," Herzl began to recite—what else—Psalm 137, the primordial injunction against forgetting Jerusalem and urtext for Zionism's territorial components. The Uganda Proposal was never seriously pursued: an exploratory commission was approved at the 1903 Congress, but the proposal ultimately was voted down at the Seventh Congress in 1905. Within the framework of Zionism—again, consider the term itself—Jews are always-already spatialized as being *of*, and therefore as eventually being *in*, Zion. Like other diaspora Jews, European Zionists at the turn of the twentieth century remained ardently committed to the idea of return, imagined in terms of the land itself, where their ancestors had flourished in antiquity as a more-or-less cohesive polity.

The injunction against forgetting Jerusalem yields at least two notions of return. But there is an important distinction between them: one concept of return is spatialized in terms of heavenly Jerusalem and involves a return to God, whom Jews believe once actually dwelled in the Temple of Jerusalem's inner sanctuary, the Holy of Holies (*Kodesh ha-Kodashim*); the other is spatialized in terms of terrestrial Jerusalem and is committed to the formation of a Jewish polity in the particularized space of Palestine. What early Zionists sought to stimulate was a shift from the former to the latter, and a mobilization of colonial and, later, national resources toward achieving the ultimate migration. Within the development of Zionist thought came an intensified attachment to the idea of actual return to terrestrial Jerusalem and, by extension, greater Palestine.

---

[23] For a succinct summary of developments surrounding the Uganda Proposal, see Penslar (2020: 185–92).

Tel Aviv as Heavenly Jerusalem

As this chapter nears its close, it is worth exploring a more contemporary setting, in which there is not always complete and total animosity between residents of Jerusalem and Tel Aviv. On a symbolic level, they may indeed represent opposite orientations to what it means to be Jewish in the modern world and in Israel more specifically (Hankins 2015: 73), but the two cities are interconnected and connected with other cities outside of the Tel Aviv-Jerusalem binary in the functioning of the region's political and economic geography. In 2006, Jerusalem-based hip-hop fusion group Hadag Nahash[24] released a song that expresses this interconnection in what was intended to be an anthem for the twenty-first-century Jerusalemite, "Here I Come" (*Hine Ani Ba*). In the song and its video, the group's members play on the long-standing oppositional thinking about Tel Aviv and Jerusalem established in the Yishuv and produced through political and musical discourse in the intervening years.

Here I come . . .
Jerusalem, a city like an explosion
Walking on the mall feels like the ingathering of the exiles
A thousand cultures, everyone has a brother and nine sisters
Arabs are okay, Haredis are in the study-room
All are set on and receiving God's frequency
After Teddy Jerusalem dies down
From day to day Tel Aviv sparkles more
Friends either left or got closer to the creator of the heavens
Gray, boring, there's no sea
Thoughts about leaving
It took me three years to make the decision
I'll pack my stuff into the suitcase
From the village to the city, a downhill descent

Tel Aviv—here I come
I'm coming—here I come
I'm coming to sweat—here I come
Because you're the only one, I swear

[24] The name "Hadag Nahash" translates rather whimsically to "Snakefish," but the name is pun on *nahag ḥadash*, meaning "new driver" and a commonly seen bumper sticker on Israeli cars.

I went toward the coastal plain
What a shock I'm in for
And now that I'm finally in Tel Aviv
I fit right in to the scene, all is clear, it's good
Whoa, so many breasts my eyes got burnt
After two years of Sodom and Gomorrah
I don't recognize myself in the mirror
Getting to know, mingle, blend in, make friends with
All the owners of the clubs
Now that I'm in, I know that it doesn't sparkle
So much noise, so much soot, give me grass, give me a tree
The whole day is wasted on "shalom," "shalom"
The rent costs a fortune, the humidity and craziness
And then it hit me
Paradise was in my hands
Thoughts about leaving
It took me three years to make the decision
I'll pack my sins into the suitcase
From the city to the village, toward . . .

Jerusalem—here I come
I'm returning to you—here I come
To your walls—here I come
Because you're the only one, I swear

I returned to Jerusalem, here the hummus is good, for sure
Give me calm, give me quiet, some yawning won't hurt
When was the last time I put a note in the Kotel, took time to make
    some food
Or made new friends
This city gives me back control over my life
Spend time with myself instead of doing useless stuff
Let's breathe some "mountain air as clear as wine"
Let's go Beitar, let's go life in the village
The main thing is to be happy

Here I come . . .
Tel Aviv—here I come!

I'm coming—here I come!
I coming to sweat—here I come!
Because you're the only one, I swear!

הִנֵּה אֲנִי בָא...

יְרוּשָׁלַיִם, עִיר שָׁוָה פִּיצוּץ
הוֹלֵךְ בַּמִּדְרָחוֹב מַרְגִּיש כְּמוֹ קִבּוּץ גָּלוּיוֹת
אֶלֶף תַּרְבֻּיּוֹת, לְכָל אֶחָד יֵשׁ אָח וְתֵשַׁע אֲחָיוֹת
עֲרָבִים בְּסֵדֶר חֲרֵדִים בַּחֶדֶר
וְכֻלָּם פֹּה קוֹלְטִים אֶת אֱלֹהִים - בְּתֶדֶר
אַחֲרֵי טֶדִי יְרוּשָׁלַיִם דָּעֲכָה מַהֵר
מִיּוֹם לְיוֹם תֵּל אָבִיב נִצְּחָה יוֹתֵר
חֲבֵרִים עָזְבוּ אוֹ הִתְקָרְבוּ לְבוֹרֵא שָׁמַיִם
אֵפֶר, מְשַׁעֲמֵם, אֵין יָם
מַחְשָׁבוֹת עַל עֲזִיבָה
שָׁלוֹשׁ שָׁנִים לָקַח לִי לְקַבֵּל תַּ'הַחְלָטָה
אָרַז תַּ'חֲפָצִים לְתוֹךְ הַמִּזְוָדָה
מֵהַכְּפָר לָעִיר בְּכִוּוּן הַיְרִידָה

תֵּל אָבִיב - הִנֵּה אֲנִי בָא
אֲנִי מַגִּיעַ - הִנֵּה אֲנִי בָא
בָּאתִי לְהַזִּיעַ - הִנֵּה אֲנִי בָא
כִּי אַתְּ הַיְחִידָה אֲנִי נִשְׁבַּע

יָצָאתִי לְכִוּוּן מִישׁוֹר הַחוֹף
אֵיזֶה שׁוּק אֲנִי עוֹמֵד לַחֲטֹף
וְעַכְשָׁו כְּשֶׁאֲנִי בְּתֵל אָבִיב סוֹף סוֹף
מִשְׁתַּלֵּב עִם הַנּוֹף, הַכֹּל טָרִי וְזֶה טוֹב
וַוי, כַּמָּה שָׁדַיִם, נִשְׂרְפוּ לִי הָעֵינַיִם
אַחֲרֵי שְׁנָתַיִם שֶׁל סְדוֹם וַעֲמוֹרָה
לֹא מְזַהֶה אֶת עַצְמִי בַּמַּרְאָה
מַכִּיר, מִתְעָרֵב, מִתְמַזֵּג, מִסְתַּחְבֵּק עִם
כָּל הַבְּעָלִים שֶׁל הַדִּיסְקוֹטֶקִים
מֵבִין, זֶה לֹא נוֹצֵץ in, עַכְשָׁו כְּשֶׁאֲנִי
כַּמָּה רַעַשׁ, כַּמָּה פִּיחַ, תֵּן לִי דֶּשֶׁא, תֵּן לִי עֵץ
כָּל הַיּוֹם מִתְבַּזְבֵּז עַל שָׁלוֹם, שָׁלוֹם
הַשְּׂכִירוּת הוֹן הַלְּחוּת וְשִׁגָּעוֹן
וְאָז נָפַל הָאַסִימוֹן,

גַּן עֵדֶן הָיָה לִי בַּיָּדַיִם
מַחְשָׁבוֹת עַל עֲזִיבָה
שָׁלוֹשׁ שָׁנִים לָקַח לִי לְקַבֵּל תְּ'הַחְלָטָה
אוֹרֵז תֵּ'חֲטָאִים בְּתוֹךְ הַמִּזְוָדָה
מֵהָעִיר לַכְּפָר לְכַוֵּון

יְרוּשָׁלַיִם - הִנֵּה אֲנִי בָּא
חוֹזֵר אֵלַיִךְ - הִנֵּה אֲנִי בָּא
אֶל חוֹמוֹתַיִךְ - הִנֵּה אֲנִי בָּא
כִּי אַתְּ הַיְחִידָה אֲנִי נִשְׁבָּע
חָזַרְתִּי לִירוּשָׁלַיִם, פֹּה הַחוּמּוּס טוֹב זֶה בָּדוּק
תֶּן לִי רֹגַע, תֶּן לִי שֶׁקֶט, לֹא יַזִּיק אֵיזֶה פָּהוּק
מָתַי פַּעַם אַחֲרוֹנָה שֶׁמָּתִי אֵיזֶה פֶּתֶק בַּכֹּתֶל, הִשְׁקַעְתִּי בָּאֹכֶל,
עָשִׂיתִי חֲבֵרִים חֲדָשִׁים,
הָעִיר הַזֹּאת תַּחֲזִיר לִי תֵּ'שְׁלִיטָה בַּחַיִּים
נִתְעָרְבֵּב עִם עַצְמִי בְּמָקוֹם לְעָרְבֵּב מַיִם
נִנְשֹׁם קְצָת אֲוִיר הָרִים צָלוּל כַּיַּיִן
יָאלְלָה בֵּיתָ"ר, יָאלְלָה חַיִּים בַּכְּפָר!
הָעִקָּר לִהְיוֹת מְאֻשָּׁר

הִנֵּה אֲנִי בָּא...

תֵּל אָבִיב - הִנֵּה אֲנִי בָּא
אֲנִי מַגִּיעַ - הִנֵּה אֲנִי בָּא
בָּאתִי לְהַזִּיעַ - הִנֵּה אֲנִי בָּא
כִּי אֶת הַיְחִידָה אֲנִי נִשְׁבָּע

The narrator of this song—spread across the multiple voices of the band, whose members alternate lines—feels torn between Jerusalem and Tel Aviv and the different lifestyles and identities they enable. The most striking contrast here is when the narrator refers to Jerusalem as a "village" (*kfar*) and Tel Aviv as a "city" (*ir*)—a distinction suggesting that the former offers a small, closed social system while the latter is characterized by openness and social possibility.

Originally from Jerusalem, the narrator feels the unbearable weight of history, religion, and violence there. At his coming of age, he finds himself in a position where members of his social group have either moved away, presumably to Tel Aviv, or become devout to such a degree as to be off-putting. After three years of deliberation, he decides to move to Tel Aviv in search of a better life. As he arrives, he feels the pull of Tel Aviv's charms, with its beautiful scenery and vibrant social life. Once he achieves insider status in the community, however, he becomes disillusioned with the problems of living in an overdeveloped urban environment, especially due to its cost of living, close proximity of people and pollution, and distance from nature. He makes the decision to move back to Jerusalem. The chorus leading into the next verse uses parallelism with the first one, exchanging Tel Aviv for Jerusalem. It also employs clichés from the field of Jerusalem song, including the word "return" (_hozer/lahzor_) and a mention of the city's walls (_homot/homotaykh_)—marking the narrator's familiarity with and affinity for Jerusalem's symbolic nature. In the spoken verse we learn that he joins in with the city's own social life, as he roots for the Jerusalem Beitar soccer club (after referring to Teddy Jerusalem stadium earlier) and sings the words to Naomi Shemer's 1967 song, "Jerusalem of Gold" ("mountain air as clear as wine"), which is discussed in Chapter 4. After an instrumental interlude, the band repeats the first chorus with "Tel Aviv—Here I Come!" until the outro, suggesting that the narrator, for all his desire to make a nobler life in Jerusalem, has given in to the sin and temptation offered by Tel Aviv.

The video for "Here I Come" yields some clues for how the band resolves the tension created by the opposing forces of Tel Aviv and Jerusalem. The video opens on a rotating black box whose etchings and pockmarks resemble the giant stones of the Western Wall. The resemblance is confirmed in the next sequence, which begins with an image of the Western Wall. The band appears rapping over a backdrop of rapidly changing but easily recognizable images of the city of Jerusalem, such as the Old City walls and the Dome of the Rock. When the lyrics shift to Tel Aviv, we see images of that city: skyscrapers and bustling streets. Some of these scenes are processed so that frames alternate between positive and negative exposure, creating the sense of flashing lights one might see in a dance club. When the lyrics turn back to Jerusalem, images of that city return. The band members stand together, with vocalist Guy Mar in the center assuming a meditative pose with his eyes closed.

As images of the city change behind him, the black box returns in spliced-in single frames, as if the object is intended to have a subliminal influence on either Mar, the narrator, or the music video's audience. When Mar finally opens his eyes, he sees the Western Wall in front of him. His eyes and the camera scan upward, and the stone wall transforms into a steel and glass skyscraper. The camera view shoots through one of the building's windows to reveal a raging dance party, as the final Tel Aviv chorus repeats. While out on the packed dance floor, Mar seems to have dropped something, and he tries reaching through dancing legs to retrieve it. Finally, we see him pick up a pair of miniature black stones, resembling the rotating box from earlier. Mar looks disturbed. When the video cuts to the final scene, all of the band members, paired up with women from the club scene, appear inside a large box whose sides have fallen down. As the music stops, they look around to see they are in a room full of these boxes, which are arranged haphazardly around some sort of cosmic warehouse. The video ends.

The song's sonic and visual components together musically synthesize an argument that reverberates in Nitzan-Shiftan's thinking:

> [T]he old dichotomies between Tel Aviv and Jerusalem no longer describe dependent, complementary halves, as the ancient and modern silhouettes of the national body. Rather, they function as antagonistic weights that pull this body apart—one stretches modernity to its most radical ends, the other retreats into a reactionary fundamentalism that halts life with irreducible essentialist truths. (Nitzan-Shiftan 2007: 94)

In losing himself in Tel Aviv, the narrator has gone further by destroying Jerusalem, represented by the Western Wall, whose symbolic stone blocks contain the city's population. The song does not simply resolve the tension by upholding Jerusalem at the end; rather, it plays on a preexisting discursive tension, established in a much earlier era, in order to demonstrate the positive and negative qualities that characterize each city. Jerusalemite identity and social life are constructed as aspirational; the narrator wants to adhere to the "village" life. Tel Aviv is constructed as a place to which one might succumb—and, indeed, the narrator does succumb, at the expense of all things holy.

Reflections on Forgetting

In the previous chapter, I chronicled the development of Jerusalem's poetics of place from the writing of the Hebrew Bible through *Haskala* (Jewish Enlightenment) in nineteenth-century Europe into the twentieth-century Zionist settlement of Palestine and the creation of the State of Israel, establishing the city's centrality to Jewish understanding of self and other, home and exile, and other dualities. In the current chapter, I have shown that the images of place territorializing Hebrew song were predominantly images of rural Palestine, particularly deserts and green valleys, and images of the new Hebrew city of Tel Aviv.

But it's not quite so simple. My argument is not that Jerusalem's absence proves that Israeli Jews did not care about Jerusalem but rather that prior to Israel's conquest of Jerusalem in 1967, the Israeli public was not necessarily longing for control over the Old City and East Jerusalem. This claim revises the idea of a divinely ordained Jewish teleology but also the insidious idea of a secret Jewish plot to take the city, both representing popular beliefs that circulate as facts on the ground. To readers who are unaccustomed to thinking outside of the Israel-Palestine conflict's dominant ideological frameworks, this chapter's exposition might read like critical acrobatics meant to justify Israel's claim to Greater Jerusalem, whose occupation violates international law and to which there is little evidence of Zionist musical attachment in an overt sense. For, if Jerusalem's liberatory poetics were applied to Tel Aviv and other spaces, would this not, in fact, strengthen the state's claims to ruling over the entirety of Palestine in fulfillment of Jewish prophecy and a continuous demonstration of attachment to the terrestrial territory itself? Not exactly; my point has been that Jerusalem's long-standing status as the poetic spatialization of Jewish religious and political liberation was manifested differently in the political context of Ottoman and British Palestine and that Jerusalem still managed to cast its shadow over much of that musical activity. In turn, this framed how other spaces within the Zionist territorial imagination, such as Tel Aviv, would be musically contemplated after 1948 and into the twenty-first century.

My claim that Jerusalem was adumbrated within Zionist music about other spaces is rooted in ontology, on the one hand, and in the relations between memory, history, and forgetting, on the other. In his essay "Ontologies of Music" (1999), Philip V. Bohlman describes "adumbration" as an ontological condition of music wherein "music itself is not present, but its effects or the recognition of its presence elsewhere are; it is recognized because of the shadow it has cast" (19). He goes on to claim that adumbration "may be recognizable only through the objects it leaves or the processes it unleashes" (19). This last statement clearly implies a role for temporality in the nature and experience of music, for music must have sounded previous to its having left objects or having unleashed processes.

A broader philosophical accounting for the experience of things (including music) that exhibit such an ontological condition may help explain the functioning of adumbration within Zionist cultural production. In Husserl's phenomenology of objects, adumbration (*Abschattungen*) signifies both foreshadowing and shadow-casting, such that a thing might not only leave a faint cast of itself, as in Bohlman's ontological formulation, but might also prefigure another thing—a thing on which that faint cast may or may not be inscribed or apparent. So to extend one of Bohlman's examples, "when Islamic thought claims that recitation of the Koran is not music" (Bohlman 1999: 19), a person who hears Qur'anic recitation must have a preconception of what music is in order to have the ability to distinguish one from the other as two distinct forms of vocalization having radically different ontologies and ethics of audition (see also Nelson 1985: 32–51). This example may seem obvious, but it relates directly to Jerusalem—not only via the city's soundscape, which certainly includes the recitation of the Qur'an within Islamic spaces, but also via how Jerusalem both prefigures alternative spaces of Jewish political liberation and casts its shadow on the manner in which those spaces are musically represented. In my claim about how Jerusalem casts its shadow *within* songs in which the city's explicit representation is absent or rare, in accord with pre-state Zionism's spatial ethos, "Jerusalem" stands in for "music" in Bohlman's definition of adumbrated ontology. To restate the argument in such terms, I have demonstrated that in the ethos of Zionist music before the founding of the state in 1948, a representation of Jerusalem itself may not be present, but its effects or the recognition of its presence elsewhere are.

One might use a similar formulation to describe *forgetting* itself. In *Memory, History, Forgetting* (2004), philosopher Paul Ricoeur takes on the nebulous relation between the three titular temporal forms. The ultimate philosophical aim of Ricoeur's writing about forgetting was to connect it to the act of forgiveness, which was an end that bound the entirety of his study with the specter of the Holocaust and therefore connected his work on time and narrative to his work on recognition; such investigations are related to my project, albeit indirectly, for they are instructive about the interaction of memory, history, and forgetting in the context of an Israeli-Palestinian conflict approaching resolution (sadly, this is not the case at the time of writing). But for my investigation into the nature of "forgotten" Jerusalem, here I focus more specifically on Ricoeur's understanding of how forgetting and memory are linked together, which is not as obvious as it may seem in their common usage in English and Hebrew alike (in the latter language, the respective gerunds are *shkhiḥa* and *zikaron*).

By his own admission, Ricoeur's investigation is "inaugurated, accompanied, and tortured" by "a dialectic of presence, absence, and distance" (2004: 419). In reading these phrases, which appear in a section titled "Forgetting and Effacing Traces" (418–27) from his chapter on the historical condition produced by forgetting, one might also apply the same language to Jewish exile itself, which was inaugurated, accompanied, and tortured by a dialectic of presence (within), absence (from), and distance (away from) Jerusalem. In this configuration, Jerusalem stands in for what we might call "the past," in the general sense in which Ricoeur uses the term throughout his investigation. But can temporality (the past) be transmogrified as spatiality (the city) by such theoretical magic? My point in this chapter is that it can and has been, via Zionist musical manifestations of Jerusalem as a liberatory space. After all, Ricoeur uses the term "distance" to refer to time's passage when distance is actually a spatial variable.

As I have shown, the spatial ethos of Yishuv cultural production persists in the territorial imagination of twenty-first-century Israel, most especially in how Tel Aviv and Jerusalem are set at odds in musical discourse. The two neighboring cities, and the nonurban spaces with which they form geographical contiguities, represent for many Israelis distinct ways of inhabiting the same national identity. As sociologist Uri Ram argues, "Critics are right to argue that Jerusalem and Tel Aviv belong to the same system, and despite their blatant antagonism, they belong to the same Zionist colonialist project. Yet despite this commonality between the cities, each of them indicates a distinct potential" (Ram 2005: 32). He may be right in seeing a dangerous provinciality as Jerusalem's defining quality. But as I have argued in this chapter, both of those "distinct potentials," each with its own narrative of spatial redemption, demonstrate how cosmopolitan and world-wary the crisis over Jerusalem really is.

3

Haunted Jerusalem

Musical Memorialism and the Politics of Bereavement

I've come back to this city where names
are given to distances as if to human beings
and the numbers are not of bus routes
but: 70 After, 1917, 500
B.C., Forty-eight. These are the lines
you really travel on.

And already the demons of the past are meeting
with the demons of the future and negotiating about me
above me, their give-and-take neither giving nor taking,
in the high arches of shell orbits above my head.

A man who comes back to Jerusalem is aware that the places
that used to hurt don't hurt anymore.
But a light warning remains in everything,
like the movement of a light veil: warning.

שַׁבְתִּי אֶל הָעִיר הַזֹּאת שֶׁבָּה נִתְּנוּ
שֵׁמוֹת לַמֶּרְחַקִּים כְּמוֹ לִבְנֵי אָדָם
וּמִסְפְּרֵי קַוִּים לֹא שֶׁל אוֹטוֹבּוּסִים,
אֶלָּא 70 אַחֲרֵי 1917, חָמֵשׁ מֵאוֹת
לִפְנֵי הַסְּפִירָה, אַרְבָּעִים וּשְׁמוֹנֶה. אֵלֶּה הַקַּוִּים
שֶׁבָּהֶם נוֹסְעִים בֶּאֱמֶת.

וּכְבָר שְׂדֵי הֶעָבָר נִפְגָּשִׁים
עִם שְׂדֵי הֶעָתִיד וְדָנִים עָלַי מֵעָלַי
נוֹשְׂאִים וְנוֹתְנִים, לֹא נוֹשְׂאִים וְלֹא נוֹתְנִים,
בַּקְּמוּרִים גְּבוֹהִים בְּמַסְלוּלֵי פְּגָזִים מֵעַל רֹאשִׁי.

City of Song. Michael A. Figueroa, Oxford University Press. © Oxford University Press 2022.
DOI: 10.1093/oso/9780197546475.003.0004

אָדָם שֶׁשָּׁב לִירוּשָׁלַיִם חָשׁ שֶׁהַמְּקוֹמוֹת
שֶׁכָּאֲבוּ שׁוּב אֵינָם כּוֹאֲבִים.
אֲבָל אַזְהָרָה קַלָּה נִשְׁאֶרֶת בַּכֹּל,
כְּמוֹ צָעִיף קַל נָע: אַזְהָרָה.

—Yehuda Amichai, from "Jerusalem 1967" (1968)[1]

The body, one may say, belongs to the land, while the land is felt to
acquire contours that resonate with the bodies buried within it.
　　　　—Don Handelman and Lea Shamgar-Handelman (1997: 90)

In his poem cycle, "Jerusalem 1967," Yehuda Amichai sought to capture the
manifest cultural changes wrought by the Six-Day War in his home city. In the
second section, which serves as an epigraph to this chapter, the poet demonstrates how the utterance of numerals iconizing years has an indexical quality
that betrays the existential concomitance of place and cultural memory in
Jerusalem. "70 After" refers to 70 CE, when the Romans destroyed the Second
Jewish Temple; 1917 was the year of the Balfour Declaration, in which the
British Empire officially expressed support for a Jewish national home in
Palestine; "500 B.C." connotes the Jews' return to Israel after the Babylonian
exile; "Forty-Eight" is short-hand for the 1948 War of Independence, known
among Palestinians as *al-Nakba* (the Catastrophe). In comparing these numer-
ical expressions to modern bus routes traveling the city ("These are the lines /
you really travel on"), the poet demonstrates how violent narratives are marked
by a sense of nonlinear temporal motion, a sense that in turn affects how people
traverse space itself. As Hebrew literature scholar Ranen Omer-Sherman writes:

> In this lightly mocking stanza, blending the sense of temporal confusion that
> Jerusalem bestows on everyone at times, there is a pervasive sense of shared
> fate with all the other hapless inhabitants, all woefully out of step with the city's
> own uncanny logic of time, that is, its impenetrable cyclicality, its "other" logic
> of death and destruction, rebirth and renewal. (Omer-Sherman 2006: 222)

Memories of violence in the city evoke powerful emotions and betray the
fragility of peace. Amichai and his artistic contemporaries in literature and
music understood well the political expediency of narrative expression in

---

[1] Original poem in Amichai (1968: 9–10). Translation by Stephen Mitchell; in Alter (2015: 81–82).

Israeli society and have deployed it during and after times of war for commemoration, critique, or other political ends. In turn, their publics project their political desires onto poems and songs by performing them in ritual contexts that commemorate those violent historical moments or else call into question the moral legitimacy of this memorialism. Poets and musicians have been critical to establishing territorial sovereignty as a matter of public debate, as they used their social and symbolic capital to represent places in ways that resonated within multiple political domains, most especially for the public bereavement of those who died in service to the nation and to provide metacommentary on bereavement practices themselves.

In this chapter, I discuss the memorialization of wartime violence in Israeli musical practice. It is about what comes *after* war, what solidifies and transfers the memory to be instantiated time and again across multiple hearings and performances. Even after a ceasefire, as Amichai writes, "a light warning remains in everything / like the movement of a light veil: warning." As I have established in the preceding chapters, within dominant formations of Israeli national culture music has been a preeminent form of expression for constructing, or contesting, such localized emotional styles, social structures, and cultural routines. This is perhaps nowhere more evident than for purposes of commemoration and bereavement. Scholars of commemoration forms within Israel have long understood that commemoration and bereavement have a dynamic history according to changing tastes, relationships to national culture, religious affiliation, and especially the nature of the memory being commemorated (see, e.g., Handelman and Shamgar-Handelman 1997; Kaplan 2009). As such, it would be impossible to characterize in broad strokes some underlying structural commonality that unifies all such practices in music. Instead, I show how the poetics of bereavement are complex and given to transfiguration according to musicians' political or aesthetic agendas; their genealogies link the everyday with the extraordinary, and intense sorrow with biting critique or even irreverence.

Jerusalem's Memorial Landscape

Multiple groups in the region have used some form of musical memorialism to lionize national martyrs who sacrificed themselves for the land and whose "present absence" embodies military victory or defeat (Handelman and Shamgar-Handelman 1997). The morality of martyrdom in service of conquering, keeping, or taking back the territorial homeland is written into foundational myths of both Israeli and Palestinian national identity. In the case of Israeli nationalism, as Handelman and Shamgar-Handelman write,

> The soldier-citizen is thought to offer his life so that the state and its citizens will live. Just as the state exists through the viable constitution of its territory, so military death is intimately related to the land that such death is said to protect and propagate in some way. Therefore, in modern nationalism an intimate relationship is struck between the body of the dead soldier and the substance of the land he battled to defend. (1997: 90)

To that end, every Israeli knows by heart Joseph Trumpeldor's dying words: "It is good to die for our country" (*Tov lamut be'ad artsenu*).[2] Trumpeldor was memorialized in song by Abraham Broides (see Chapter 2) and the political firebrand Ze'ev Jabotinsky, as well as nonmusically through a 1926 roaring lion monument erected over the common grave he shares with the seven other casualties of the Battle of Tel Hai in the Kfar Giladi cemetery, where Tel Hai Day is still observed annually on the eleventh day of Adar in the Hebrew calendar. Trumpeldor has remained strongly resonant throughout the public sphere as the archetype of national death, which is linked explicitly to land and is a critical subject for commemoration in music, monument, and ritual.[3]

In a sense, this practice links Israelis with the region's (and the city's) other groups. After 1948, for example, Palestinian singers operating across several genres (e.g., *'atābā*, *shurūqīya*, and *muraba'*) developed a complex poetics of bereavement that combined the mourning of personal and collective loss with feelings of humiliation and anger at how the Arab states failed to liberate Palestine in the war. The articulation of indigenous values—chiefly, *sumud* (steadfastness or rootedness) and *sabr* (patience), both of which are explicitly connected to the land—intermingled with the commemoration of spaces of Palestinian cultural life that were lost in the war.[4] And, of course, the politicization of the *dabke* line dance ushered in by the folk revivalism that accompanied two Intifadas indicates that "Palestine will always remain under our stamping feet" (*Filasṭin rāḥ bizāl taḥt aqdāmna*), as the Palestinian

---

[2] This phrase is a play on Horace's words, "dulce et decorum est pro patria mori," from *Odes* (iii.2.13).

[3] For more on the importance of Trumpeldor and Tel Hai to Israel's national mythology, see Zerubavel 1995: 39–47, along with Chapter 2 of this book.

[4] For analyses of several such examples, see McDonald (2013: 62–72). For an account of how the Nakba altered Palestinian musical life more generally, see Jalal, Boulos, and Bursheh (2013).

intellectual Abu Hani told David McDonald in the latter's ethnography of the "poetics of Palestinian resistance" (McDonald 2013: 20).

As one of the most important urban centers of the Armenian diaspora, Jerusalem is also an important site for the commemoration of the Armenian Genocide (1915) on April 24 each year. According to Sylvia Alajaji's research, the centennial commemoration in 2015 involved a coordinated, worldwide series of concerts called "With You, Armenia" that began in Jerusalem, with other concerts held in New York, Italy, London, and Vienna (Alajaji 2020). Jerusalem is critical for such commemorative efforts, even though the mass-murder of Armenians at the hands of the Ottoman Empire took place in the Anatolian region of the empire (now Turkey), not in the Vilayet of Syria, of which the Sanjak of Jerusalem—long home to a sizable Armenian community—was a part. The city thus serves for Armenians as a diasporic outpost of what is essentially "a nation-state-centered discourse, where the diaspora appears through the country of Armenia" (Alajaji 2020: 231).[5] A monument to the victims of the Armenian Genocide of 1915 and the Armenian Legion of 1917 provides a silent testament to collective trauma as it sits in the Armenian Cemetery just outside the Zion Gate leading out of Jerusalem's Armenian Quarter.

Locally in Jerusalem, the dead haunt the living not only in music but also in the built environment's memorialist ethos. The prevalence of tombs and cemeteries is so great that the city's geography sometimes seems to be organized around them. Ancient Jewish custom was to bury the dead outside the city walls, but as Jerusalem started to expand beyond the Old City's boundaries in the mid-nineteenth century, ancient and medieval burial grounds eventually became swallowed by the modern city's geography. The tombs of the Kings, the Sanhedrins, and other Second Temple-era figures thus dot the landscape of modern East Jerusalem neighborhoods. Mamilla Cemetery, a historic Muslim graveyard in City Center that is home to Sufi shrines and other burial plots dating from early and middle-period Islamic history, sits directly across the street from the ritzy Mamilla Mall and several upscale hotels.[6] One can purchase a new wristwatch and then walk to the gravesites

---

[5] In the cited essay, and in what amounts to an effective postcolonial critique, Alajaji examines the repertory choices of these concerts, arguing that the heavy emphases on European concert repertory "position this [pan-Armenian] discourse strategically within a sonic framework that shifted decisively away from the world of the Ottoman Other, ostensibly eliminating non-Western elements of the self" (2020: 231).

[6] Mamilla Cemetery has also been the focus of considerable controversy since 2008, when plans were announced for the Museum of Tolerance Jerusalem, associated with the Simon Wiesenthal Center, to be built atop some of the gravesites; see Makdisi (2010).

of Salah ad-Din's ministers in less than three revolutions of the seconds-hand; such is the confluence of consumer capitalism and religious tourism in Jerusalem.

Up the road from there, at the intersection of King Solomon Street and Jaffa Street—at the very seam of East and West Jerusalem, the external walls of the Jerusalem municipal building are covered in pockmarks from Jordanian gunfire in the 1948 and 1967 Wars. Some twenty-five meters away, the Old City walls record the returned Israeli shots. This has been the site of violence, which has now grown silent but remains forever visible. When I asked architect Moshe Shapiro about the conservation of these bullet holes, he indicated that they served a memorial function: "They show what we have passed [endured]" in order to secure Jerusalem for the Jewish people (Shapiro 2017). There and elsewhere throughout the city, the built environment provides visual evidence of gunfire and conquest, the silence of the dead monumentalized in the very spaces where they died so noisily.

Looming east of the Old City is the Mount of Olives, a central focus of Jewish funerary practices that is now the home to Palestinian villages and Israeli settlements as well as many important Christian landmarks, such as the Church of Mary Magdalene. Located across the Kidron Valley—itself home to funerary monuments to Absalom, the Prophet Zechariah, and the Hezir family of temple priests—the Mount of Olives has been used as a burial site since King David's conquest of Jerusalem in circa 1000 BCE (David himself is purported to have been buried on Mount Zion to the west). Given its panoramic view of the Temple Mount, the Mount of Olives was a traditional location for observing the Jewish holidays of Sukkot and Tisha B'Av, the latter of which commemorates the 70 CE destruction of the Second Temple and, with it, ancient Israelite civilization. Although Jewish pilgrimage to the Mount of Olives has waned since the establishment of the State of Israel (Christian pilgrimage still persists), its image as a monument to individual and communal death in Jewish antiquity continues to mark the East Jerusalem landscape. The Palestinian village of Silwan at the mountain's southern ridge has been a notable site of conflict in the early decades of the twenty-first century, as the Israeli government has taken actions to destabilize Palestinian life there, especially through home demolitions, and long-standing residents and settlers clash in the streets or through acts of vandalism.[7]

---

[7] For data on home demolitions in Silwan, see https://www.btselem.org/planning_and_building/east_jerusalem_statistics.

Mount Herzl, to the west of the city, is the paramount monument of remembrance for Israeli modernity. Named for Theodor Herzl (1860–1904), the chief architect of political Zionism and "Visionary of the State" (*Hozeh ha-Medina*), it was chosen to be the central monument to Israel's deceased leaders in 1949, shortly after the establishment of the state and the end of the Independence War. As the seat of national remembrance—its other name is *Har ha-Zikaron* (Mount of Remembrance)—it is the resting place for the great majority of Israel's national heroes, from Herzl himself (whose remains were exhumed from a Viennese grave and brought to Jerusalem) to leaders of the Israeli government, such as past prime ministers Golda Meir and Yitzhak Rabin and iconic Jerusalem mayor Theodor "Teddy" Kollek. A whole section on the mountain's northern slope is dedicated to the National Military Cemetery, whose "synthesis of body and land" Handelman and Shamgar-Handelman characterize as being "the exemplar of the presence of national death" (1997: 90). They posit a synecdochic relationship between each unadorned grave—uniform headstones flatten the hierarchy of the living military—and the territory that each soldier is believed to have died protecting.

On the southern slope of Mount Herzl is Yad Vashem, a museum that commemorates victims of the Holocaust—the ultimate, and actualized, expression of Jewish death at the hands of the outside world. Israeli politicians have often found it effective to connect the Holocaust and its imagery to Israeli political issues. In 2014, amid negotiations with the Palestinian Authority over a possible two-state solution to the conflict, Netanyahu and Deputy Foreign Minister Ze'ev Elkin attempted to strengthen the Israeli position by referring to the pre-1967 borders, which most international parties accept as the starting position for territorial negotiations, as "Auschwitz Borders," alluding to the infamous Nazi concentration camp and to an often repeated statement made by Abba Eban to a German interviewer in 1969:

> We have openly said that the map will never again be the same as on June 4, 1967. For us, this is a matter of security and of principles. The June map is for us equivalent to insecurity and danger. I do not exaggerate when I say that it has for us something of a memory of Auschwitz. We shudder when we think of what would have awaited us in the circumstances of June 1967, if we had been defeated; with Syrians on the mountain and we in the valley, with the Jordanian army in sight of the sea, with the Egyptians who hold our throat in their hands in Gaza. This is a situation which will never be repeated in history. (quoted in Blum 2014)

Netanyahu's and Elkin's uses of this term suggest that the threat of external extermination dictates the necessity of possessing Jerusalem, and with it the rest of the West Bank, as well as other territory in Israel/Palestine. The memories of the dead are critical to this calculus, and they are preserved not only in political pronouncements but also in musical commemorations, ritual performance in Jerusalem's public space, and the memorial landscape itself.

In the exposition that follows, I explore how Israelis musically memorialize national heroes who haunt sites of violence in Jerusalem and its surrounding environs, in order to examine how people remember times of war and internalize a sense of personal agency and political will within narratives of the violent past. It is not that this memorial repertory shapes Jerusalem's soundscape any more than it does other Israeli and Palestinian cities. There are plenty of songs that consecrate battle grounds in Tel Aviv and Ramallah (and elsewhere). For that matter, Jerusalemites sing memorial songs set elsewhere, and people in other cities sing memorial songs set in Jerusalem; I have experienced this firsthand at concerts located all around the country. Musical memorialism is about *national* bereavement. But for a large part of the region's population, Jerusalem serves as the main epicenter of the international conflict, and so focusing on examples of musical memorialism that locate national death and bereavement there is essential to understanding how Jerusalem fits into an Israeli national identity framework, and vice versa.

Many of these memorial songs exemplify the poetics of Jerusalem song in a general sense. As I established in Chapter 1, some songwriters use anthropomorphism or personification to endow material icons of the city with human bodily elements and emotions. A striking example of this practice is a song about a site at the epicenter of Jerusalem's conflicted space, and the most important religious site conquered during the 1967 War: "The Kotel" (*Ha-Kotel*, i.e., the Western Wall), written by Yossi Gamzu with music by Dov Seltzer. The song's lyrics personify the Western Wall, using this poetic move as a vehicle for engaging with the loss of life involved in liberating the Wall itself:

> A girl stood facing the *Kotel*
> She brought her lips and chin closer
> She said to me: "the shofar's blasts are strong,
> But the silence is even stronger."
> She said to me: "Zion, the Temple Mount."
> She quieted me: "the reward and the right."

And what shone on the peak at sunset
Was the purple of royalty.

[Refrain]
The Kotel: hyssop and despair,
The Kotel: lead and blood.
There are people with hearts of stone,
There are stones with human hearts.

The paratrooper faced the Kotel,
The only one left from the platoon
He said to me: "Death has no image, but it has a diameter—
Only nine millimeters."
He said to me: "I'll shed no tears"
And lowered his gaze back down.
But my grandfather, God knows,
Is buried here on the Mount of Olives.

[Refrain]

Standing in black, facing the Kotel,
An infantry soldier's mother,
She said to me: "My boy's eyes are glowing,
Not the candles on the wall."
She said to me: "I'm not writing
Any note to tuck between the cracks
Because what I gave to the Kotel just last night
Is greater than mere words."

[Refrain]

עָמְדָה נַעֲרָה מוּל הַכֹּתֶל
שְׂפָתַיִם קְרֵבָה וְסַנְטֵר
אָמְרָה לִי: "תְּקִיעוֹת הַשּׁוֹפָר חֲזָקוֹת הֵן,
אֲבָל הַשְּׁתִיקָה עוֹד יוֹתֵר"
אָמְרָה לִי: "צִיּוֹן הַר הַבַּיִת"
שָׁתְקָה לִי: "הַגְּמוּל וְהַזְּכוּת"
וּמַה שֶּׁזָּהַר עַל מִצְחָהּ בֵּין עַרְבַּיִם,
הָיָה אַרְגָּמָן שֶׁל מַלְכוּת.

[פִּזְמוֹן:]
הַכֹּתֶל—אֵזוֹב וְעַצֶּבֶת,
הַכֹּתֶל—עוֹפֶרֶת וָדָם.
יֵשׁ אֲנָשִׁים עִם לֵב שֶׁל אֶבֶן,
יֵשׁ אֲבָנִים עִם לֵב-אָדָם.

עָמַד הַצַּנְחָן מוּל הַכֹּתֶל,
מִכָּל מַחְלָקְתּוֹ רַק אֶחָד
אָמַר לִי: "לַמָּוֶת אֵין דְּמוּת אַךְ יֵשׁ קֹטֶר—
תִּשְׁעָה מִילִימֶטֶר בִּלְבָד"
אָמַר לִי: "אֵינֶנִּי דוֹמֵעַ"
וְשָׁב לְהַשְׁפִּיל מַבָּטִים...
אַךְ סַבָּא שֶׁלִּי, אֱלֹהִים הַיּוֹדֵעַ,
קָבוּר כָּאן, בְּהַר הַזֵּיתִים.

[פִּזְמוֹן]

עָמְדָה בִּשְׂחֹרִים מוּל הַכֹּתֶל,
אִמּוֹ שֶׁל אֶחָד מִן הַחַיִּ"ר.
אָמְרָה לִי: "עֵינֵי נַעֲרִי הַדּוֹלְקוֹת הֵן
וְלֹא הַנֵּרוֹת שֶׁבַּקִּיר."
אָמְרָה לִי: "אֵינֶנִּי רוֹשֶׁמֶת
שׁוּם פֶּתֶק לִטְמֹן בֵּין סְדָקָיו.
כִּי מַה שֶּׁנָּתַתִּי לַכֹּתֶל רַק אֶמֶשׁ,
גָּדוֹל מִמִּלִּים וּמִכְּתָב".

[פִּזְמוֹן]

Each stanza narrates the experiences of three individual characters—a young girl, a male paratrooper (the lone survivor of his infantry), and a grieving mother—who all encounter the Western Wall after the war. The characters are representative of divergent relationships to the territorial expansion resulting from the war: the girl sees in the Western Wall Jewish royalty and splendor, the site of the Temple, and the beauty of the city unmarred by the recent violence; the paratrooper sees the opposite, as the site is associated with the death of all of the rest of his platoon; the mother indicates her bereavement over the sacrifice of her son, who was a soldier in the war—she even forgoes the traditional practice of pressing a prayerful note between the cracks of the wall's giant stones, seeing instead his spirit manifested in the re-instatement of Jewish access to the holiest site in Judaism.[8]

The refrain, which appears between each character's verse, adds a fourth character: the Western Wall itself. Through inversion, the final two lines of the refrain suggest that "There are people with hearts of stone, / There are stones with human hearts." The wall's personification becomes a vehicle for castigating people who uncritically celebrate the war victory without re-flecting on the losses of life, and perhaps political challenges, that come with it. The poignant vocal melody, sung by the Darom Duo, is accompanied by discordant harmonic motion (primarily through a rising sequence of sec-ondary leading tones) to emphasize the refrain text's ironic tone. After the war, personal stories of real loss intersected with a larger national narrative of conquest and redemption. In "The Kotel," as in examples of apostrophe discussed in Chapter 1, Jerusalem is given human form—if not explicitly incarnate, then at least characterized by a sonic materiality that places the city in the roles of listener and mourner. The city itself thus attains a cer-tain level of metaphorical agency and, like its mourning people, is capable of experiencing grief, empathy, and despair in the wake of violence that itself has altered the city's cultural geography.

"The Kotel" is part of a broader memorial repertory that is subject to in-vestigation in this chapter. Analyzing this repertory reveals a strong linkage of bereavement and land in Israeli national culture but a relative lack of con-sensus about the political and religious tenability of that linkage in the face of changing historical circumstances. This is perhaps nowhere more apparent than in songs locating national death and bereavement in Jerusalem between 1948 and 1967.

Memorial Observance

The memorialization of war operates not only on the level of metaphor but also in ritual practice. Each spring, Jewish Israelis observe a cycle of national holidays that annually affirm a narrative teleology establishing the State of Israel. The first holiday is Holocaust Remembrance Day (*Yom ha-Shoah*); six

---

[8] As Dana Olmert points out, in modern Hebrew literature between the 1940s and 1990s the image of bereaved mothers who "do not question the ideology that sends their sons to war and into their deaths" (2013: 3) renders them canonical figures, against whom later authors such as Orly Castel-Bloom would push; see Olmert (2013).

days later marks Memorial Day (*Yom ha-Zikaron*); and the day following that is Independence Day (*Yom ha-Atsma'ut*). This seasonal ritual, which sociologist Danny Kaplan characterizes as "a movement from the catastrophe of the Holocaust (and the exile in general), through the sacrifices of life made in the struggles for rebuilding and liberating the nation, and peaking with the establishment of the state of Israel" (Kaplan 2009: 325), embodies a messianic narrative of "destruction to resurrection" that confirms the historical inevitability of the state's founding and, for some, a moral impetus to the state's policies and military practices. The synthesis of catastrophe (at the hands of the outside world) and sacrifice (through the bravery of national subjects) through redemption (the creation of the state) creates an opportunity for musicians to draw on rich symbolic and emotional resources for their performances; as such, the commemorative mode of ritual is facilitated powerfully by the musical invocation of historical events. The spring holidays are accompanied by concerts organized around the country—in schools, pubs, and public squares throughout major cities. The agents involved in planning and executing public events facilitate a sense of communal sentiment in an attempt to confirm the political-theological narrative.

Memorial Day presents an intimate counterpart to the relative inebriety of Independence Day celebrations. As with all Jewish holidays, observances begin at sundown the prior evening. In Jerusalem, official ceremonies are held at the Western Wall and Yad Le-Banim, a site near the government quarter that memorializes fallen soldiers who died fighting on the Jerusalem front. The ceremony is primarily for parents who have lost children (Yad Le-Banim means "Memorial for Children"), and it is customarily attended by a host of senior bureaucrats, including the prime minister, chair of the Knesset, head of the Supreme Court, chief rabbi, and mayor of Jerusalem. At the Western Wall, the mayor customarily joins the president, army chief, and an assortment of other VIPs, including families of fallen soldiers and terror victims, for an official opening ceremony. These official ceremonies involve prayers, political speeches, and poetry readings. The readings often conform to a canonic repertory of poems, especially ones written in the aftermath of wars, such as Haim Gouri's "Bab El Wad" and "Friendship" and Nathan Alterman's "The Silver Platter" and "Elifelet"—poems that, much like the grave sites on Mount Herzl, sanctify the bodies of soldiers who fought for the Jewish national cause.

During the day, most businesses, including music venues, are closed, and many people gather for prayer in military cemeteries around the country.

Mainstream radio and television outlets devote their programming to retrospective segments and limit their musical playlists to a repertory of "memorial day songs" (Kaplan 2009: 323). The constant presence of memorial music is rendered conspicuous when people mark the day with silence by stopping their cars and standing still in the streets as the city's alarms ring out, in a collective performance of remembrance. The memorial music played over radio and television and at the evening concerts is no less unisonant, but the repertory is highly varied in style, authorship, and poetic content. One might hear classic songs—known widely through mass media dissemination and programming in school dining room assemblies—commemorating martyrs of the 1948, 1967, or 1973 Wars alongside imported songs whose associations with Israeli national bereavement have accrued long after their composition for a much different context. As an example, cover versions of Leonard Cohen's "Hallelujah" (1984) seem ubiquitous in the twenty-first-century Israeli memorial repertory.

Against the backdrop of this eclectic collection of memorial songs, two songs that memorialize the dead in service of securing Israeli possession of Jerusalem have become canonic for, and iconic of, musical memorialism in Israel: Haim Gouri's "Bab El Wad" (1949) and Yoram Toharlev's "Ammunition Hill" (1968).

"Bab El Wad"

About halfway between Jerusalem and Tel Aviv, a parade of eviscerated military vehicles has sat, decomposing on the side of Highway 1, since the 1948 War. This monument commemorates a site of violence during the early months of the War, the Battle for Jerusalem. Some of the fiercest fighting for the city occurred there, approximately fifteen miles west of Jerusalem's western entrance, where Jewish forces attempted to break the Arab blockade in order to establish passage to alleviate the city's critical shortage of food, water, and supplies. At the time, the road running through this area, which passed through a narrow valley whose Arabic name is Bab El-Wad, was the only known point of entry into Jerusalem from the western territory controlled by Jewish fighting groups. This gave the area its strategic military value for both Israel and Jordan. Conquering Jerusalem necessitated control over this passageway, and so it determined the stakes of the casualty-heavy Latrun and Bab El-Wad battles.[9] After three failed campaigns, the Haganah successfully built a by-pass road to the north, called Burma Road, which served as a supply line for the besieged city. The iron skeletons that continue to sit roadside there serve as a monument to remind passersby of the fighters' sacrifice amid overwhelming odds.

Since the 1948 War, this place has become broadly emblematic of the Siege of Jerusalem and represents a modern story of Jewish determination and survival under the direst circumstances. It is also the contextual backdrop for the 1949 poem "Bab El-Wad" by Haim Gouri. In addition to being a poet, Haim Gouri (1923–2018) was a soldier who fought in the Palmach, an elite striking force, during the 1948 War. After the war, he became the leading voice of his generation of poets, most especially with the release of his 1949 volume *Flowers of Fire* (*Pirḥey Esh*), which helped to define the poetics of the "State Generation" (*Dor Ha-Medina*).

The text for "Bab El-Wad" operates on multiple referential levels to recall soldiers' memories and memories of soldiers:

> Here I pass, standing by the stone.
> A black asphalt road, rocks and ridges.
> Evening slowly descends, sea wind blows
> First starlight over *Bayt Maḥsir*.
>
> Bab El-Wad,
> Remember our names evermore,
> Convoys broke through, on the way to the city.
> Our dead lay on the side of the road.
> The iron skeleton is silent like my comrade.
>
> Here pitch and lead fumed under the sun,
> Here nights passed with fire and knives.
> Here sorrow and glory live together
> With a burnt armored car and the name of an unknown.
>
> And I walk, passing here silently, silently
> And I remember them, individually, individually
> Here we fought together on cliffs and boulders
> Here we were one family.

---

[9] See Morris (2008: 219–31), for an in-depth account of these battles.

A spring day will come, the cyclamens will bloom,
Red of anemone on the mountain and the slope.
This is what will follow in our path that we walked
Do not forget us, Bab El-Wad.

פֹּה אֲנִי עוֹבֵר. נִצָּב לְיַד הָאֶבֶן,
כְּבִישׁ אַסְפַלְט שָׁחֹר, סְלָעִים וּרְכָסִים.
עֶרֶב אַט יוֹרֵד, רוּחַ יָם נוֹשֶׁבֶת
אוֹר כּוֹכָב רִאשׁוֹן מֵעֵבֶר בֵּית-מַחְסִיר.

בָּאב אֶל וָאד,
לָנֶצַח זְכֹר נָא אֶת שְׁמוֹתֵינוּ.
שַׁיָּרוֹת פָּרְצוּ בַּדֶּרֶךְ אֶל הָעִיר.
בְּצִדֵּי הַדֶּרֶךְ מוּטָלִים מֵתֵינוּ.
שֶׁלֶד הַבַּרְזֶל שׁוֹתֵק, כְּמוֹ רֵעִי.

פֹּה רָתְחוּ בַּשֶּׁמֶשׁ זֶפֶת וְעוֹפֶרֶת,
פֹּה עָבְרוּ לֵילוֹת בְּאֵשׁ וְסַכִּינִים.
פֹּה שׁוֹכְנִים בְּיַחַד עֶצֶב וְתִפְאֶרֶת,
מִשְׁרָיִן חָרוּךְ וְשֵׁם שֶׁל אַלְמוֹנִים.

וַאֲנִי הוֹלֵךְ, עוֹבֵר כָּאן חֶרֶשׁ חֶרֶשׁ
וַאֲנִי זוֹכֵר אוֹתָם אֶחָד אֶחָד.
כָּאן לָחַמְנוּ יַחַד עַל צוּקִים וָטֶרֶשׁ
כָּאן הָיִינוּ יַחַד מִשְׁפָּחָה אַחַת.

יוֹם אָבִיב יָבוֹא וְרַקֶּפוֹת תִּפְרַחְנָה,
אֹדֶם כַּלָּנִית בָּהָר וּבַמּוֹרָד.
זֶה אֲשֶׁר יֵלֵךְ בַּדֶּרֶךְ שֶׁהָלַכְנוּ
אַל יִשְׁכַּח אוֹתָנוּ, אוֹתָנוּ בָּאב אֶל וָאד.

The poem draws on the spatial ethos of Yishuv cultural production, such as
the *Shirey Halutsim* (pioneer songs) and *Shirey Erets Israel* (Songs of the Land
of Israel) discussed in Chapter 2. It is filled with naturalistic imagery drawn
from stone, star, sun, and sea, mixed with references that indexed the violent memories of soldiers who fought in the war: iron, lead, fire, knives, and
armor. Gouri never mentions the name of Jerusalem, preferring the euphe-
mism "the city" (*ha-ir*), but as Eliyahu Hacohen writes, "Every child in the
country knew what he meant" (Hacohen 2018: 60).

The word "here" (*po* and, later, *kan*) opens the majority of the poem's lines, locating the narrator and listeners at Bab El-Wad. Through a casual simile in the refrain's closing line, the very vehicle carcasses that sit on the highway between Jerusalem and Tel Aviv today appear in this 1949 song as a metonym for anonymous fallen soldiers, making their "absence present so that it serves the agency of the living" (Handelman and Shamgar-Handelman 1997: 87). The dead and the living are, in the words of the song, "one family here."

By the penultimate verse, the song's narrative undergoes a shift in perspective from the first-person singular to the first-person plural, underscoring a connection between individual and collective experience. The narrator sings on behalf of the nation, frames the event in terms of a shared social memory of violent trauma and collective grief, and implores listeners to remember the dead. But just who should be remembered is rendered ambiguous, as Haim Rechnitzer (2008) points out. In the lyrics, the dead are characterized as both "unknown" and as people the narrator remembers "one by one," suggesting that they were his known comrades. Rechnitzer argues that the term for "unknown," *almoni*, "functions similarly to the English use of 'one' pointing to a general third person who can be assigned any 'real' name by the readers"; its use here "allows the readers to fill in the names of the soldiers they have personally known to have died in the wars, creating a personalized memory while retaining a shared experience" (Rechnitzer 2008: 44). This slippage creates an opportunity for ritualized remembrance, as people who read the poem, or who participate in singing the song version of "Bab El-Wad" on national holidays, connect personal memories of fallen soldiers with the collective commemoration of national death more generally, thus reinforcing the sense of personal investment in the national project. The line, "A spring day will come, the cyclamens will bloom," was especially prescient: every spring during Memorial Day and Independence Day, people lay wreaths at the memorial site in ritual observance of the two holidays that together capture the fact that both "sorrow and glory live together." The text is not merely mimetic but also narrative; it tells a familiar story with vivid sensory detail and in the present tense. The narrator's very memories are triggered by the landscape. The reader remembers along with the narrator.

This was precisely the motive behind the poem's musical arrangement. Shaike Yarkoni, a central figure in the Haganah, the Jewish paramilitary unit that became the core of the Israel Defense Forces after 1948, had the idea to set Gouri's poems "Bab El-Wad" and "Ha-Reʿut" to music (Sarfatti 2012).[10] The project to realize "Bab El-Wad" in song included an arrangement by Shmuel Fershko, a Polish composer-pianist who already had made a name for himself in the 1940s cabaret scene of Tel Aviv, and a now-iconic vocal performance by Yaffa Yarkoni, a then-peripheral figure in the national music scene and spouse of Shaike Yarkoni. The musical setting (Figure 3.1) involves one major formal change to the poem: the original strophes have been re-organized into a verse-chorus-verse form, and the second stanza serves as the refrain (beginning at the pickup to m. 11), thus highlighting the song's memorial function, with the site's name and its monumentality reiterated throughout the song ("Our dead lay on the side of the road. / The iron skeleton is silent like my comrade.").

The 1966 commercial recording of "Bab El-Wad," arranged by Alex Weiss and Gil Aldema for a large orchestral setting, provides insights into the complex cultural work that the song and its creators perform. While remaining faithful to the arrangement and general feel of the original 78RPM recording (c. 1949), the 1966 version includes bigger and more diverse instrumentation, with winds and strings, including a forward-mixed violin that articulates the main melody, as well as a rather large choir accompaniment.[11] These elements enhance the pathos and sense of gravity of the lyrics. The instrumental accompaniment involves fairly prominent modal mixture within the D-minor key (on the recording; in the original score, it is A-minor), by raising and lowering the sixth and seventh scale degrees to create moments of modal mixture (e.g., in mms. 9 and 17 of the score). During the final cadence of the song, Yarkoni flattens the second scale degree (E♭) to briefly, but finally, transform the minor key into Phrygian. These elements of modal mixture entered the *Shirey Erets Israel* stylistic lexicon through the dual streams of Ashkenazi Jewish music originating in east central Europe and the long-standing presence of modality in European compositional practice since the Baroque era (see Fleischer 2005: 157–80). Fershko would have been familiar with these procedures through his participation in Tel Aviv's

[10] "Ha-Reʿut," meaning "combat fraternity" (see discussion near the end of this chapter) was set by Sasha Argov and recorded by several of Yarkoni's contemporaries, including Shoshana Damari and Yehoram Gaon.

[11] Precisely dating the original recording is difficult, since the year does not appear on the record label and because, as Regev and Seroussi write, "In three short years, between 1949 and 1952, Yarkoni recorded an astonishing total of 400 records (78 RPM'S) for Hed Artzi, including many historical recordings of the heroic songs of the War of Independence" (2004: 84). Regarding the 1966 LP version discussed here, Zemereshet indicates that Yarkoni had been playing a similarly arranged version since at least 1959 (https://www.zemereshet.co.il/song.asp?id=754).

Figure 3.1 Original score of Shmuel Fershko's "Bab El-Wad" arrangement (courtesy of the National Sound Archive, National Library of Israel).

Figure 3.1 Continued

European–oriented cabaret scene, where composers often turned to modality (particularly Aeolian, Dorian, and Phrygian) to develop their individual compositional styles (Fleischer 2005: 158). It was commonplace for a midcentury cabaret composer like Fershko, the recording arrangers Weiss and Aldema, and *Shirey Erets Israel* more generally to evince a cosmopolitan musical style that borrowed heavily from these musical languages.

All of this stylistic complexity inflects the text with heightened poetic sensibility and its functional memorialism. Listening to Yaffa Yarkoni's performance of "Bab El-Wad," one can almost smell the crisp, dark, pine-perfumed air of calm that punctuated the sweaty daytime fighting. The singing narrator, with pronounced vocal pathos, communes with the national dead by way of the landscape. In the final verse, which begins "A spring day will come," she shifts from song to speech and intones the text in the manner of a political speech or religious incantation, before rejoining the chorus of voices in the pickup (" . . . us / Bab El-Wad"). This creates a sense of teleology in the song form, although that sense is punctuated by the use of a repeating refrain. The arrangement is rhythmically based around a fairly consistent dotted-eighth-note/sixteenth-note beat division, but Yarkoni's vocal delivery often blurs this static conception of time. Her intense vocal rubato, which mingles with vibrating swells in the violin, creates a sonic metaphor for the oblique haziness of memory and experience against the objective measure of linear time.

Yarkoni's rendition of "Bab El-Wad" enjoys pride of place within the Israeli song canon: it was one of five of her songs included on *We Grew Up Together* (*Gadalnu Yahad*), the 1998 anthology commemorating fifty years since Israel's founding, and it continues to be programmed in live cover performances in the twenty-first century. But both the song and its source poem have been criticized for the text's anonymous treatment of both Israeli soldiers and Arab enemies. As philosopher Meir Buzaglo remarks, "The nonappearance or disappearance of the Arabs from Gouri's poem erases any guilt and carries within it dehumanization of the Arab" (2003: 182, in Rechnitzer 2008: 46–47). The song thus has been taken to task through musical parodies.

In the years following the song's original release,[12] Buzaglo's father Rabbi David Buzaglo, a singer of Hebrew liturgical poems (*piyyutim*), wrote a poignant contrafact of Fershko's "Bab El-Wad" melody called "Wise Up, O

---

[12] Rechnitzer claims that "Wise Up, O Revels!" was written sometime between 1952 and 1965. No one has been able to date this or any other Buzaglo song with precision, since he did not make audio or textual recordings and we are left to the memory of the students to whom he orally taught the songs; see Rechnitzer (2008: 39).

Rebels!" (*Binu Na Mordim*), which addresses the original song's apparent political and religious deficiencies. The lyrics of the refrain are printed here:[13]

Remember a passing day was made for creation.
The angelic advocates of peace have cried loudly to God:
"But man is quick to fight!"
Remember, therefore, and call them to peace
Man, the crown of creation, has been created like a king,
so as to build the deserts, to plant the desolated places,
but he has ruined the fields of plenty
and turned citadels and palaces to rubble.

זִכְרוּ נָא יוֹם בֶּן-חֲלוֹף הוּכַן לִיצִירָה
כַּת שָׁלוֹם נָתְנָה בְּקוֹל מַר לְמֶרְיוֹ
הֲלֹא הוּא יְצִיר נַפְשׁוֹ לָרִיב נִמְהָרָה
זִכְרוּ נָא אֵפוֹא, קִרְאוּ לְכֶם שָׁלוֹם
נֵזֶר הַיְצִירָה אֱנוֹשׁ נוֹצַר כַּמֶּלֶךְ
רַק לִבְנוֹת צִיָּה לִנְטֹעַ יְשִׁימוֹן
אַךְ הוּא שָׁת בָּתָה שְׂדוֹת יְבוּל רַב עֶרֶךְ
וַיְמַגֵּר לָאָרֶץ, עֹפֶל וְאַרְמוֹן

In both "Bab El-Wad," and "Wise Up, O Rebels!" the singer-narrator commands the listener to remember, using slight variations on the imperative form of the word *lizkor* (to remember), but the terms are fundamentally different in context. While "Wise Up, O Rebels!" is specifically geared toward remembrance as a theological tenant of Judaism, "Bab El-Wad" is "a religious poem without references to God, to past tradition, or to classical Jewish texts" (Rechnitzer 2008: 42). The song associated with Gouri, Fershko, and Yarkoni represents a secular, Labor Zionist vision of Jewish modernity, whereas Buzaglo's song privileges enduring theological and ritual aspects of Judaism as the rightful pillars of a Jewish society, as his lyrics—laden with biblical references—suggest.

During a filmed conversation for Jerusalem-based cultural organization Beit Avi Chai in September of 2014, Haim Gouri and Rabbi David Buzaglo's

---

[13] My translation is adapted, with minor changes, from Rechnitzer (2008: 62). The entire text of "Wise Up, O Rebels!," including an English translation, is available there.

son, Meir Buzaglo, discussed these seemingly opposing views of national culture:[14]

> Meir Buzaglo (MB): I grew up and sang "Bab El Wad" even before I was aware of my father's poetry. And a good few years back I came upon a song that my father wrote, "Wise Up, O Rebels!," which he wrote to the melody of "Bab El-Wad." I couldn't understand, it was a riddle to me, why write Hebrew words to a song originally in Hebrew?
>
> Haim Gouri (HG): I read your late father's song and I wondered what it is in this encounter through the melody that characterizes the Israeli cultural experience. The song becomes a bridge to a totally different text. So this contradiction that is supposed to create a distance suddenly creates an encounter. . . . [after reciting the poem's opening lines] "Bab El-Wad" is a lamentation of the fallen. One thousand Jerusalemites were killed in the attacks.
>
> MB: This is unique, I think Dad did this one time—writing lyrics like this, Hebrew over Hebrew. It's the only time.
>
> . . .
>
> MB: It's a Jewish memory that wants to dialogue with your song. Father's world was all about [medieval liturgical poets] Rabbi Yehuda Halevi and Solomon Ibn Gabirol. That was his world, his sounding board. It's as if Yehuda Halevi is responding to your song. We placed it in the past; that's why it's so special.
>
> [While they listened to a contemporary cover performance of "Wise Up, O Rebels!" by Rabbi Haim Louk, Gouri expressed being moved by the song.]
>
> HG: If someone had told me that a Jewish liturgist from Morocco who immigrated to Israel had heard "Bab El-Wad" and the melody captured his soul, I'd think, "it's a fairy tale" . . . We're the Palmach! What does that have to do with you [Rabbi David Buzaglo]? They're the same voices from different pasts and we create culture [*tarbut*]. If there's anything that scares me, it's a world without cultural associations. The correct formula is: know your brother better—his culture, his poetry, his liturgy. What's nice about this story is that it's a call for mutual curiosity. If we could find in this divided nation, with all its disagreements, some common ground that creates our identity . . .

[14] The video can be accessed here: https://www.youtube.com/watch?v=3GiXBhsEYsc.

MB: It's being taught in schools. It's such a beautiful encounter between Israeliness and Judaism that it's a true gift.

. . .

MB: Father takes it [the Midrash] to a national dimension. Meaning, we want peace and we use God's name, which is peace itself.

HG: Suddenly you hear that the cultural mission for thousands of years of the people of Israel has been peace and human dignity. This all comes together through the melody. That kind of thing happens once every thousand years!

The eventual "encounter through the melody," as Gouri characterized the intersecting genealogies of "Bab El-Wad" and "Wise Up, O Rebels!," was a musical synthesis of opposing views of national culture vis-à-vis religion. Those views coexist across the two song versions, as Rabbi David Buzaglo critiques the glorification of war and death in Labor Zionism, and perhaps even the moral legitimacy of the violence involved in realizing the dream of statehood. "Wise Up, O Rebels!" is a thoroughly critical text, and yet Gouri quite graciously viewed the dialectic it formed with "Bab El-Wad" as "a call for mutual curiosity." He and Meir Buzaglo understood the frictions between the two songs as being an embodiment of domestic Israeli social problems that are rooted in nationalism and religiosity, and to be sure, they saw this musical encounter as an opportunity to view those as compatible forces within Israeli society by virtue of their rootedness in the eternal "cultural mission" mythologized and enshrined by Zionism.

Like Rabbi David Buzaglo, Yaffa Yarkoni articulated a critical view, albeit from a nonreligious perspective, on violence in service of the nation in her public political pronouncements, particularly those made near the end of her life. Yarkoni's performance of "Bab El-Wad" and other war-music repertory, such as "The Finjan" (also a Gouri poem), catapulted her to national stardom and earned her a nickname: "The War Singer." It was an epithet that she absolutely detested, as her daughter Tami Sarfatti emphasized when I interviewed her in February 2012 in Ramat Aviv, a northern suburb of Tel Aviv:

She didn't like [the "War Singer" nickname] at all. On the one hand, she thought it was very important to appear in front of soldiers—there are many, many people who remember her appearing in front of the army . . . especially after '73 [Yom Kippur War], which was a more traumatic war and

less victorious [than those in 1948 and 1967]. She was always very willing
to sing for anyone, in the sense of making them feel good, but not songs for
the troops to march to. Nothing in that sense, but in the sense of bringing
them a taste of home to the front. And I think that for part of Israeli society
after '73, it was a kind of awakening from the euphoria of '67. . . . I heard
recently a live interview with her on the radio, after she got the Israel Prize
[in 1998].[15] She said—it was after Rabin's assassination [in 1995]—she took
very hard the assassination. She very much believed in him. . . . She said,
I have no sentiments about Israel. I think we should be a small state.' She
said it in '98. . . . It was a different time. It was a hegemony of right-wing
people. (Sarfatti 2012)

The dissonance between Yarkoni's cultural persona and her private views apparently was borne out in her musical choices. When I asked Sarfatti whether
her mother was, at heart, a political singer in the way the public has constructed her, Sarfatti told me,

She began by singing songs that were kind of dance music, like European
dance music, what we call *salonim* . . . not ideological songs, but tangos and
things like that that were played in all kinds of cafes in Tel Aviv [including
one owned by her mother], which was in a way almost . . . a very different
culture, a Bohemian culture. "Bab El-Wad" was recorded in the '50s. In that
respect, [she] was constructed as "the voice of Israel." Only then did she receive this legitimacy; only then did the so-called State Generation embrace
her. Before then, she was considered an outsider to the ideals of the kibbutz,
to the ideals of Mapai.[16] [She represented] in a way, you know, European
life, with jazz music and things like that. She was reconstructed retroactively. (Sarfatti 2012)

It was important for Yarkoni, as for the caretakers of her legacy, to emphasize
her cosmopolitanism as being antithetical to the provincial nationalism of other

---

[15] The Israel Prize is the highest cultural honor awarded by the State of Israel. Several musicians
have received it, including Paul Ben-Haim (1957), Mordechai Seter (1965), Josef Tal (1970), Hanoch
Avenary (1994), Noam Sheriff (2011), and others. In 1998, Yaffa Yarkoni became the first female musician to receive the prize.

[16] Originally formed in Palestine in 1930, Mapai was the dominant political party in Israel during
the early decades of statehood, eventually merging with Ahdut Ha-Avodah and Rafi to form the
Labor Party in 1968. "Mapai" is a Hebrew acronym for "Mifleget Poalei Erets Yisrael," lit. "Worker's
Party of the Land of Israel."

cultural forces, such as the agricultural settlements, political parties, and even poets from the State Generation. Yarkoni expressed this sentiment throughout her later years, particularly in her denouncement of the Israeli government's culpability in, and response to, the Second Palestinian Intifada (2000–2005): "For 51 years ... I am singing about Israel all over the world, telling stories about how it was before—the first war, the second war, every war. War, war, war. They call me the singer of wars. I don't like this name. I want to be the singer of Israel" (LA Times 2012).

Upon Yarkoni's death in January 2012, Israeli politician Tzipi Livni characterized her in a way that, on the surface, satisfied Yarkoni's desire to represent national identity rather than nationalist violence: "She was a synonym to Israeliness, her face and her voice crossed generations of Israelis who were raised on her songs. Yafa [sic] Yarkoni was one of the strongest symbols of Zionism—along with other singers of her time she helped shape the soundtrack of the country. Her death is a great loss to Israeli culture. May her memory be blessed [zikhrona livrakha]" (Haaretz 2012). Livni's eulogy raises the question: What exactly is "the soundtrack of the country?" The implication here is that Israel's soundtrack is militarized through an abundance of war songs, or at least songs about violence. Strictly speaking, this is not true. Israelis have produced songs on as wide a range of topics as any society; many commercial albums feature memorial and war songs alongside love songs and general Zionist songs. But throughout this book is evidence that war and memorial songs are held in particularly high regard as icons of Israeliness, charged with doing the work of articulating a national political consciousness.

Accordingly, and in spite of her discomfort with her nickname, Yarkoni's "War Singer" reputation kept her in demand for recording contracts as well as for live and televised performances during the many wars that raged during her lifetime and on annual holidays such as Memorial Day. In 1973, for example, she appeared on a television program dedicated to songs of the 1948 War that was produced by the music industry mogul Gil Aldema and radio personality Rivka Michaeli.[17] In keeping with other music television during the mid-1970s, such as Dan Almagor and Eliyahu Hacohen's program *I Sang to Thee, My Country!* (*Sharti Lakh Artsi*), the program featured popular musicians from around the country singing and discussing Israeli song in a participatory environment meant to evoke what Oz Almog has termed "the culture of the circle" (Almog 2000: 226–54)—that is, a culture drawing on the

---

[17] Both Aldema and Michaeli play important roles in the next chapter.

communal ethos of early Zionism associated with the pioneers and kibbuts residents of the Yishuv. In other words, these musicians, led by Yaffa Yarkoni, participated in ritual observance of the state's founding mythology—the very mythology, as Tami Sarfatti pointed out in our interview, that had been used to marginalize Yarkoni before her foray into war song.

This founding mythology has also been a source of play for musicians who do find its effects, either within Israeli society or outwardly projected as dominance over the Palestinian population, to be unsavory or immoral. The band Habiluim, for instance, created a grotesque parody of "Bab El-Wad" for the opening track to their 2007 album *Bereavement and Failure* (*Shikkul ve-Kishalon*), much of which is devoted to sending up the hegemony of memorialism within Israeli culture. The "Bab El-Wad" track sticks out, however, because it is the most egregiously irreverent take on quasi-sacred national symbols, using what Oded Erez—riffing on the philosophy of Michel de Certeau (1984)—calls "the practice of everyday quotation" (Erez 2015). The song's title, "Bab El-Wad 38א," is rendered like a street address, indicating that through use, repetition, and difference (like the names of real streets) the subject memorialized in the original song "slowly loses its original semantic value," becoming "more than a place" (Erez 2015: 177).[18] The banal, everydayness of this magnificent act of musical memorialism—the original song—is a fitting characterization of Israel's and Jerusalem's commemorative landscape. Erez lends further wisdom here:

> With Habiluim, we meet the sign "Bab El-Wad" as a text, even before listening, though not as a mythical battle site or as a war and canonical memory but rather as what Israeli daily life might have brought us: as a street name, a kind of currency that has lost its semantic value, or a "liberated space" that the song would populate or reside within. (Erez 2015: 177)

In the lyrics, which depict a bizarre airline flight, the two band members Noam Inbar and Yammi Wisler lampoon the dread that Israelis carry with them, with dark jokes about Sudden Infant Death Syndrome (SIDS) and the Holocaust film *Schindler's List* (1993), among other taboo subjects. The song's bridge and chorus comment most directly on the original "Bab El-Wad":

---

[18] This and other citations of Erez (2015) are my translation of the original Hebrew.

I'm not here to entertain you
And this is no ancient Circassian dance
I'm moving my hands
To point to the emergency exits

And those afraid to watch can get
A colorful sack to cover your head with
And here are headphones with songs of old
That always make things pleasant

Bab El-Wad
Bab El-Wad
They will not start without us
Bab El-Wad

אֲנִי לֹא כָּאן לְבַדֵּר אֶתְכֶם
וְזֶה לֹא רִקּוּד צֶ'רְקֶסִי קָדוּם
אֲנִי מְזִיזָה אֶת הַיָּדַיִם
לְכַוֵּון שֶׁל יְצִיאוֹת הַחֵירוּם

וּמִי שֶׁמְּפַחֵד לְהִסְתַּכֵּל יָכוֹל לְקַבֵּל
שַׂק לָרֹאשׁ בְּכָל מִינֵי צְבָעִים
וְיֵשׁ גַּם אָזְנִיּוֹת עִם שִׁירִים שֶׁל פַּעַם
שֶׁתָּמִיד עוֹשִׂים נָעִים

בָּאבּ אֶל וָאד
בָּאבּ אֶל וָאד
לֹא יַתְחִילוּ בִּלְעָדֵינוּ
בָּאבּ אֶל וָאד

The singer assumes the position of the flight attendant, who seeks to keep the passengers docile by offering them a pair of headphones playing "songs of old," in this case represented by Yaffa Yarkoni's "Bab El-Wad," which appears in the Habiluim song via a distorted sample, warbling and slowed down to match the dragging, sardonic tempo of its new musical setting. The presence of Yarkoni's voice as a sound-recording artifact is conspicuous; the unnatural pitch, timbre, and envelope of this otherwise familiar sound produces a schizophonia that serves the political ends of the song itself. As Erez poignantly summarizes, "The symbol of Bab El-Wad dominates the cultural space at its feet, within which it repeatedly appears, like a sculpture carved in stone, or like the 'iron skeleton' laid in the roadside statehood: a monument" (Erez 2015: 179).

Implied in the song's lyrics and musical signification is the idea that these passengers are anxious about impending tragedy in no small part due to the musical memorialism that they have internalized as an everyday reality and yet which also becomes their salve. "Bab El-Wad" stands in for Habiluim as the memorial song par excellence—a reputation that it earned through consistent programming and rejuvenation in the fifty-eight years between its initial release and the Habiluim parody. The stakes of internal Israeli parodies of militarization come further into focus in my discussion of "Ammunition Hill" that follows.

Ultimately, "Bab El-Wad" is a core component of the memorial repertory that is sung perennially, both at official state and municipal ceremonies where large crowds gather in auditoriums or public spaces (or tune in on radio, television, and online) at run-of-the-mill concerts that are not themselves framed as commemorative events. The dynamics of audience participation in performances of this song reveal much about the affective and collective power of the memorial repertory:

Metula (Israel-Lebanon border town), May 2012

I attended the annual Festival Shira, a two-day event that included academic lectures, discussions with poets, poetry readings, and musical performances. This year happened to focus in part on the work of Haim Gouri, who was present at the festival (the other featured poet was Tuvia Ruevner). During a roundtable discussion on the dual legacies of Hebrew poetry and Israeli song, Shlomo Gronich, who was one of the panelists, stood up from the table and walked stage right toward the piano. Gronich regularly had been performing his own arrangement of "Bab El-Wad" since the 1970s. After taking his seat, he began to play the chords from his arrangement, in what seemed to be an impromptu performance.

When he started singing the iconic melody of the first verse (intact from Fershko's original arrangement), the audience applauded, in recognition of the song and its classic status. Gradually, people began to sing along with Gronich, demonstrating their familiarity with the lyrics and melody. People gave each other knowing glances to communicate their shared knowledge. By the time we reached the song's refrain, where on the original Yarkoni recording a unison chorus enters, most of the people in the auditorium were singing together, cued by a gesture from Gronich, who dropped the left-hand part of his piano accompaniment to raise an open palm and signal audience participation. At this point, I joined in with the singing. A man sitting further down my row glanced at me with a smile as he continued singing, and then refocused his attention on Gronich and the audience seated ahead of us. Although some voices quieted during subsequent verses and rejoined the others during refrains, the palpable sense of welcome communal participation carried throughout the entire remainder of the song.

The song's end was met with loud audience applause, reciprocated by Gronich (directed, via facial and extended-arm gestures, toward the audience) and the other speakers, an assortment of Israeli musical and literary figures, sitting on the stage. This shift in musical field—from the presentational to the participatory (see Turino 2008: 23–65)—is characteristic of memorial events. While I learned that these moments are typical and frequent, the remarkable breakdown in field, frame, and social hierarchy proved to be an important key to understanding the musical transmission of social memory in Israel. Such performances of collectivity become especially pronounced when musicians commemorate moments of violence.

Certainly, the scene just described was nothing if not quotidian. This type of collective participation in group singing is so integral to Israeli national culture, as I discussed in Chapter 2, that it would hardly seem remarkable to any of the participants themselves. It is what people do at concerts. But this is precisely the premise of Habiluim's parody of the song: as a quasi-sacred national symbol, "Bab El-Wad" invites acclimation to musical memory; the song is thus both an act of commemoration (a process) and a memorial unto itself (an object), whose original meanings may be lost, agglomerated, or deliberately reprogrammed.

The song's objectivity-in-ubiquity is especially heightened when the occasion is auspicious. One can scarcely make it through Memorial Day without hearing the song played or performed multiple times across multiple venues. It is also one of the "siren songs" that are played to "engineer national sentiments" (Kaplan 2009: 319) in the aftermath of military and paramilitary/terrorist violence in Israel. Kaplan writes that this repertory forms "[a] linkage between the representation of commemoration and the representation of emergency . . . [that is] persistent in Israeli music programming" (321). This linkage is a part of the everyday in Jerusalem, as a crucial site of conflict in the country and in the region. Like the cemeteries and monuments located throughout the city, musical memorialism, too, forms an important part of Jerusalem's commemorative landscape.

Returning to the iron skeletons that physically memorialize the battle site, like the many instantiations of "Bab El-Wad" performed on Memorial Day, Independence Day, and during times of crisis, everyday activities such as the drive between Jerusalem to Tel Aviv betray the violent history that enabled the very ability for Israelis and foreign visitors like myself to traverse the sovereign space. Traveling through the territory, a spoil of war, invites one to consider how musical renderings of landscape are woven into the spatial imaginary of Israeli nationalism.

"Ammunition Hill"

Safra Square, Jerusalem, August 2013

I board the Jerusalem light rail and head north. As the route curves around the Old City and its Damascus Gate, I glimpse a view of occupied East Jerusalem. The parking lot in front of the Damascus Gate is filled with Palestinian taxis and food trucks making deliveries to the various markets along Sultan Suleiman Road, named for the sixteenth-century Ottoman ruler who built up the Old City walls as we find them today. Here is also the central station for Palestinian buses that run to the occupied territories in the East, North, and South. This area is bustling and emits a noisy mixture of machinery, vehicle emissions, haggling, and sounds from commercial and religious activities, such as the Muslim call to prayer (adhan), lofting over the Old City walls and the surrounding East Jerusalem hotels. The train speeds further north, riding the dividing line between East and West Jerusalem. Whereas for years the realities of uneven urban development have meant that public transit has been almost wholly segregated, the new light rail route has resulted in increasingly mixed crowds gathering at its stops. Eventually, we reach the stop for Ammunition Hill.

Ammunition Hill (*Givʿat Ha-Taḥmoshet*) is an Israeli memorial, a museum and archive, a destination for Israeli school field trips and for tourists, and a venue for induction into the Israel Defense Forces. Originally the site of a British Mandate-era police station, it was the setting for a particularly intense battle during the Six-Day War that was critical to Israel's success in securing Jerusalem and opening a contiguous Jewish territory between West Jerusalem and Mount Scopus, where the Hebrew University had been built but sat relatively dormant when the city was divided as a result of the 1948 War. The battle at Ammunition Hill has come to be remembered for its fierceness and for the unbearably close proximity between Israeli and Jordanian soldiers trading shots and watching each other die. The tides turned when Israeli paratroopers blew up the Jordanians' massive concrete bunker and overtook their position. The official body count holds that thirty-six Israelis and seventy-one Jordanians were killed in the battle. Memories of this violence elicit strong emotional responses from people who lived through the war and those who relive it through musical commemoration of the battle.

The battle was memorialized in a popular 1968 song, "Ammunition Hill," recorded by the Central Command Variety Ensemble. Written by lyricist Yoram Taharlev and melodist Yair Rosenblum, the song is structured around prose narratives of the battle, taken from quotations of military figures, that are punctuated by the singing of a monophonic chorus, which advances the dramatic plot. The lyrics are excerpted below:[19]

> *It was the second morning of the war in Jerusalem. The sun started rising in the east. We were deep in the middle of the battle of Ammunition Hill. It was a fierce battle. The Jordanians fought fiercely. It was a well-fortified area. At one point of the battle I had only four soldiers with me. We came up there with two companies. I didn't know where the others were, because communications with Dudik, the company commander, got disconnected at the beginning of the battle. At that moment I was sure that everyone was killed.*

At 2:00, 2:30 AM
we entered through the rocky ground
to the fields of fire and mines
of Ammunition Hill.

In front of fortified bunkers,
and 120mm cannons
100-some guys
on Ammunition Hill.

---

[19] Text translated in collaboration with Daniel Taharlev.

The pillar of dawn hadn't risen yet
and already half the company was laying in blood.
But we were already there
on Ammunition Hill.

Between the fences and mines,
we left only the medics behind
and we ran senseless
to Ammunition Hill.

At that moment a grenade was thrown from outside. Miraculously we
weren't hurt. I was afraid the Jordanians would throw more grenades.
Someone had to run from above and watch. I didn't have time to ask for a
volunteer. I sent Eitan. Eitan didn't hesitate for a moment. He went above
and started firing his machine gun. Sometimes he would overtake me and
I'd have to yell to stay in the same line as me. That's how we moved about
thirty meters. Eitan would cover from above and we would clear the bun-
kers from within, until he was hit in the head and fell inside.

We went down to the tunnels,
to the nooks and the rails
and to death in the trenches
of Ammunition Hill.

And no one asked where we're heading.
Whoever was first just fell.
You needed a lot of luck
on Ammunition Hill.

Those who fell were dragged to the back,
so they wouldn't disturb the others passing—
until the next one fell
on Ammunition Hill.

Maybe we were lions,
but if you wanted to live
you should not have been
on Ammunition Hill.

We decided to try and blow up their bunker with the bazooka. It made a few scratches on the concrete. We then decided to try and blow it up with explosives. I waited above them until the guy who went to get the explosives came back. The guy at the back would throw me the packs, and I would put them one by one at the entrance to their bunker. They had a system: first they would throw a grenade, then they shot from their automatic weapons, and then they would rest. So between the shots and the next grenade I'd run to the bunker's entrance and place the explosives. When I initiated the explosive, I tried moving as far as possible. I had only four meters to move because there were Jordanians all over the place. I don't know why I got the Medal of Honor; all I wanted was to get home alive.

At 7:00, 7:20,
at the police academy
we gathered all the rest
from Ammunition Hill.

Smoke rose from the hill.
The sun was rising in the east.
The seven of us returned to the city
from Ammunition Hill.

The seven of us returned to the city.
Smoke rose from the hill.
The sun was rising in the east
over Ammunition Hill.

From fortified bunkers,
the story of our brothers, the men
who remained there twenty years old
on Ammunition Hill.

היה אז בוקר היום השני למלחמה בירושלים. האופק החוויר במזרח. היינו
בעיצומו של הקרב על גבעת התחמושת. לחמנו שם זה שלוש שעות. התנהל
קרב עקשני. קטלני. הירדנים נלחמו בעקשנות. זה היה יעד מבוצר בצורה
בלתי רגילה. בשלב מסויים של המלחמה נשארו לידי ארבעה חיילים בלבד.
עלינו לשם בכוח של שתי פלוגות. לא ידעתי היכן האחרים כיוון שהקשר עם
דודיק המ״פ ניתק עוד בתחילת הקרב. באותו רגע חשבתי שכולם נהרגו.

בשתיים, שתיים ושלושים
נכנסו דרך הטרשים
לשדה האש והמוקשים
של גבעת התחמושת.

מול בונקרים מבוצרים
ומרגמות מאה עשרים
מאה וכמה בחורים
על גבעת התחמושת.

עמוד השחר עוד לא קם
חצי פלוגה שכבה בדם
אך אנו כבר היינו שם
בגבעת התחמושת.

בין הגדרות והמוקשים
השארנו רק את החובשים
ורצנו אבודי חושים
אל גבעת התחמושת.

באותו רגע נזרק רימון מבחוץ. בנס לא נפגענו. חششתי שהיורדנים יזרקו
רימונים נוספים. מישהו היה צריך לרוץ מלמעלה ולהשגיח. לא היה לי
זמן לשאול מי מתנדב. שלחתי את איתן. איתן לא היסס לרגע. עלה למעלה
והתחיל להפעיל את המקלעון. לפעמים היה עובר אותי והייתי צריך לצעוק
לו שיישאר בקו שלי. ככה עברנו איזה שלושים מטר. איתן היה מחפה
מלמעלה ואנחנו טיהרנו את הבונקרים מבפנים, עד שנפגע ונפל פנימה.

ירדנו אל התעלות
אל הכוכים והמסילות
ואל המוות במחילות
של גבעת התחמושת.

ואיש אי אנה לא שאל
מי שהלך ראשון נפל
צריך היה הרבה מזל
על גבעת התחמושת.

מי שנפל נסחב אחור
שלא יפריע לעבור
עד שנפל הבא בתור
על גבעת התחמושת.

אולי היינו אריות
אך מי שעוד רצה לחיות
אסור היה לו להיות
על גבעת התחמושת.

החלטנו לנסות לפוצץ את הבונקר שלהם בבזוקה. הבזוקה עשתה כמה
שריטות לבטון. החלטנו לנסות בחומר נפץ. חיכיתי מעליהם עד שחזר
הבחור עם חומר הנפץ. הוא היה זורק לי חבילות-חבילות, ואני הייתי מניח
את החבילות אחת אחת בפתח הבונקר שלהם. להם היתה שיטה: קודם זרקו
רימון, אחר כך ירו צרור, אחר כך נחו. אז בין צרור לרימון, הייתי ניגש לפתח
הבונקר שלהם ושם שם את חומר הנפץ. הפעלתי את חומר הנפץ והתרחקתי
כמה שיכולתי. היו לי ארבעה מטר לתמרן, כי גם מאחורי היו ליגיונרים. אני
לא יודע למה קיבלתי צל״ש. בסך הכל רציתי להגיע הביתה בשלום.

בשבע, שבע ועשרים
אל בית הספר לשוטרים
אספו את כל הנשארים
מגבעת התחמושת.

עשן עלה מן הגבעה
השמש במזרח גבהה
חזרנו אל העיר שבעה
מגבעת התחמושת.

חזרנו אל העיר שבעה
עשן עלה מן הגבעה
השמש במזרח גבהה
על גבעת התחמושת.

על בונקרים מבוצרים
ועל אחינו הגברים
שנשארו שם בני עשרים
על גבעת התחמושת.

In many ways, this song has become emblematic of the bravery and might of the Israeli army. Notably, the phrase "pillar of dawn" (*amud ha-shaḥar*) was intended as a reference to the Israelites' journey out of Egypt in Book of Exodus, wherein "The LORD went before them in a pillar of cloud by day, to guide them along the way, and in a pillar of fire by night, to give them light, that they might travel day and night" (Exodus 13:21). Throughout the narrative, delivered in plain language, the soldier-narrator faces overwhelming odds yet persists and ultimately prevails. Just as important, his combat brothers are not so lucky, and by the end of the second stanza the story is really about memorializing the dead.

"Ammunition Hill" is a song whose musical elements illustrate a form of "military mimesis" employed by songwriters in the aftermath of the Six-Day War. A march-like rhythm on the snare drum and the accordion's quickly alternating bass-chord figure maintain a quick tempo throughout. The lyrics' form is instructive here, too: the majority of vocal production is oriented toward the spoken delivery of prose, as if the speaker is debriefing the audience on the battle's events in a dispassionate manner. The tension breaks only for the melodic entrance of the unison chorus. Lawrence Zbikowski writes that mimesis is "highly conditioned by the choice of cross-domain mappings through which discourse about music is structured; in turn, these mappings reflect the global models of a given cultural perspective and historical moment" (2002: 74). In other words, mimesis of various kinds can reveal the close relation not only between musical sound and text but also between music and musical discourse.

Musical discourse is critical to how people connect national loss to national land, for example in the festivities of Jerusalem Day (*Yom Yerushalayim*), which takes place each spring on the 28th of Iyyar according to the Jewish calendar (usually in April or May of the Gregorian calendar). On this day, people do not stop their cars and step out onto the streets to bow their heads in silence while sirens sound around the city, as they do on Memorial Day. They project a celebratory, if not flagrant, tone into the cityscape itself through violent processions in and around the Old City, as I documented in Chapter 1. Meanwhile, members of the military and national and municipal governments are compelled to attend official Jerusalem Day events around the city. It is at these events that "Ammunition Hill" perennially facilitates the commemorative mode of public ritual by musically narrating the historical events leading to Jerusalem's capture.

Ammunition Hill itself is a main venue for official ceremonies to commemorate Jerusalem Day. A performance of the memorial song at its memorial site during Jerusalem Day 2009 demonstrated how musical memorialism, when appropriated by government figures, can be used to invoke a teleology of modern sovereignty via violent conquest. Attended by dignitaries, such as Prime Minister Benjamin Netanyahu and President Shimon Peres, and members of the press, the ritual performance was staged in a way that highlighted the military mimesis of the original recorded version of the song. Bereted soldiers flanked an empty stage, while the audience watched from bleachers arranged in a semicircle. As the musicians began, two rows of soldiers entered the stage in a coordinated march. They halted, turned, and remained still for much of the performance. The audience joined in singing the refrain lines at the end of each verse: "Ammunition Hill" (with various prepositional prefixes attached, such as "on" and "from," according to the lines' function in each particular verse). A torch flame and memorial wreaths on the ground below suggested that the violent deaths chronicled by the song's lyrics were not in vain. This was a spectacle of might, intended to strengthen the resolve of Jewish Israelis to retain control of Jerusalem by employing the graphic realism of a memorial song, serving the ends of both popular nationalism and the state apparatus on a controversial holiday so strongly associated with the extreme flanks of both nationalism and the state. Whether performances are styled in the pathos of Jerusalem song or actively reflect a call to arms, when it comes to Jerusalem they all commemorate a sense of loss and renew narratives of consequential historical events that lead teleologically to the city's status quo in the present.

Other Israeli artists have sought to turn these symbols of nationalism and militarism inward, via parody or other forms of deconstruction, in order to draw attention to the uneasy relation between expressions of dominance and the desire to live a normal life not shaped by a state of emergency. The dual roles of these parodies form part of "a long tradition of Jewish humour emanating from moments of crisis . . . in an attempt to rally Israelis around an intimate memory of bodily sacrifice" (Figueroa 2016: 14). Often deploying taboo humor, they can serve the purpose of domesticating national myths (Alter 1987), solidifying social bonds while serving as a form of surrogate agency in a situation where little agency exists (Nevo and Levine 1994), or for struggling over competing notions of locality (Sebba-Elran and Milo 2016), among other functions.[20] More often than not, such deconstructive treatments serve the purpose of a more serious critique of top-down notions of sociality that emanate from the militarization of national symbols.

According to choreographer Roy Assaf (b. 1982), "Ammunition Hill" entered Israelis' "DNA" by way of, but partially dissociated from, its commemorative function. Assaf's best-known and most-toured work, "The Hill" (2012), features a five-minute-long edited recording of its namesake song. Assaf's core aesthetic in this piece is his play with the tension created between sounds and movement, not necessarily a politicized engagement with past war. The piece nevertheless illuminates much about the place of violence in Israeli social memory through a form of musical eclecticism that renders even the most harrowing memories of violence banal until reenacted.

I attended a concert featuring "The Hill" in October 2017. The performance blasted open with a recording of the Israel Defense Forces march, "Tsahal Tso'ed," a rather generic military march written in 1963 by Yoav Talmi (b. 1943) in an international style, with requisite melodic sequences, alternations of featured instrumental groups, and tidy cadences, all in a moderate tempo to facilitate procession in parades and ceremonies. Its playing in "The Hill" has garnered criticism from right-leaning Israelis, as it includes a moment when two of the three dancers grab their buttocks with both hands and wiggle their hips in time to the march. This creates some distancing from the song, whose routinized ritual playing is typically performed with controlled body movements aligned with the music's militaristic ethos. The dancers seemed to parody the song's staidness with their booty-shaking. This was, in fact, an act of lampoonery, but Assaf told me that he meant to poke fun not at Israeli nationalism per se but rather at the self-seriousness of Israeli national identity and its semisacred emblems, such as the song "Ammunition Hill." This accords with my analysis of Habiluim's parody of "Bab El-Wad" earlier, where the song's status as a musical memorial evacuates the object of some of its original meaning—like Certeau's street names or Erez's spent coins—and allows for new meanings to accumulate or be created anew in future iterations.

As Assaf said during our interview, "I am attracted to symbols and stereotypes—codes that everybody knows how to read—and playing with

---

[20] See also Meir Ariel's parody of "Jerusalem of Gold" discussed in Chapter 4 and a brief introduction to the Israeli sketch comedy troupe *Nikui Rosh*, who were among the most notoriously irreverent groups in this regard, in Figueroa (2016: 8–9).

them. It's beyond culture, it's DNA" (Assaf 2017). He based the booty-shaking movements on a real memory from his time as a paratrooper in the IDF, when, during a formal military ceremony, two of his friends began surreptitiously, and ironically, "boogying" to the march song. During our conversations, he characterized this moment of the show, perhaps with right-wing criticism in mind, as a kind of laughing-with (i.e., well-intentioned familiarity) rather than laughing-at (i.e., mockery) the Israeli military's place of pride in national culture. For Assaf, the social component of social memory is based on relationships rather than on any abstract notion of collectivity. In the context of "The Hill," this move foregrounds a youthful irreverence, which humanizes the dancer-soldiers before they are sent to die in the battle for Ammunition Hill.

As a choreographer, Assaf seems particularly reliant on arm styling for communicating thematic material. Much of the opening song is danced by a duet, whose hands remain locked together while the dancers twirl and contort into various poses of embrace and near-separation. The soldiers remain connected in spite of it all, highlighting the confraternal bonds facilitated by military life. Meanwhile, the third dancer has been standing still at the rear, house-left corner, and eventually begins to fall forward, as the erstwhile duet rushes to catch him before he hits the floor. Assaf develops this idea further during the climactic song, "Ammunition Hill," whose accordion-laden bars play in an extended loop, gradually increasing in volume, before breaking into the iconic prose lyrics. The choreography here focuses more directly on depictions of battle violence, as each dancer appears to play multiple characters from both armies. The scenes are quite cinematic, as the dancers seamlessly transform between pockets of fighting, each with different physical scenarios, from hand-to-hand to gun-oriented combat. As the soldier-characters fall dead or wounded, they are caught by brothers-in-arms and, in some cases, dragged to safety as in a real battle scene. These moments are punctuated at one point by a fleeting moment of celebratory line dance drawn from the modern Israeli folk dance tradition.

The final song is somewhat jarring due to its complicated relation to the war context: the Bee Gees' "I Started a Joke." Having been released on the Australian band's 1968 album *Idea*, one year after the Six-Day War, the song is only slightly anachronistic as period music, but its clever deployment of sentimental pop stylistic signifiers, combined with an alienated lyrical voice, seem to signal Assaf's ambivalence toward the thematic material of "The Hill." The brief lyrics end on a sour note: "Till I finally died, which started the whole world living / Oh, if I'd only seen that the joke was on me." The song's melody and lyrics, along with the choreographed succession of dead bodies hitting the ground, highlight the injustice of individual martyrdom for a cause with complicated moral implications. This idea moves to the foreground in the piece's final moments, when the music subsides and gives way to a synthesized sonic palette of buzzing, bell-like tones moving through filtered swells and washes of whooshing white noise that seem to indicate the passing of artillery shells. A shell-shocked lone soldier stands in frozen horror while the larger battle scene unfolds around him. At the end, a cornet—perhaps the ultimate sonic signifier of military death—enters prominently then trails off, before the lights abruptly cut to black.

During our conversations, Assaf told me emphatically that he did not originally set out to create a piece about war. The idea to use "Ammunition Hill," the very song and memorialized battle site for which the piece was eventually named, occurred to him very late in the creative process. Assaf began with choreographic sketches and then searched for music to focus the steps into an overarching narrative. His other options were quite different, stylistically speaking. Among the other pieces he considered for the "Ammunition Hill" section of the piece was an excerpt from Bach's Goldberg Variations (BWV 988). The Austro-German classical ethos originally ran deep, as "Tsahal Tso'ed" was actually a replacement for Assaf's original selection of Franz Schubert's "Du bist der Ruh" (D 776), as recorded by Argentine mezzo-soprano Bernarda Fink (2008). What is striking about the soundtrack selection process is that the various pieces Assaf considered for inclusion seem to bear virtually no structural musical resemblance to one another. But Assaf told me that, as a dancer, he perceived a beat—a fragment of rhythm isolated from all other musical parameters, including, perhaps, meter—that transcended the stylistic diversity of the musical repertory that he repeatedly referred to in our interview as his "library," defined cheekily as "the availability of stuff in my mind" (Assaf 2017). It was by serendipity, therefore, that he pulled "Ammunition Hill" and "Tsahal Tso'ed" from the metaphorical stacks and developed a war theme for this show rather than some other theme that would have displayed the impressive cultural capital, represented by Bach and Schubert, that accompanies his educated, bourgeois class identity.

Throughout his interview statements to me and during postconcert talkbacks, Assaf seemed to invite the psychoanalytic retrospection of others rather than claim agency for programmatic politics in his creative expression. He told me, "Sometimes I feel disappointed in myself for not being an

activist. . . . I have devoted myself to making connections between movement and music [rather than to political causes]." And, in fact, he suggested,
"Maybe, sub-consciously, I want to stimulate something," although he would
not disclose what that something might be. I pushed him further about the
connection between the soldiers' booty-shaking during "Tsahal Tso'ed" and
the violence and death of "Ammunition Hill," asking "What is this piece
really about?" After a moment of pondering, he answered, "ahuvat ha-
lohamim," literally meaning "warriors' love" but more idiomatically referring to an internalized responsibility for one's fellow soldier; it is meant to
be the webbing that holds together the military's individuals into a cohesive
unit. *Ahuvat ha-lohamim* is related to *re'ut*, an overtly masculinized concept
of friendship that I briefly mentioned in connection to Haim Gouri's poetry
(including the poem named "Ha-Re'ut"). In his analysis of *re'ut* in Israeli society, Danny Kaplan argues that "some of these emotions [associated with
male friendship] can only be experienced through a sense of loss, and that
by entering the public discourse they transform into rituals of passionate
commemoration, suggesting a dynamics of collective necrophilia" (Kaplan
2006: xi). Implied in the term's contemporary usage is the idea that military
service, which is compulsory for most Israeli citizens, is a core site of nation-
building in Israel.[21] It is the highest form of friendship and a model for national social relations; a soldier's death is a national death, and an ex-soldier's
trauma is a national trauma. There can be no *re'ut* without death and bereavement (see Figueroa 2020: 136–37).

Roy Assaf was referring to a more specific emotional quality in his work;
unlike *re'ut*, which is a type of combat fraternity that models national social relations more generally, *ahuvat ha-lohamim* has specific associations
with active soldiers and thus is compartmentalized within a military setting.
He commemorates life during the time of service rather than its ending in
death. In light of this understanding, one might interpret Assaf's use of the
phrase to indicate that his depictions of wartime violence in "The Hill" are
meant to emphasize the pastness of military life rather than to generate a
model of citizenship based on combat-unit relations. In Israel, conscription
is mandatory and thus military service is a rite of passage into adulthood
for most people (Palestinians and Orthodox Jewish citizens usually receive
exemptions). This shared experience, both real (among members of the same

---

[21] Military service is compulsory for all Israeli citizens except for ultra-Orthodox Jews and
Palestinian citizens of Israel. Other minority groups, such as the Druze, also serve in the army.

company or brigade) and imagined (among Israelis in general), is part of the social "DNA," to use Assaf's words, of Israeli society. Those experiences are triggered, relived, negotiated, and renewed through the varied performances of memorial songs such as "Ammunition Hill" and "Bab El Wad," whose programming in a diversity of performance environments—from recording studios, concert halls, and poetry festivals to Jerusalem's public spaces and monuments themselves—and at regular intervals on holidays continually reinstate the emergencies that threaten Jewish survival and control over the homeland territory. To use another of Roy Assaf's metaphors, the reverence of national death is a large volume in the library of national affect. Like actual books, people interpret and use such texts (and, as I have shown, their musical realizations) in many different ways. The memorial repertory thus becomes a site of contesting identity, politics, history, and the morality of war itself.

* * *

The memorial repertory performed annually in Jerusalem, and elsewhere in Israel, sonically marks the passage of time between the violent past and the commemorative present. In performing war songs such as "Bab El-Wad" and "Ammunition Hill," in addition to the considerably larger repertory concerning violence before and after the 1948–1967 period, people who did not live through those wars now have the opportunity to bear the burden of Israel's violent history, to experience the viscerality of those wars and to internalize the threats faced by their ancestors. But those songs also provide symbolic and musical material for parody, play, and critique. This diversity of musical responses to war and emergency provides a context for socialization into a longer history of militarized relations that create solidarities in the face of continued threats, as the State of Israel remains in a perpetual state of tension with many of its neighbors in the region (including perceived internal threats), or for processing the grief involved in more immediate personal losses in the crisis. War songs locating national death in Jerusalem provide a critical repertory for public bereavement and for political discourse. They have been called upon to rally people to the military cause, protest unjust war, celebrate victory, commemorate national death, challenge national myths, and teach the repertory of symbols and sensibilities to new generations of Israelis.

4

Gilded Jerusalem

"The Song That Took a City"

Binyenei Ha-Uma, May 15, 1967

It was Independence Day, and a crowd gathered in Jerusalem's International Convention Center (Binyenei Ha-Uma) for the annual Israel Song Festival.[1] As artists, military chiefs, and other members of Israel's cultural elite filled their seats, a tense atmosphere settled over the crowd. For the past several weeks, rumors of war dominated the airwaves of state radio, as border skirmishes with Arab military and paramilitary groups created a state of emergency. Israelis were living in fear that their young country could be annihilated within weeks or even days—a tiny nation of three million citizens surrounded by mighty regional powers such as Egypt and Syria seemed to have little chance of surviving the kind of attacks promised in the heated rhetoric of the countries' leaders.[2] (Little did they know that the war to come would solidify their country's unquestionable regional dominance through a preemptive attack wiping out the capabilities of the Egyptian Air Force.) Earlier that night, the news spread that Egyptian President Gamal Abdel Nasser, in a show of strength, amassed some 100,000 Egyptian troops and 900 tanks in the Sinai Peninsula and closed the Straits of Tiran to Israeli vessels, initiating what has come to be known as "the Waiting Period" (*Tkufat ha-Hamtana*) in Israel and, ultimately, the event that the Israeli state claimed to be casus belli for the Six-Day War in June.

---

[1] The Israel Song Festival was a musical competition that ran from 1960 to 1980, with songs judged based on their having "advanced an original Hebrew song" that reflected "the accomplishments of Israeli society and the culture of the Jewish people." The Israel Broadcast Authority revived the festival in 2012. For more on music festivals in Israel, see Regev and Seroussi (2004: 113–33).

[2] Although ordinary citizens on all sides felt dread at what they believed to be an impending war, there is some evidence to suggested that such fear was manufactured for political ends, or at least exaggerated in the public discourse as broadcast and print media in Israel, Egypt, and Syria stoked these fears (see Shemesh 2008, Segev 2005: 225–46).

City of Song. Michael A. Figueroa, Oxford University Press. © Oxford University Press 2022.
DOI: 10.1093/oso/9780197546475.003.0005

Settling into seat thirty-seven of row nine, songwriter Naomi Shemer joined her neighbors in nervous contemplation. Those who could not attend listened at home to the live broadcast on state radio. The idea of war on Israel's doorstep inspired an already notoriously news-obsessed public to listen intently for any breaking news that might occur. As the lights dimmed and the curtain lifted, this anxious nation took a breath. The country was transfixed. The concert progressed with songs by some of the most popular singing groups in the country, among them Hedva and David, Chava Alberstein, the Parvarim, Ron Eliran, Michal Tal, and Mike Burstyn (see Figure 4.1). The final song of the competitive portion of the night, Burstyn's "Who Knows How" (*Mi Yodeʾa Kama*), was a crowd favorite. Then came the time for votes to be counted.

For the 1967 installation of the song festival, the producers commissioned five noncompeting songs to be performed during the tally. Singer Shuly Nathan was part of a lineup that included established musicians Hedva Amarni, Shimon Israeli, Hadassa Siglov, and the Parvarim. It was an honor for Nathan, who had been just a humble soldier with a guitar whom Naomi Shemer plucked out of an amateur singing contest on the radio. When her turn came, she entered the stage and began unceremoniously. Plucking out the D-minor accompaniment on her nylon-stringed acoustic guitar, Nathan's unseasoned vibrato rang out as she sang a never-before-heard song by Naomi Shemer: first a few verses, then the refrain, then a few more verses and another refrain. As she entered the final refrain, she knew her biggest challenge was approaching: an emphatic note at the top of her range, held as a fermata on the final syllable of the word *kinnor* (lyre). She intoned the high

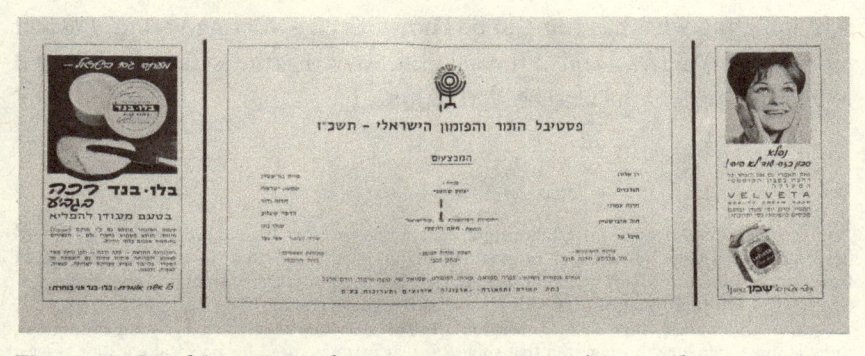

Figure 4.1 Israel Song Festival 1967 concert program (Naomi Shemer Papers, National Library of Israel).

E without flaw, paused, and repeated the final word, ending on a tonic D before playing her way out. The performance was such a success that the crowd demanded an encore before they left the building, and on her second performance, around midnight, the crowd was with her, singing along with the refrains. Before she could finish, the crowd exploded in applause so loud that it distorted the ambient microphones that captured the now-iconic live recording (Jerusalem Song Festival 1967). By morning, Shuly Nathan became a household name. Mike Burstyn's song may have won first prize at that year's song festival, but "Jerusalem of Gold" was the song that defined 1967.

During my time in the field, "Jerusalem of Gold" was a common point of reference with nearly every person with whom I discussed my research on Jerusalem song. I was often asked the question, "Have you heard 'Yerushalayim shel Zahav'?," as my colleagues and interlocutors tried to assess my seriousness of purpose; if I had not known the song, the implication was that I clearly would not have known where to begin my project. How striking to me it was that a single song, written so late in Jerusalem's musical history, would serve as a beginning point in that history's narrative, but this is because in a modern Israeli context the song did no less than initiate a renaissance of the Jerusalem song genre itself.

In this chapter, I discuss the genesis, performance history, and critical responses to "Jerusalem of Gold," arguing that the song's process of canonization, along with the Israeli public's variegated response to its representational ethics, demonstrates a lack of consensus on the status of Jerusalem and its inhabitants within Israeli political imaginaries.

"Jerusalem" by Design

Earlier installations of the Israel Song Festival took place in Tel Aviv, but beginning in 1965 the producers at the national broadcast authority Kol Israel (Voice of Israel)[3] moved the festival to Jerusalem, in part due to the entreaty of Jerusalem's mayor, Theodore "Teddy" Kollek (1911–2007). Kollek's lobbying was part of a slate of projects he sponsored in an attempt to assert the importance of Jerusalem to Israeli culture. To celebrate the song festival taking place there in 1967, Mayor Kollek commissioned five songs to be performed

---

[3] There is also a homophonic meaning for this word: "All Israel."

during the festival's segment devoted to counting votes. Each song would be required to deal explicitly with the subject of Jerusalem.

Perhaps the most surprising choice for this assignment was Naomi Shemer. It was surprising not because she was unknown—she had already begun to make a career for herself with hit songs such as her 1963 "The Eucalyptus Grove" (*Hurshat ha-Eukaliptus*)—but because she had little personal connection to the city of Jerusalem. Shemer was raised at Kvutsat Kinneret, in the Lower Galilee region of northern Israel, and was professionally based in Tel Aviv, the center of the Israeli culture industry. When festival producer Gil Aldema called her to propose the project, Shemer initially refused, citing her lack of familiarity and personal connection with the city. Aldema responded to her hesitation by employing reverse psychology, reportedly telling Shemer to write about whatever topic she wanted.[4]

Several days later, her anxiety apparently at ease, Shemer called Aldema to accept his invitation to write a song about Jerusalem and requested some time to conduct preparatory research. She spent the next week traveling around Jerusalem, where she toured the streets and markets and consulted poets and religious leaders who were familiar with Jerusalemite literary idioms. Within a few weeks, Shemer drafted a short tune with just two stanzas and a refrain:

> The mountain air is clear as wine,
> And the smell of pines
> Carries on the winds of twilight
> With the sound of bells.
> The trees and stones in hibernation,
> Captured in a dream.
> How deserted lies the city,
> And at its heart—a wall.
>
> [Refrain:]
> Jerusalem of gold,
> Of copper, and of light,
> For all your songs
> I am a lyre.

[4] This story was recounted to me by Aldema's friend Dan Almagor during a May 2012 interview.

אֲוִיר הָרִים צָלוּל כַּיַּיִן
וְרֵיחַ אֲרָנִים
נִשָּׂא בְּרוּחַ הָעַרְבַּיִם
עִם קוֹל פַּעֲמוֹנִים
וּבְתַרְדֵּמַת אִילָן וָאֶבֶן
שְׁבוּיָה בַּחֲלוֹמָהּ
הָעִיר אֲשֶׁר בָּדָד יוֹשֶׁבֶת
וּבְלִבָּהּ חוֹמָה

[פזמון:]
יְרוּשָׁלַיִם שֶׁל זָהָב
וְשֶׁל נְחֹשֶׁת וְשֶׁל אוֹר
הֲלֹא לְכָל שִׁירַיִךְ
אֲנִי כִּנּוֹר

The simple text was set to a simple melody, to be accompanied by simple chordal accompaniment on guitar or piano, highlighting the song's uncluttered lyricism (Figure 4.2).

Figure 4.2 "Jerusalem of Gold" melody manuscript (Naomi Shemer Papers, National Library of Israel).

Shemer excitedly played the draft of the song for her friend, the actress and radio personality Rivka Michaeli (b. 1938). In her feedback, Michaeli criticized the lyrics for only dealing with Jerusalem on a metaphorical level—the text could arguably have applied to any Mediterranean city with pine trees and walls of stone. She implored Shemer, "Why don't you write something about the Old City? My family lived there for hundreds of years, and we had to leave during the War of Independence. Where is the Old City my father has been dreaming about for nineteen years?" (Nathan 2012). The 1948 War had divided the city, with Jordan controlling East Jerusalem, including the Old City and its religious monuments. In the mid-1960s, Israeli-controlled West Jerusalem functioned as a small town that catered primarily to students at the Hebrew University and the Orthodox enclaves of the city's religious neighborhoods. Michaeli urged Shemer to convey a realistic sense of Jerusalem that included the Old City as she and other Israelis\remembered it. Shemer went back to work while beginning to search for a singer to perform the song.

She found her singer's name scribbled on a piece of scrap paper in her desk drawer. Several months earlier, Shemer and her daughter Lali had been listening to a radio program that showcased amateur musicians from around the country. All of a sudden, Lali called her mother into the room and said, "Listen to this voice!" Impressed, Shemer told her daughter, "When they say her name at the end of the song, write it down and place it in our secret drawer. We're going to need her one day." The singer was a young soldier in the Israel Defense Forces named Shuly Nathan (Figure 4.3).

While Shemer was preparing for the song festival—crafting new verses and brainstorming singers—she recalled hearing Nathan on the radio and immediately had Gil Aldema's office contact Nathan. Relating this story to me in 2012, Nathan remarked, "The directors of the festival said, 'No, you cannot use an amateur singer for the festival,' but Naomi told them, 'If you don't let her sing it, I will not give you a song.' That was my luck!" (Nathan 2012). Shemer's posturing paid off, Nathan agreed to the gig, and the two of them spent the next few weeks rehearsing together.

Nathan's performance on the night of May 15 suggests that Shemer had taken Rivka Michaeli's advice and dealt with the controversial subject of the Old City in two new verses following the original first verse.

Figure 4.3 Shuly Nathan in *Yediot Aḥronot* daily newspaper, June 27, 1967 (Naomi Shemer Papers, National Library of Israel).

How is it that the wells dried up
The market square is empty,
And no one visits the Temple Mount
In the Old City.
And in the caverns in the rock
The winds howl.
And no one goes down to the Dead Sea
On Jericho Road.

[Refrain]

But I come today to sing to you
And fasten you with crowns,
I am the least of all your children
And last of the poets.
Because your name will scorch my lips
Like a seraph's kiss.
If I forget thee, o Jerusalem,
All in gold.

[Refrain]

אֵיכָה יָבְשׁוּ בּוֹרוֹת הַמַּיִם
כִּכָּר הַשּׁוּק רֵיקָה
וְאֵין פּוֹקֵד אֶת הַר הַבַּיִת
בָּעִיר הָעַתִּיקָה
וּבַמְּעָרוֹת אֲשֶׁר בַּסֶּלַע
מְיַלְּלוֹת רוּחוֹת
וְאֵין יוֹרֵד אֶל יָם הַמֶּלַח
בְּדֶרֶךְ יְרִיחוֹ

[פזמון]

אַךְ בְּבוֹאִי הַיּוֹם לָשִׁיר לָךְ
וְלָךְ לִקְשֹׁר כְּתָרִים
קְטֹנְתִּי מִצְּעִיר בָּנַיִךְ
וּמֵאַחֲרוֹן הַמְשׁוֹרְרִים
כִּי שְׁמֵךְ צוֹרֵב אֶת הַשְּׂפָתַיִם

כְּנְשִׁיקַת שָׂרָף
אִם אֶשְׁכָּחֵךְ יְרוּשָׁלַיִם
אֲשֶׁר כֻּלָּהּ זָהָב

[פזמון]

The text here is more specific than in the original first verse. Earlier references to a generic ancient city now lead into concrete geographical locations in Jerusalem—the Temple Mount and Jericho Road—and she mentions the Old City by name. The Old City of the verses is empty, destitute, lonely, and devoid of a human presence, while the chorus recalls a shining city whose memory is borne by the singer—in this case, by Shuly Nathan—in spite of the physical city's supposed barrenness. The lyrics furthermore place the singer in line with the singers and poets of yore, and it is not only through calling places into being that the lyrics trade on the symbolic ecology of Jerusalem.

Shemer's words serve as a virtual anthology of timeworn, carefully selected references to Jerusalem in Jewish literary history. Canons of Jewish poetry and liturgy appear alongside well-known lyrical gestures from synagogue and holiday rituals. In the first verse the line, "How deserted lies the city," is from the opening verse from the Book of Lamentations, which chronicles the destruction of Jerusalem and its First Temple by Nebuchadnezzar in 586 BCE. Lamentations, known in Hebrew as *Eikha* ("How [did it happen]!"), is recited annually on Tisha B'Av, the Jewish holiday commemorating the destruction of the Temple. The book's tone is emotionally distraught, and as the text is ascribed to the Prophet Jeremiah, who witnessed the siege firsthand, it provides an intimate portrait of tragedy. As such, it also has provided intertextual possibilities for other Hebrew poets, most notably as an important allusion in Uri Zvi Greenberg's *Vision of One of the Legions* (*Ḥazon Eḥad ha-Ligyonot*, 1928; see Ginsburg 2014: 156). In "Jerusalem of Gold," this line draws a direct parallel between the ruins of First Temple–era Jerusalem to the Jordanian-controlled Old City, which was off-limits to Jews.

The final phrase of the refrain, "I am a lyre for all your songs" (*Le-khol shirayikh ani kinnor*), is an explicit allusion to the closing line of Yehuda Halevi's "Zion, Do You Wonder" (*Tsiyon Halo Tishali Le-Shalom Asirayikh*), which is a masterclass in apostrophe to Jerusalem: "I am a mourner who weeps for your poverty / and when I dream of the return I am a lyre to thy songs." Finally, and most recognizably, the line "If I forget thee" comes from Psalm 137, verse 5, and has appeared on innumerable instances in music and poetry about Jerusalem since the Middle Ages, including in Halevi's work.[5] Shemer would return to the same poetic well in other songs, too; for example, in her 1977 song, "By the Rivers of Babylon" (*Al Naharot Bavel*), Shemer quotes the whole first verse of Psalm 137 in the refrain, and of course the title comes from the psalm's opening line.

"Jerusalem of Gold" takes its title and main metaphorical device from the Talmudic story of Rabbi Akiva, who in destitution longed to buy his wife a golden diadem shaped like the city of Jerusalem, as was the custom among the wealthy across much of the Near East in the early centuries CE.[6,7] For the Jerusalem-shaped diadem, there were three common choices of materials, according to the wealth of the family: gold, copper, and leather. Shemer cleverly erased what would have been a glaring class distinction by playing on the quasi-homophonic words 'or and 'or, meaning "leather" and "light."[8] In so doing, she transformed all of the terms from items in a list of descending value into vague imagery meant to hyperbolize the city's beauty. Flattening the prestige of the materials meant that, when it came to Jerusalem, anyone

---

[5] The ritual injunction against forgetting Jerusalem is discussed at length in Chapter 2.

[6] The text in translation:

> The daughter of Kalba Savu'a betrothed herself to R. Akiva. When her father heard thereof, he vowed that she was not to benefit from aught of his property. Then she went and married him in winter. They slept on straw, and he had to pick out the straw from his hair. "If Only I could afford it," said he to her, "I would present you with a golden Jerusalem." [Later] Elijah came to them in the guise of a mortal, and cried out at the door. "Give the some straw, for my wife is in confinement and I have nothing for her to lie on." "See!" R. Akiva observed to his wife, "there is a man who lacks even straw." [Subsequently] she counseled him, "Go, and become a scholar." So he left her, and spent twelve years [studying] under R. Eliezer and R. Joshua. At the end of this period, he was returning home, when from the back of the house he heard a wicked man jeering at his wife, "Your father did well to you. Firstly, because he is your inferior; and secondly, he has abandoned you to living widowhood all these years." She replied, "Yet were he to hear my desires, he would be absent another twelve years. Seeing that she has thus given me permission," he said, "I will go back." So he went back, and was absent for another twelve years, [at the end of which] he returned with twenty-four thousand disciples. Everyone flocked to welcome him, including her [his wife] too. But that wicked man said to her, "And whither art thou going?" "A righteous man knoweth the life of his beast," she retorted. So she went to see him, but the disciples wished to repulse her. "Make way for her," he told them, "for my [learning] and yours are hers." When Kalba Savu'a heard thereof, he came [before R. Akiva] and asked for the remission of his vow and he annulled it for him. From six incidents did R. Akiva become rich. (from *b*.Nedarim.50a)

[7] This practice has undergone something of a revival over the past few decades in Israel.

[8] Generally speaking, it is not considered strong poetic practice in Hebrew to rhyme or alliterate *aleph* and *ayn*, which are the initial consonants of 'or and 'or respectively, since those consonants traditionally had distinct pronunciations, aleph being a glottal stop and ayn being a voiced pharyngeal fricative. For the majority of modern Hebrew speakers, they are pronounced the same and would appear to be orthographically, rather than phonologically, distinct and therefore appropriate for homophony. This would not be the case, however, for speakers of Yemeni or Mizrahi Hebrew dialects nor for adherents to classic Hebrew poetic convention.

might one day wear a crown of gold. The ancient marital custom, furthermore, was always considered to be a metaphorical act of redemption. According to Talmud scholar Yael Levine Katz, "[The] symbolic act on the part of Rabbi Akiva in the generation following the destruction of the Second Temple (70 CE) was a manifestation of his more profound yearning for the rebuilding of Jerusalem and the Temple" (Levine Katz n.d.). As with Shemer's allusions to Lamentations and Psalms, here she maps the past onto the present political context in a way that resonated with her Israeli listening public. By singing along with these words, listeners in 1967 could imagine themselves as modern rebuilders with the power to restore Jerusalem to its former glory as capital of the Jewish people, at a time when outright destruction at the hands of the Egyptians seemed to loom right around the corner.

The lyrical power of "Jerusalem of Gold" resided not only in Shemer's powerful deployment of symbolism but also in the song's lexical composition and syntactical organization. Like much of Shemer's early work, the song tells a story through "the employment of long, well-connected syntactic structures . . . [that] present a narrative based on a clear sequence of events (Reshef 2012: 165). According to linguist Yael Reshef, during the early part of Shemer's career she was an innovative poet in the sense that she helped to popularize the use of a narrative style through a "a moderate measure of literariness" (Reshef 2012: 167). This was, to be sure, a time when poetic composition tended toward an elevated register of the language that was rooted in a fragmented syntax:

> Until the late 1960s, she was at the forefront of a fundamental linguistic-stylistic change in the character of the Hebrew song, which manifested itself in the transition from an archaic, classicized linguistic style to a more contemporary-oriented language. By contrast, from the late 1960s on her work took a conservative turn, when certain modes of expression she had initially eschewed were reintroduced into her work. (Reshef 2012: 158)[9]

"Jerusalem of Gold" appeared near the end of this early period, prior to Shemer's conservative turn, both poetically and politically, in the late 1960s and 1970s. In the song, she deftly weaves the intertextual references

---

[9] Reshef's argument here contradicts that of Shemer's most vociferous critic, Dan Miron, who writes that the songwriter "never brought about a living and continuous connection between the standard poetic language, learned at school, and the living language with its rhythms and intonations" (Miron 1987: 135, transl. in Reshef 2012: 158; see also Reshef 2012: 169–70).

described earlier into plain language, organized into a clear sequence that builds throughout the song, climaxing at the final refrain.

Owing in large part to the song's intertextuality and narrative flow, audience members and radio listeners alike experienced a profound sense of historical responsibility to the city and its sacred spaces. As the playwright and poet Dan Almagor relayed to me, "[After Nathan's performance] we just sat there, feeling guilty—all of us. For nineteen years we ignored it [Jerusalem]—even those of us who lived there for school—but now, it felt like: This is our city, and we should take it back" (Almagor 2012). Beginning the next day, the Israeli authorities seized the opportunity to use the song to rally public support for war with the neighboring Arab states. Both Naomi Shemer and Shuly Nathan were enlisted to perform for army reserves being called to duty around the country. In the few weeks between the Israel Song Contest and the Six-Day War, state radio played the live recording of "Jerusalem of Gold" several times daily, and the song provided a consistent soundtrack for the Waiting Period.

Writing a few months after the war, journalist Linda Gottlieb went as far as to call it "the song that took a city" (Gottlieb 1967).[10] Like the Israeli army, "Jerusalem of Gold" rose to immediate success, and its status as an epoch-defining song truly began to solidify in the aftermath of the Six-Day War.

The Wall, the Shouk, and the Fallout

Having swiftly defeated the Egyptian Air Force on June 5, the first day of the war, Israel turned its sights onto Jordanian-controlled East Jerusalem. After a brutal day of fighting, Israeli forces undertook a dramatic siege in the Old City. Over the radio, Lieutenant General Motta Gur announced, "We're sitting right now on the ridge and we're seeing the Old City. Shortly we're going to go in to the Old City of Jerusalem that all generations have dreamed about. We will be the first to enter the Old City" (Balfour 2015: 260). Breaking through the Lion's Gate to the East, the battalion advanced through a rain of Jordanian gunfire and made their way to the Temple Mount/Noble Sanctuary

---

[10] A similar phrasing was used in a December 4, 1967, spread in *Yediot Aḥranot*. The Hebrew word "kavash" has some additional resonances here. Literally "conquer," it is used to refer to the Occupation but also metaphorically to indicate a conquering of the heart or the musical charts. The slippage between these potential uses, as they pertain to the song, may not have been intentional. The point is the power attributed to the song by these commentators.

Figure 4.4 Rabbi Shlomo Goren and soldiers on the Temple Mount, June 7, 1967 (Getty Images).

and the Moroccan Quarter, butted up against the Western Wall.[11] The radio blared, "The Temple Mount is in our hands! I repeat, the Temple Mount is in our hands!" (Balfour 2015: 261). After securing the area, General Uzi Narkiss and Rabbi Shlomo Goren led speeches and prayers for fallen soldiers and in thanksgiving for victory. Goren sounded the shofar, a symbolic act with multiple resonances at that moment.[12] It signaled the promise to rebuild the Temple in Jerusalem and the ingathering of the exiles in this land—a process presumably begun by the founding of the State of Israel nineteen years prior and completed with the conquest of Jerusalem. Afterward, the soldiers spontaneously began singing the national anthem "Hatikva" and "Jerusalem of Gold" in unison at the Western Wall (Figure 4.4). The event captured on the news radio broadcast that day has since come to symbolize the euphoria of that historic moment.

[11] A few days after the war, the Jerusalem municipality would bulldoze the Moroccan quarter to create the Western Wall plaza that would provide access for large numbers of worshipers, thus displacing the erstwhile residents in the process; see Abowd 2000.

[12] The shofar, fashioned from a ram's horn, is traditionally blown during synagogue services to announce the Jewish holidays of Rosh Hashanah and Yom Kippur, among a few other contexts.

Inspired by the soldiers' actions and filled with newfound zeal, Naomi Shemer responded to this new development by appending the song with a pair of stanzas celebrating Israel's victory and the new life she believed that Jews could now breathe into the abandoned spaces of longing she once elegized:

> We returned to the wells,
> To the market, and to the square.
> The shofar rings on the Temple Mount
> In the Old City.
> And in the caverns of stone,
> A thousand suns will shine.
> We'll go back down to the Dead Sea
> On Jericho Road.

חָזַרְנוּ אֶל בּוֹרוֹת הַמַּיִם
לַשּׁוּק וְלַכִּכָּר
שׁוֹפָר קוֹרֵא בְּהַר הַבַּיִת
בָּעִיר הָעַתִּיקָה
וּבַמְּעָרוֹת אֲשֶׁר בַּסֶּלַע
אַלְפֵי שְׁמָשׁוֹת זוֹרְחוֹת
נָשׁוּב נֵרֵד אֶל יָם הַמֶּלַח
בְּדֶרֶךְ יְרִיחוֹ

She premiered the new verses herself, performing for troops in Jerusalem on June 7 and then in newly occupied Bethlehem on June 10.[13] Through the use of parallelism, the new lines answer the lonely calls of the original verses: dry cisterns flow again with water, dark caverns are filled with light, and newfound joy is born from the possibility that a collective "we" (Jewish Israelis) might take the Dead Sea Highway (Jericho Road) together. The line, "The shofar rings on the Temple Mount," refers not in a general sense to the ritual meaning of the shofar, but to the actual blowing of the instrument by Shlomo Goren at the Western Wall on June 7. Thus, Shemer positions the Six-Day War as the teleological conclusion of a long narrative of Jewish history from the destruction of the First Temple, through diasporic wandering, into present-day Greater Israel, which now included most of the bible lands and Jerusalem.

---

[13] A recording of her Bethlehem performance was tacked onto the final track of the album *Naomi Shemer Sings Her famous Jerusalem of Gold* (1968).

This postwar messianic fervor was widespread, yet not all Israelis hailed the war as a moral victory. "Jerusalem of Gold" caused Naomi Shemer to fall out of favor with the left-leaning literary elite who spoke out against the song's compliance with right-wing Israeli military policy. Just one day after the war ended, author Amos Oz (1939–2019), who at that time was writing for the daily newspaper *Davar*, launched a bellicose critique of Shemer's poetic rendering of space. Consider the following lines:

> How is it that the wells dried up
> The market square is empty,
> And no one visits the Temple Mount
> In the Old City?

אֵיכָה יָבְשׁוּ בּוֹרוֹת הַמַּיִם

כִּכַּר הַשּׁוּק רֵיקָה

וְאֵין פּוֹקֵד אֶת הַר הַבַּיִת

בָּעִיר הָעַתִּיקָה

Here, Shemer erases the human presence from the Old City's spaces. In his article, Oz reminded his readers that the market square and the Temple Mount were not empty prior to Israeli occupation but full of Arabs who lived, worked, and worshiped there. Indeed, the market square (*shuk/sūq*) was, and is today, one of the liveliest places in the city—an open-air market filled with the noise of chaotic transactions, polyglot conversations between visitors, and static-filled radios blaring Islamic sermons. For Oz, these spaces were not empty voids waiting to be occupied by the Jewish people by way of violent conquest but instead a complex human geography to which no group had an inherent right of sovereign control. Shemer's vision of terrestrial Jerusalem bore little resemblance to the city's urban landscape but rather replicated tropes from heavenly Jerusalem that fitted poorly to the city that Jerusalemite listeners knew. As geographer Daniel Bertrand Monk points out, Shemer's self-defense, which she published in an article twenty years after the song first appeared, "would hinge upon an argument concerning the autonomy of the artwork." He summarizes her claims thusly: "she didn't have the *actual* Jerusalem in mind, or even the nineteen-year interval of its divided status, but had composed a work referring to the sum total of all histories, a mythic Jerusalem instead" (Monk 2005: 177; see Shemer 1987). Here, the conceptual schism between metaphorical and material Jerusalem serves the purpose of a neo-Romantic conception of art that absolves the artist from responsibility for their effects on the realm of social and political life. As Monk argues, by way of rhetorical questioning, "If Shemer aimed to present a telescopic, or suprahistorical view of Jerusalem (her 'sum of all Jerusalems'), *then why would the 1967 victory necessitate a new stanza?*" (Monk 2005: 177, emphasis in original).

This song about metaphorical Jerusalem produced a strong resonance within the political realm, as it was sung at the moment of military conquest and in subsequent commemorative events. Metaphorical Jerusalem, as I argued in Chapter 1, overlays the material space of the city and helps to drive its-violent history. Oz's and Monk's remarks on "Jerusalem of Gold" thus resemble critiques that anthropologists such as Patrick Wolfe have leveled at settler colonialism. As Wolfe writes, "settler society required the practical elimination of the natives in order to establish itself on their territory. On the symbolic level, however, settler society subsequently sought to recuperate indigeneity in order to express its difference—and, accordingly, its independence—from the mother country" (Wolfe 2006: 389). In the song, Shemer's representations of Jerusalem serve both functions: they eliminate Palestinians from view in an exposition that treats a possible return to Jerusalem as a negation of exile. It is no surprise, then, that the song and its creator drew a litany of criticism from figures across the Israeli political spectrum.

One prominent critique took the form of a parody song, which drew very close parallels that made its relation to the original unmistakable: Meir Ariel's "Jerusalem of Iron" (*Yerushalayim shel Barzel*). The lyrics are printed here:

> In your darkness, Jerusalem,
> We found a loving heart,
> When we came to widen your borders
> And to overwhelm the enemy.
> We became satiated of all his mortars,
> Then suddenly dawn broke.
> It just arose, not yet even white,
> And it was already red.
>
> Jerusalem of iron,
> Of lead, and of darkness,
> Haven't we set
> Your walls free?

The strafed battalion broke forward,
Everything was blood and smoke.
And a mother came, and another mother,
In the congregation of bereavement.
Biting their lips, indefatigable,
The battalion continued fighting,
Till at the end, the flag flapped
Above the Museum of antiquities

Jerusalem of iron,
Of lead, and of darkness,
Haven't we set
Your wall free?

The king's army dispersed,
The sniper in his tower is silent.
Now it's possible to go to the Dead Sea
On Jericho Road.
Now it's possible to go the Temple Mount
And the Western Wall.
Here you are in the twilight,
Almost all of you, gold.

Jerusalem of gold,
Of lead, and of dream,
Will forever between your walls
Be peace.

בְּמַחְשַׁכַּיִךְ יְרוּשָׁלַיִם
מָצָאנוּ לֵב אוֹהֵב
עֵת בָּאנוּ לְהַרְחִיב גְּבוּלַיִךְ
וּלְמַגֵּר אוֹיֵב
מִקּוֹל מַרְגֵּמוֹתָיו רָוִינוּ
וְשַׁחַר קָם פִּתְאוֹם—
הוּא רַק עָלָה, עוֹד לֹא הִלְבִּין הוּא
וּכְבָר הָיָה אָדֹם

יְרוּשָׁלַיִם שֶׁל בַּרְזֶל
וְשֶׁל עוֹפֶרֶת וְשֶׁל שָׁחוֹר

הֲלֹא לְחוֹמוֹתַיִךְ
קָרָאנוּ דְּרוֹר

הַגְּדוּד, רָגוּם, פָּרַץ קָדִימָה,
דָּם וְעָשָׁן כֻּלּוֹ
וּבָאוּ אִמָּא אַחַר אִמָּא
בִּקְהַל הַשַּׁכּוּלוֹת
נוֹשֵׁךְ שְׂפָתָיו וְלֹא בְּלִי יֶגַע,
הוֹסִיף הַגְּדוּד לִלְחֹם
עַד שֶׁסּוֹף סוֹף הָחֳלַף הַדֶּגֶל
מֵעַל בֵּית הַנְּכוֹת

יְרוּשָׁלַיִם שֶׁל בַּרְזֶל
וְשֶׁל עוֹפֶרֶת וְשֶׁל שָׁחוֹר
הֲלֹא לְחוֹמוֹתַיִךְ
קָרָאנוּ דְּרוֹר

נָפְצוּ כָּל גְּדוּדֵי הַמֶּלֶךְ,
צַלָּף—נָדַם צְרִיחוּ
עַכְשָׁו אֶפְשָׁר אֶל יָם הַמֶּלַח
בְּדֶרֶךְ יְרִיחוֹ
עַכְשָׁו אֶפְשָׁר אֶל הַר הַבַּיִת
וְכֹתֶל מַעֲרָב
הִנֵּה הִנֵּךְ בְּאוֹר עַרְבַּיִם,
כִּמְעַט כֻּלָּךְ זָהָב

יְרוּשָׁלַיִם שֶׁל זָהָב
וְשֶׁל עוֹפֶרֶת וַחֲלוֹם—
לָעַד בֵּין חוֹמוֹתַיִךְ
יִשְׁכֹּן שָׁלוֹם

Just as Naomi Shemer portrayed the city as a fantastical splendor of Jewish antiquity, Ariel chose to emphasize the grit and horror of 1967, the very modern
war that he and his comrades fought to realize that vision in the present, even
if—through the closing line of the refrain ("Haven't we set your walls free?")—
he tempers such imagery with a triumphant tone. As Yossi Klein Halevi points
out, even though Ariel "had intended to rebuke Naomi Shemer's naïveté . . .
he too couldn't help celebrating Jerusalem" (Klein Halevi 2013: 103). Besides

the obvious play on Shemer's title, in his version Ariel employs the poetic device of antithesis to maintain the connection of his song to hers. Any native speaker of Hebrew would note the refrain's rhyming replacement of Shemer's words: *zahav/barzel* (gold/iron), *nehoshet/oferet* (copper/lead), *or/shahor* (light/darkness; this also rhymes with *kinnor* [lyre] in Shemer's refrain). Beyond these textual parallels, Ariel used a similar sung melody and guitar accompaniment to the original recording made by Shuly Nathan.

"Jerusalem of Iron" formed a pair with "Jerusalem of Gold," and their parallels stem from much more than the poetic and musical content of the two versions. None other than Rivka Michaeli, the radio deejay who pushed Naomi Shemer to include specific references to Jerusalem in her lyrics, was responsible for disseminating Ariel's "Jerusalem of Iron" to a wider public. Ariel first premiered the song at a June 12, 1967, concert at the Hebrew University amphitheater on Mt. Scopus to commemorate the war victory. To the audience, he was just an unknown soldier at the mic, just as Shuly Nathan had been at the Israeli song contest four weeks earlier. And just like at Nathan's performance, what began as a premiere ended in a moment of communal singing, despite the audience having never heard or read the lyrics (see Klein Halevi 2013: 105–108). After witnessing this moment, Michaeli took Ariel backstage and compelled him to sing the song once more, this time into her tape recorder, which she took to the radio station to broadcast nationwide. Even the "overnight success" narrative of Meir Ariel's parody version parallels the original song.

The popularity of "Jerusalem of Iron" among Shemer's dissenters grew rapidly in the aftermath of the war. Reflecting on the song three decades later in 1996, Meir Ariel reportedly attributed his earlier sentiments to "combat shock and whisky" (Levine Katz n.d.). Although this sentiment would seem to contradict the politics of his original message, which injected a realistic picture of violence into the fanfare and celebration of 1967, the stakes were perhaps more personal for Ariel. His biographer Nissim Calderon (2016) reports that the songwriter always regretted the fact that "Jerusalem of Iron"—more so than his original compositions such as "The Snake's Slough" (*Neshel ha-Nahash*, 1988)—is so widely recognized as his lasting contribution to the Israeli song canon. This is a fascinating phenomenon, considering that "Jerusalem of Iron" circulated only briefly on the radio and then as a simple EP, while the majority of Ariel's output over the next three decades enjoyed the support of major recording studios, distributors, and labels, such as NMC Music Ltd., once a subsidiary of CBS and home to many of Israel's major musical figures, such as Chava Alberstein and Ehud Banai. Despite Ariel's status and privilege as a successful commercial musician, his participation in the events of 1967 and his connection to "Jerusalem of Gold," however antagonistic it may have been, overshadow his other contributions to Israeli public culture. These issues transformed into specters that would haunt Meir Ariel, in spite of his efforts to establish political distance from the crisis over Jerusalem.

Victory Albums and Jerusalem Song Revival

Immediately following the 1967 War, musicians and producers rushed to record and release albums celebrating Israel's domination of the Arab enemy on land and in the skies, almost instantaneously establishing a "nostalgia industry of the Six Day War" (Monk 2005: 178). By October of that year, no fewer than twenty commercial recordings devoted to the war had been released, with titles such as *Israel's Victory 1967* (various), *Six Days in June* (various), *Songs after the 6-Day War* (Geula Gill), *Songs of the War and Victory* (various), and *To Zahal with Love* (Yaffa Yarkoni) (see Billboard 1967). Most of these albums are compilations of recordings made by various artists, highlighting the collective, cooperative spirit that Israeli culture brokers wished to promote during this period. Some record labels released flexi-disc mailers so that Israelis could share their musical triumphalism with the world through the post. There is considerable content overlap between many of these albums, forming a veritable archive of war songs that remain associated with 1967 today. Naomi Shemer's "Jerusalem of Gold" appears on each one of them, even lending its name to some album titles. This included a pair of records called *Jerusalem of Gold: Songs of the Six-Day War* and *Jerusalem of Steel: More Songs of the Six-Day War* (Figure 4.5).

With this pair of albums, record label Hed Artzi and producer Benny Amdursky chose to present a bilateral treatment of the war, even though *Jerusalem of Steel*, named for Meir Ariel's song (*barzel* translates to both "iron" and "steel"), is not an album of protest songs. But unlike many other albums marking the war's end, *Jerusalem of Steel* does include songs that confront the complex realities of violence and its aftermath, even if they are not critical of the war itself. The featured songwriters accomplish this cultural work with strikingly intimate language and imagery, as in "Ammunition Hill" and "Ha-Kotel," both discussed in the previous chapter.

Along with victory albums, an outpouring of albums devoted to Jerusalem song itself appeared in the wake of "Jerusalem of Gold." This form of anthologism has been a powerful presentational frame that Israelis have employed to create musical narratives about Jerusalem. Much like popular literary anthologies devoted to Jerusalem (see, for example, Hammer 1995), many Israeli and Euro-American record labels were keen to capitalize on the post-1967 Jerusalem craze and released compilation albums. Many songs appear on more than one of the albums, either through the same recording or through different recordings by multiple artists. In effect, these anthologies do the work of shoring up the Jerusalem song renaissance initiated by Naomi Shemer and, in so doing, produced a ready-made canon for the genre that would serve as reference recordings for multiple versions of the songs contained therein.

Lyrically speaking, the newly anthologized repertory drew on many of the discursive patterns and citational practices addressed in the preceding

Figure 4.5 Album covers for *Jerusalem of Gold* and *Jerusalem of Steel* (1968).

Figure 4.5 Continued

chapters. A particularly revealing example is a 45-RPM EP that singer
Hadassah Sigalov recorded shortly after the war under the title *Nashir Lakh
Yerushalayim*, translated into English on the album cover as "Songs for Thee
Jerusalem" but more properly translated as "We Sing to You Jerusalem."
using in both possible translations, the city is addressed in the feminine-
gendered, second-person declension of *la* (to): *lakh*.[14] In keeping with other
victory albums, the cover art for this EP depicts jubilant Israeli soldiers, guns
strapped to their backs, dancing the iconic *hora* folkdance (see Figure 4.6).

---

[14] The album metadata completely omits a date of publication, on both the physical object and in
any archival records. I would estimate its release at late 1967 or early 1968, as with many Six-Day War
victory albums, but it could have appeared anywhere between 1967 and 1969, given the broader context of victory-album record production.

JR 5038
נשיר לך ירושלים
SONGS FOR THEE JERUSALEM
ירושלים של זהב
JERUSALEM SHEL ZAHAV
sung by   שרה
HADASSAH SIGALOV   הדסה סיגלוב

Figure 4.6 Album cover for Hadassah Sigalov, *Nashir Lakh Yerushalayim* (c. 1967–1968).

The visual presentation suggests that the soldiers constitute the "we," indicated in the album title, who sing to Jerusalem, the listener at their backs.

The four-song track list includes covers of songs that were already well known at the time of release. Side A includes Naomi Shemer's "Jerusalem of Gold" and Avigdor Hameiri's "From the Summit of Mt. Scopus" (alternatively titled on the sleeve as "Jerusalem"), two songs whose genealogies involve dense intertextual webs and liberal use of the poetics of longing, including the signature device of apostrophe.

The third song on Sigalov's *Nashir Lakh Yerushalayim* provides a break from the apostrophic lyrics found throughout the rest of the album and instead highlights the spatial ethos of Jerusalem song that connects the city to its environs (see Chapter 2). The song is identified on the sleeve by the title

"Tomb of Rachel" (*Kever Raḥel*), but it is better known by the name "In the Fields of Bethlehem" (*Be-Shadmot Bet Leḥem*). Written by Abba Constantin Shapiro (lyrics) and Hanina Krachevsky (music), every element of the recording drips with pathos, from the vibrato-heavy organ accompaniment to the slow attack envelope of Sigalov's voice, as she swells through lyrics that pay tribute to the tomb of the matriarch Rachel, located in south Jerusalem near Bethlehem but never referenced by name. The final song on the album, "If I Forget Thee Jerusalem," is a musical setting of Psalm 137, whose inclusion solidifies the album's apostrophic motif and its close adherence to canonicity. It is, like the opening song "Jerusalem of Gold," a form of meta-apostrophe, as Sigalov not only sings to Jerusalem but also sings about singing to Jerusalem.

The renewal of Jerusalem song engendered by Sigalov's album and the various albums discussed earlier would reach beyond the domain of the Israeli recording industry and national media to the very halls of government itself.

The Anthem Debacle

"Jerusalem of Gold" has been instrumentalized to political ends since its inception. In December 1967, Knesset member Uri Avnery submitted a bill to change the national anthem from "Hatikva" to "Jerusalem of Gold." This is often hailed as a real achievement for Naomi Shemer and cited as proof of the song's universal appeal within Israeli society, since Avnery is generally considered a great bastion of the Left—perhaps its most vocal figure since the collapse of the Labor movement after 1977. Naomi Shemer's music, by contrast, is associated primarily with right-wing political parties, including the extremist settler group Gush Emunim.[15] *Yediot Aḥronot* columnist Nahum Barnea wrote in June 2004, just weeks after Shemer's death,

> The land of Israel was for her a one-nation land, devoid of conflicts, devoid of minorities. . . . A one-sided deal for Jews alone. Even the wars to which we went out on [sic] with her songs were one-sided. It was not an enemy

[15] A line from her song "For All These Things" (*Al Kol Eleh*), "Al na ta'akor natua" (Do not uproot what has been planted), became a political tagline for Israeli settlers at the illegal outpost of Yamit in the Golan Heights—land that also changed hands in 1967, until the settlement was evacuated in 1982.

facing us, but a virgin land waiting to be conquered. (cited and translated in Colton 2004)

Given Shemer's poor standing among the Israeli Left, during an interview I asked Uri Avnery to clarify his purpose in suggesting "Jerusalem of Gold" as a new national anthem. He told me:

My purpose has been for a long time, and still is, to get rid of "Hatikva" as the national anthem. I believe "Hatikva" is a very bad national anthem. It excludes the Arabs, which are twenty percent of the citizens of Israel. It belongs to a period at the beginning of the Zionist movement, a hundred years ago. It was inappropriate for the State of Israel. I'd been looking for some time for an opportunity to convince the Knesset to change it, and after the Six-Day War I thought I had an opportunity because "Yerushalayim shel Zahav" became a very popular song. It had all of the attributes of a national anthem, so I submitted a bill in the Knesset to change it, to change "Hatikva" for "Yerushalayim shel Zahav." Of course I did not agree to all the text of "Yerushalayim shel Zahav," but I thought that once we have the decision, a resolution in the Knesset to change the national anthem, the words of "Yerushalayim shel Zahav" could be changed to be more suitable. (Avnery 2012)

Israel did not, in fact, have an official national anthem until 2004, when the Knesset sanctioned "Hatikva" as a part of the Flag, Coat-of-Arms, and National Anthem Law (Seroussi 2015). But the song had already been the de facto anthem and was sung at all official government events as well as in schools and other contexts that called for a national anthem; thus, most people simply assumed it was official. Owing to this confusion about the status of "Hatikva," Avnery continued his preparations for the bill.

Speaker of the Knesset Kadish Luz instructed Avnery to secure Naomi Shemer's permission before proceeding, so he met with her to discuss the possibility. After what Avnery detected as hesitancy, Shemer agreed to the idea and allowed him to pass the message on to Speaker Luz. Looking back on this moment forty-five years later, Avnery attributed Shemer's initial reluctance to fear of being caught "plagiarizing" the melody:

Later on, before Naomi Shemer died, she confessed that she did not write the melody of the song but took it from a Basque song. This must've been the reason for the hesitation which I detected in our conversation. I think she was all her life after '67 tortured by the idea that somebody someday would discover that she'd stolen the melody. (Avnery 2012)

I will take up this question of plagiarism later, but suffice it to say that Avnery expressed relief that, due to a procedural complication, his bill was never put to a motion. Still, in his mind the lasting memory of the bill stands as a symbolic referendum on the exclusionary nature of "Hatikva" and not, contrary to popular belief and scholarly consensus (see, e.g., Gavriely-Nuri 2007), an affirmation of the equally dubious meanings that have accrued to "Jerusalem of Gold."

Although "Jerusalem of Gold" never became the Israeli national anthem, there is no question that it rivals "Hatikva" in domestic and international popularity, both songs being charged with articulating the core values of the various strands of Zionism embodied by the mature state. At the same time, it is the clearest musical expression of the elision of Jewish attachment to metaphorical Jerusalem, as a space of religious liberation and political self-determination, with an implicit justification of violence—through both force and exclusion—toward Jerusalemites who do not fit into that vision.

With this critique in mind, shortly after the war Yeshayahu Leibowitz published an article in *Haaretz* mounting a stunning critique of the widespread euphoria gripping Israeli society across Jewish social sectors, suggesting sarcastically that the state should convert the Western Wall plaza into a giant, open-air discothèque. In the article, he coined the portmanteau *Diskotel* (*Discothèque* and *Kotel*) to indicate what he considered the "idolatry" (*avoda zara*) of overtures to the "liberated" monuments' supposed religious significance (which he denied). He called the phenomenon of Israeli Jews driving to visit the Western Wall and other sites during the religious festival of Shavu'ot, during which driving was forbidden by Jewish law and yet was facilitated by the government's opening of parking lots, a "degradation of the Torah and of Judaism" (*bizayon Torah ve-Yahadut*).[16] As geographer Daniel Bertrand Monk and musicologist Tanya Sermer conclude in their respective accounts of this criticism of Naomi Shemer's representational politics, by Leibowitz and others (including Amos Oz), the newly liberated

---

[16] An excerpt of the article appears in translation, as quoted here, in Monk (2005: 175; also Sermer 2015: 58–59).

Western Wall would nevertheless "become the primary symbol of Jewish unity" (Sermer 2015: 59).[17]

With the song's release shortly before the Six-Day War of 1967, "Jerusalem of Gold" became a cultural force in its own right—one that helped to place its subject, Jerusalem, at the center of debates about Israeli identity after the war. After the city's several years of relative obscurity in the national discourse, it seemed to appear out of the blue—at least for the secular, Labor Zionist majority—and at a most fortuitous moment, when Israelis believed themselves to be under threat of extinction and feared that the dream of modern Jewish sovereignty over Judaism's historical homeland would be short-lived. Naomi Shemer energized the public in preparation for the June war, which seemed inevitable beginning on the very night that the song premiered, when Egyptian President Gamal Abdel Nasser closed the Straits of Tiran to Israeli ships and amassed troops on the Egypt-Israel border in Sinai. The song also seemed in hindsight to prophesize one outcome of the war: the unification of Jerusalem under Israeli rule and consequent occupation of Palestinian and Arab territories. Naomi Shemer also foresaw another controversy stemming from the song: a debate about the melody's originality that would serve as a proxy for the ideological war over occupation.

Gold or "Counterfeit?"

In the spring of 1962, five years before the 1967 debut of "Jerusalem of Gold," Naomi Shemer and a group of fellow musicians, including Dan Almagor, Benny Amdursky, and Nechama Hendel, went to a small jazz club in Jaffa to see Spanish singer Paco Ibáñez perform.[18] Among the songs that Ibáñez played that night was "Pello Joxepe," a Basque folksong about a man who denies being the father of his spouse's child. A quick listen reveals an almost pitch-for-pitch resemblance between the two melodies, their opposing meters notwithstanding. Figure 4.7 includes a transcription of each melody.

[17] It is worth noting that Hillel Cohen offers a somewhat different perspective on the place of the Western Wall within post-1967 interpretations of Zionism, arguing that "the level of Israeli unity around the claim that the Jews must assert their rights on the Temple Mount seems to be lower than on the Palestinian side" (Cohen 2017: 16). This argument, however, is rooted in a view of the Israeli public as an essentially secularized one, and this is debatable with the increasingly conspicuous presence of religiosity in Israeli culture and politics over the past several decades, most especially in the rise to prominence of the *dati-le'umi* community discussed in Chapter 1.

[18] Dan Almagor related this story to me during our June 2012 interview.

Figure 4.7 Transcribed melodies for "Jerusalem of Gold" and "Pello Joxepe" (key signatures normalized for comparison).

What both melodies have in common is a pitch contour of 5-1-5-4 / 4-6-5-4 that eventually arrives at a half cadence in the fourth measure. In "Jerusalem of Gold," Naomi Shemer further tonicizes the iv chord (D-minor) in the second measure of the transcription by employing a secondary dominant in the accompaniment (the guitar plays A7, or V7/iv). The second phrases of both melodies use an identical contour to arrive at a 3-2-1 motion, outlining a perfect cadence to complete the phrase.[19] The similarities between melodic and harmonic content are undeniable.

Shemer chose not to disclose this musical borrowing until she sent a confessional letter to Gil Aldema in 2004, shortly before her death. In the letter, she describes a scene in which she and singer Nechama Hendel—who had been with her the night of the Ibáñez performance—visited together in Shemer's home, eating, telling jokes, and singing. She wrote, "Apparently, Nechama sang the well-known Basque song to me, and it went in one ear and out the other. . . . In winter 1967, when I was working on 'Jerusalem of Gold,' the song must have crawled into me without my knowing" (Shemer 2004). Despite the fact that the tune was memorable enough to be transmitted from a performance by Ibáñez to a casual singing by Hendel to a near-complete interpolation in the verses of "Jerusalem of Gold," Shemer circumvented the question of ethical responsibility by appealing to the complexities of musical memory. It is also unclear why she chose not to mention her attendance at Ibáñez's performance, especially since she had gone there with so many companions whose own

---

[19] "Pello Joxepe" did not appear on any of Ibáñez's commercially available recordings until 1999 (Ibáñez and Imanol 1999), but comparison is possible because he uses a traditional Basque melody and text.

memory of the event made Shemer's transgression an open secret among the group (Almagor 2012).

In the letter, she goes on to point out musical differences between her song and the lullaby, such as the distinction between major and minor modes, as if assuaging her guilt by grasping at claims to originality. She acknowledges the close resemblance of the melodies as a mistake but not as constituting an act of plagiarism:

> I consider the entire affair a regrettable work accident—so regrettable that it may be the reason for me taking ill. . . . I also didn't know that an invisible hand dictated changes in the original to me. . . . It turns out that someone protected me and provided me with my eight notes that granted me the rights to my version of the folk song. But all this was done, as I said, unwittingly. (Shemer 2004)

Here, Shemer is referring to the upper limit of borrowed consecutive pitches permitted by Israeli copyright law; if anything, it reads as an unwitting admission of shrewd intentionality, which may or may not have been the case in reality.[20]

All of Shemer's friends and colleagues whom I interviewed believe that she took the melody knowingly, or at least that she realized her subconscious mistake very early in the song's career. Most striking is their common incredulity about the extent to which the secret weighed on her conscience, since they do not believe her actions to have been unethical. After all, "Pello Joxepe" is a folksong with no attributed authorship, and popular songwriters from Israel and elsewhere freely borrowed from folksong melodies. This is not to say, however, that both supporters and detractors of Shemer's work have not pressed the issue. When Gil Aldema, who had been producer of the Israel Song Festival in 1967, submitted Shemer's confession letter to the *Haaretz* daily newspaper one year after her death,[21] the issue snowballed into international press coverage, prompting debates within Israel over what constitutes musical and literary originality and over the ideological ramifications of borrowing acts (see Meltzer 2012). To be sure, there is a long history within Israeli musical practice, particularly in the "composed folk" traditions

---

[20] For an overview on research related to music and copyrights/intellectual property, see Collins (2008; Frith and Marshall 2004; McCann 2001).

[21] This was according to Shemer's wish for the letter to be published, which she expressed in the closing lines of the letter, and with the written permission of her family.

discussed in Chapter 2 and in composed art music traditions (see Shelleg 2014: 78–93), of appropriating melodies from unidentified sources, either from those that people brought with them from points of migration (e.g., from Russia, Latvia, Poland, and other countries in east central Europe) or from sources local to Palestine (e.g., from Bedouin, Arab, Greek, and other Mediterranean contexts). But by 1967, the Israeli music industry had long shifted toward attributed authorship in the vein of global popular music, with artistic labor—customarily distributed between performer, lyricist, arranger, and/or composer, who were often different individuals—credited in detail on most records published by Hed Arzi and CBS, the two major labels at the time.

Of course, many anthems—national or not—appropriate their melodies from other sources; Israel's current national anthem "Hatikva," for instance, is based on "Carul cu boi," a Romanian folk tune.[22] In her assessment of the Naomi Shemer's "plagiarism" crisis, political scientist Dalia Gavriely-Nuri claims, "[T]he revelation did not cause any damage to the song's status" (2007: 105). It is true that the enormous cultural resonance of "Jerusalem of Gold" continues well into the twenty-first century in spite of this controversy, but many of Shemer's critics, particularly those who question the song's representational politics, have seized on the controversy to discredit her through accusations of plagiarism.

Distributed Canonization

"Jerusalem of Gold" has a singular presence within Israeli public culture, and the song has been utterly pervasive over the past half-century since its release. The afterlife of the song is colored by the checkered reception I detailed in the previous section, serving as a touchstone for people operating across the political spectrum. It also has enjoyed frequent reinstantiation through cover versions rendered in live performances and on commercial recordings, ranging in style from 1960s pop pastiche (Geula Gill, 1968) to instrumental harmonica solo (Larry Adler and Hedva & David, 1968) to *Musiqa Mizraḥit* (Zehava Ben, 2003) to house remix (Offer Nissim and Rita, 2005) to

[22] There are also widespread, erroneous claims that "Hatikva" was based on Italian ("La Montovana"), Polish ("Pod Krakowem"), and Ukrainian ("Kateryna Kucheryava") sources. See Seroussi (2015) for an overview of the song's multiple origin hypotheses.

electronic opera (Maya Ackerman, 2015), and many more. It appeared in the soundtrack to Stephen Spielberg's film *Schindler's List* (1993)[23] and even in the concert repertory of Kurdish-Armenian pop star Zara.[24] The song also has been quasi-sacralized as part of the Reform synagogue hymn repertory and is commonly found in *siddurim* (prayer books) throughout the Anglophone Jewish diaspora.[25] There are far too many instantiations of the song, diverse in stylistic content and political resonance, to catalog without distracting from the main purpose of this genealogical investigation. What is clear is that the song has remained at the top of the Israeli song canon through its distribution across those diverse instantiations while maintaining its remarkably flexible identity.

One rendition of "Jerusalem of Gold" in particular stands out as evidence for the song's canonical, and indeed anthemic, status. The program for Independence Day in 1998, Israel's Jubilee Year, included a majestic performance by the renowned mezzo-soprano singer of popular Israeli and traditional Yemenite music, Ofra Haza. Haza, who hailed from the Hatikva neighborhood of South Tel Aviv, launched her international career in 1983 with her second-place performance of "Hai" (Alive) at the Eurovision Song Contest in Munich. She went on to record several albums during the 1980s and 1990s for Israeli, European, and American record labels, attaining a level of international popularity that was rare at that point for Israeli musicians. Indeed, her voice was so widely recognized across the globe that it was sampled in a popular remix of US rappers Eric B. and Rakim's 1987 hit, "Paid in Full," which went on to rank number ten in *Rolling Stone* magazine's "50 Greatest Hip-Hop Songs of All Time" (2012).[26] By 1998, a moment of reckoning with

[23] When *Schindler's List* was initially released in Israel, audiences objected to the use of Naomi Shemer's song for this scene. They often responded with laughter that would otherwise seem inappropriate at such a moment in the film, drawing attention to the anachronism of the song with the Holocaust and with Spielberg's easy linkage of the destruction of European Jewry with the birth of the Jewish state. The filmmakers quickly replaced "Jerusalem of Gold" with David Zehavi's setting of the poem "Eli Eli" by Hannah Szenes for future releases of the film in Israel.

[24] Zara is not Israeli or Jewish—she is a convert to Russian Orthodox Christianity—but on December 16, 2009, she performed at the invitation of the Jewish community of St. Petersburg at their annual Chanukah celebration at the Ice Palace Concert Hall, delivering a nearly note-for-note rendition of Ofra Haza's otherwise idiosyncratic interpretation of the song from 1998, discussed later.

[25] "Jerusalem of Gold" appears in at least three English-language *siddurim*: *Siddur Sim Shalom* (1998: 398; American conservative movement), *Mishkan T'filah* (2007: 660–61; American reform movement), and *Forms of Prayer* (2008: 398–99; British Movement for Reform Judaism). Special thanks to Rachel Adelstein for helping me to track down these sources.

[26] This remix, recorded by British duo Coldcut, prominently features a sample of the vocal track from "Im Nin 'Alu," a Yemini song set to a seventeenth-century poem by Rabbi Shalom Shabazi that Haza recorded for her 1984 LP *Yemenite Songs*. Samples from "Im Nin 'Alu" also appear in hip-hop tracks by Public Enemy, Snoop Dogg, Nas, and others.

Israel's fifty-year history, Ofra Haza was probably the clearest choice for the marquee performance of the celebration: the Jubilee Bells Show of April 30.

The English word "jubilee" is rooted in the Hebrew word *yovel*, which has a double meaning connoting both the literal passage of fifty years and the ram's horn from which the shofar is constructed; that instrument, in turn, is historically associated with the Jewish holidays Rosh Hashanah and Yom Kippur and, in the biblical era, to mark the ushering in of a jubilee year. Yovel also shares its triliteral root with the name of Yuval, the mythological inventor of music according to Genesis 4. The Independence Day celebrations of 1998 were thus inescapably associated with music; this symbolism was not lost on the Israeli public. The Jubilee Bells Show marked the apex of a long year of musical and other arts-related performances, which, even though many did not directly mark Israel's fiftieth anniversary, had "deftly been heaped onto the anniversary bandwagon" (Schmemann 1998). According to Serge Schmemann, who was at that time Jerusalem Bureau Chief for the *New York Times*, the opportunism of state and civic bodies, who co-opted nearly all of these events to serve their message of unification, was "a fairly transparent effort to put a cheery and busy facade on a jubilee whose organization has suffered from severe infighting, and whose gloss has been tarnished by a political climate that has caused a serious drop in tourism" (Schmemann 1998).

The concert on April 30, 1998, featured a massive live audience filling Jerusalem's Givat Ram Stadium as well as an international television broadcast. The video recording of the event continues to circulate today on YouTube and other online outlets and serves as the basis of my analysis here. Haza's performance began with a stark a cappella rendition of the opening verse, followed by the easing in of a dramatic string section and piano, emphasizing the sorrowful longing of the text and indexing the tinkling guitar introduction played by Shuly Nathan in the original version. As the camera pans out, it reveals an elaborate surrounding set dominated by a scale model of Second Temple-era Jerusalem (530 BCE–70 CE), encircled by a mass of dancers wearing red and black cloaks and golden coverings on their heads (yarmulkes for the men and headbands for the women).

After the lengthy introduction, Haza launches into a heavily ornamented series of vocables, as if crying out in longing—perhaps in mimicry of the shofar but also as a signifier of Yemeni Jewish song—for the very space in which she is standing, both literally, as the performance was set in Jerusalem, and symbolically, as signaled by the Temple model. In the next verse, a pulsing bass drum and pedal-point guitar add to the urgency of the lyrics, until they break into typical rock ballad form for the chorus. This demarcation of form through dynamic and textural variation maintains suspense until the song's victorious conclusion in the supplemental postwar verses, which the crowd sang in triumphant unison with Haza over the television broadcast.

This event helped to liberate "Jerusalem of Gold" from its specific association with 1967 by sanctioning the song as the definitive anthem of a mature Israel—a successful geopolitical force whose boundaries included the territories occupied in 1967.[27] 1967, which resonated before as a defining moment that permeated daily life in Jerusalem and greater Israel, became narratively sublimated as part of Israel's past—of its childhood, as the Fiftieth Anniversary song anthology *We Grew Up Together* (*Gadalnu Yaḥad*, 1998) would have it—in a larger, miracle-based narrative of Jewish history whose teleological conclusion was Jewish sovereignty over the bible lands, in the form of the Israeli state.

* * *

"Jerusalem of Gold" is among the most polysemic cultural artifacts ever produced in Israel. As I have shown, for many listeners and commentators it signifies a poignant modern expression of the diasporic trope of longing, building as it does on its intertextual resources with a memorable, and singable, melody premiered at just the right moment in Israeli history to serve as a Zionist anthem. For Shemer's critics, it signifies an obscene statement of exclusionary politics that erases Palestinians from Jerusalem's landscape, in keeping with the poetics of erasure endemic to settler colonialism, as theorized by Wolfe (2006) and others. Such critical orientations become further differentiated with respect to the postwar verse that obscures not only the city's Palestinian presence but also the occupation itself, as it takes a purely celebratory position toward the newly "unified" Jerusalem. Shemer's jubilation at the war victory is understandable, as she wrote the verse as the war was happening around her. The verse nevertheless has taken on intensified political meaning in the intervening five decades, as the state has tightened its grip on East Jerusalem and, indeed, has expanded its territory deep across the pre-1967 armistice line. The verse now signifies a defiant statement of a renewed Jewish presence in Jerusalem, as I noted at a May 22, 2017, program devoted to the song held at the National Library of Israel, where

---

[27] Exceptions include the Sinai Peninsula, from which Israel withdrew between 1979 and 1982, following the Camp David Accords (1978) and Egypt-Israel Peace Treaty (1979), and Gaza, from which Israel would later withdraw in 2005 (seven years after the event in question).

Nathan herself performed the song and exchanged the fourth verse for the second one in that rendition. The song thus no longer served as a statement of longing but as a testament to state power, whether Shemer intended it that way or not.

The song spans a wide timeline of Israeli history—from a time when the city was divided but maintained a rather quiet modus vivendi, to the third decade of the twenty-first century, when the city remains divided along cultural and political lines but "unified" under Israeli occupation. In 1967, the question of Jerusalem's sovereignty emerged as a critical site for debates about Israeliness, and various approaches to solving the question of its future represent the divergent futures toward which different political groupings aspire.

The outbreak of the Six-Day War just weeks after the Israel Song Festival, and the important roles that Naomi Shemer, Shuly Nathan, and their song played in the events of the war, helped to enshrine all three as brokers of the war's memory and of Jerusalem's place within the historical narrative propping up Israeli rule in the city. In the ensuing decades, the song's process of canonization, plagiarism debate, and diversiform versioning created opportunities for Israelis to grapple with how the sutures sewn in 1967 have held the city together and how the lingering scars color everyday experience there. "Jerusalem of Gold" and its simultaneously celebrated and vilified composer Naomi Shemer helped to place the question of Jerusalem's status at the center of public debate. As such, at moments of reckoning with this question in the years since 1967, "Jerusalem of Gold" has continually resurfaced in variations that responded to the discourses and political situations contemporaneous to those moments.

The case of "Jerusalem of Gold" demonstrates some of the ways that musicians and musical publics alike have deployed songs to their own ends, be they overtly political or engaged in a song's politics of representation, in order to intervene in the issues embedded in the Jerusalem question—among them the ethical dilemma of occupation, the utopian erasure of otherness, and the human right of self-determination.

5

Heterotopian Jerusalem

Politics of Difference in Dan Almagor's *My Jerusalem*

Jerusalem is a city of difference. In the context of modernity's enduring nationalisms, the city is typically configured as being the urban center of two national imaginaries—Israeli and Palestinian—but in practice, those groups are both internally diverse and surrounded by several groups who do not naturally identify with the prevailing national bifurcation. Israeli Jews arrived in Jerusalem from several diasporic contexts: the Arab Middle East and the former Ottoman Empire, Iran and central Asia, South Asia, east central Europe, France, the United Kingdom, the United States, South America, Australia, South Africa, Ethiopia, and the former Soviet Union, among other places. Some come from the population of Jews who lived in Palestine before Zionist immigration began in the late nineteenth century. People identifying with these various groups occupy different sectarian and class positions, practice different cultural traditions, liturgies, and rituals, and in some cases even speak different languages, in addition to the common Hebrew tongue. And yet others identify with the *Sabra* identity—native-born Israelis whose cultural memory of exile has decreasing significance in comparison with the proliferation of a local national culture.

Like their Israeli counterparts, Palestinian Jerusalemites can be stratified along religious lines, the majority being Muslim or Christian, but the dislocating effects of the Nakba in 1948 represent the primary factor. Those who were able to remain inside the 1949–1967 borders of the State of Israel hold Israeli passports or residency cards and thus are able to work and live a somewhat stable life. A much greater number live across the dividing line and thus do not hold such papers, forcing many to operate within a Palestinian shadow economy (Sabra, Eltalla, and Alfar 2015). Those who arrived in the city from the Palestinian countryside speak with a different dialect and accent than those raised in the urban environment. Families from different villages have distinctive folk heritages, including songs, dances, and the iconic sartorial diversity visible in patterned textiles sold in the Old City's markets.

City of Song. Michael A. Figueroa, Oxford University Press. © Oxford University Press 2022.
DOI: 10.1093/oso/9780197546475.003.0006

Social stratification becomes even more pronounced at the levels of neighborhood identity, class, and political party affiliation.

The Old City is also home to sizable Arab, Armenian, Assyrian, Coptic, Georgian, and Greek Christian communities, each centered on churches or other religious institutions that serve as major components of the city's diverse religious landscape. As Abigail Wood has shown in her research on the city's sacred soundscape, difference is manifested sonically through clanging bells, liturgical chants, and pilgrim songs, creating what she calls "an acoustic mirror of perforated space and doctrinal difference" (Wood 2014: 287). Although Jerusalem is widely nicknamed the "Holy City" in Arabic, Hebrew, and English (and other languages), strong elements of secularity have pretty much always determined many aspects of social life in the city. Within modernity, Hebrew University has served as a world hub of Jewish intellectual culture divorced from the city's *yeshivot* (religious educational institutions for Jewish boys and men). The student culture that it and other institutions around the city engender are at least as palpable as the markers of religiosity that characterize everyday life in Jerusalem's small but highly energetic set of intersecting arts and nightlife scenes. Musically, too, concerts of European and Arab classical repertories, Andalusian and other Mediterranean song traditions, and participatory folk singing ensound the city's unique cultural geography throughout the space of its lived, material geography (Bohlman 1989; Tamari 2005; Beckles Willson 2013; Jawhariyyeh 2014).

The high degree to which such difference constitutes Jerusalem's urban character makes the task of musically representing the city and its multifarious meanings with any level of comprehensiveness seem impossible, if musicians wish to avoid sounding critical violence against their neighbors. The city's cultural, religious, and ideological diversity draws attention to the fallaciousness of musical representations of Jerusalem as a homogeneous utopia populated by a single group. After all, how can one accurately represent that which is fundamentally unreal? In an oft-cited lecture on heterotopia, Michel Foucault suggests,

> Utopias are sites with no real place. They are sites that have a general relation of direct or inverted analogy with the real space of Society. They present society itself in a perfected form, or else society turned upside down, but in any case these utopias are fundamentally unreal spaces. (Foucault 1986: 24)

Philip V. Bohlman reminds us that such unreality has lived in the shadow of "the real space of society" since the origin of utopian thought:

> Theologically, [Thomas] More was pushing at the boundaries of a world centered around Christianity until the sixteenth century, for he coined the word, utopia (οὐτοπός), to mean "no place." In contrast, the island he called utopia resulted from a flight of literary fancy (More [1516] 1965). Multiplying the meanings of utopia, however, is its similarity to the word, eutopia (εὐτοπός), which means "good place," the most common understanding of the term. Utopia that is "real," therefore, exists only at another time and place. *The cosmopolitanism of the utopian city is unachievable.* It is in these states that the imagined unity of utopia—all cities on More's island of Utopia are the same—give way to the difference that dominates dystopia and heterotopia. (Bohlman 2018: 159, emphasis mine)

The conundrum of utopia's unachievability resounds loudly in the *topos* of modern Jerusalem. In the aftermath of 1967 and its triumphant soundtrack—represented by "Jerusalem of Gold" as well as other postwar Jerusalem songs and memorial repertory (see also Shelleg 2014: 177–82)—musicians associated with Labor Zionist politics grappled with utopian Jerusalem's unreality, in line with the rash of Leftist rejection of these developments by figures such as Amos Oz and Yeshayahu Leibowitz, as I discussed in the previous chapter.

In Chapter 1, I examined different utopian musical Jerusalems that were endowed to varying degrees with the political capital of empires, nations, and other entities throughout world history and, more specifically, the history of Zionist settlement in Palestine/Israel. The following pages recall that discussion, as I analyze Jerusalem as a heterotopian space and reconcile its heterotopian urban possibilities with Dan Almagor's musical interventions during the Labor Zionist movement's late phase.

I consider Labor Zionism's late phase to be 1967 to 1977, the decade following its fatal injury in the Six-Day War and including the opening of the Age of Euphoria (Iddan ha-Eforia) following the miraculous war victory, that age's traumatic end during the Yom Kippur War of October 1973, and finally Labor's demise during the 1977 elections, in which the Likud party rose to power and became the dominant force in Israeli party politics and cultural politics alike. Although such a periodization is an artifice of a historian's hindsight, since historical actors from the period in question were not necessarily conscious of themselves as living within a pre-echo of Labor's demise,

I refer to this period as "late" as an analog to the term's use in the work of Frederic Jameson (1991) and others to modify "capitalism" (this is perhaps ironic given Labor's opposition to the economic relations of late capitalism). During the 1967–1977 period, when Israel's claimed territory and accompanying territorial imaginary increased dramatically and the country became a dominant regional power, Labor Zionism—the nation's very founding ideology—was becoming obsolete as it failed to reckon with the country's political-theological reorientation toward territoriality and more aggressive forms of nationalism. My historical label, therefore, is less an act of aspiration (as "late" is for neo-Marxian thought) than an acknowledgment of that ideological paradigm's process of coming to an end.

Amid the country's general political and cultural upheaval during Labor Zionism's late phase, one significant intervention into the renewed question of Jerusalem's status was Dan Almagor's musical play *My Jerusalem* (1969). Almagor wrote the show in response to a sudden, ecstatic attachment to Jerusalem after the war, when, as he recalled to me during one of our interviews, Israeli Jews "rushed to the Old City to eat and buy cheap things" without fully weighing the negative political consequences of Israel's conquest (Almagor 2012). Based on a pretense of authentically reflecting the city's cultural geography as it transitioned from partition to occupation after the war, Almagor and his collaborators musically depicted Jerusalem as a site of heterotopian cultural difference and, more to the point, a heterotopia in need of rediscovery in the wake of Israeli occupation of the city, which ushered in a wave of euphoric utopianism that would permanently transform the Zionist project in Israel/Palestine.

Almagor's purpose in *My Jerusalem* was to harness the momentum of Jerusalem song's regeneration initiated by Naomi Shemer, Shuly Nathan, and their circle, but to ground the musical representation of Jerusalem in the everyday of lived urbanity. This was not in itself a heterotopian vision. What Almagor proposed instead, was an alternative utopia to the one promoted by Shemer and others that fixated on his own personal experiences of secular Jerusalem, slotted alongside a hodgepodge of contradictory Zionist visions of Jerusalem pulled together in a documentary musical format. But as Bohlman reminds us, "the cosmopolitanism of the utopian city is," in the end, "unachievable." What I will show in the ensuing analysis is that, in the aggregate, the songs constituting *My Jerusalem* formed a heterotopian vision "capable of juxtaposing in a single real place several spaces, several sites that are in themselves incompatible" (Foucault 1986: 25). This form of heterotopia—like good-place forms of utopian thinking that erase or sublate difference—still had a liberatory aura, but here Jerusalem was spatialized and embraced as a place inherently marked by radical cultural difference generated by the forms of mobility peculiar to postcolonial modernity. Thus, in *My Jerusalem* the city is claimed as a space marked by difference while simultaneously sublimating that difference within a Zionist logic that views the city as a Jewish-national space.

As the discussion continues, I will engage the show's seeming contradictions head-on, while evaluating the political efficacy of its representational strategies during the turbulent period from 1967 to 1977, as the Labor Zionist political paradigm neared its demise. In so doing, I argue in favor of the ethics of heterotopia while critiquing its conceptual relevance in a space marked by power asymmetries.

My Jerusalem

Dan Almagor (b. 1935) is a playwright, translator, poet, leftist activist, and one of the loudest artistic voices on the issue of post-1967 Jerusalem. He also claims major responsibility for introducing Broadway heritage musicals to Israel in the mid-1960s and, later in the decade, the aesthetics of off-Broadway experimental theater (see Figueroa 2016). Almagor also has been an active agent in the preservation and transmission of Hebrew and Israeli song. Along with musicologist Eliyahu Hacohen, he served as a host for the music television program *I Sang to You, My Country!* (*Sharti Lakh Artsi*), which aired on Saturday evenings from 1974 to 1977 (and today continues to air as twice-weekly reruns on Israel's Channel One). Along with his previous works for the stage, this television show solidified Almagor's status as a major player in the Israeli cultural scene, a status he continues to enjoy in the twenty-first century as an elder statesman who lectures in various Israeli educational and media institutions on topics ranging from Hebrew song, to international theater, to cultural politics.

As I learned through my interviews with Almagor, his musical activism during the 1960s and 1970s produced a tension between his role as a broker of hegemonic Zionist culture and his critical orientation toward the violence and racism that culture sometimes has inspired. Like many of his Labor Zionist colleagues, he maintains a deep-seated ambivalence toward some of the major achievements of the Israeli state, in particular the occupation of the West Bank and Gaza Strip.[1] After the conquest and subsequent occupation of Jerusalem in 1967, Almagor felt compelled to respond to those developments in a way that would capture the radical changes to the city's cultural geography while also addressing the moral dimensions of Israel's incipient sovereignty over Jerusalem. He did so by drawing heavily on the politicized aesthetics of US fringe theater, to create a "pocket musical" featuring six actors, a simple set design, and a documentary ethos called *My Jerusalem* (1969).[2]

With *My Jerusalem*, Almagor wanted to counter the euphoric, utopian narrative associated with the song "Jerusalem of Gold" (1967) and the many victory albums appearing in its wake (see Chapter 4). As he told me during one of our interviews, "I wanted just to show . . . that it all started quite artificially, by accident, and it's mostly fake propaganda songs, unfortunately. . . . Some of them are definitely good . . . [but] the whole thing had to do with brainwashing people in the country of the local history, the local Middle Eastern history" (Almagor 2012). In his view, Naomi Shemer's song too neatly packaged Jerusalem as a space that ostensibly belonged to only one of the many social groups that composed its cultural geography as a cosmopolitan Middle Eastern city. In his own musical renderings of the city, Almagor sought to capture Jerusalem's messy history in vivid musical detail, using an experimental format that would allow for this documentary pretense, while bringing together nearly all of the myriad poetics and rhetorical strategies of Jerusalem song I documented in the preceding four chapters.

My Jerusalem opened in August 1969, just over two years after the Six-Day War ended. It was the first show performed at Jerusalem's Khan Theatre, an Ottoman-era building converted for this purpose through an initiative sponsored by Mayor Teddy Kollek in October 1967 as part of a larger effort to establish Israeli cultural institutions in the newly conquered parts of the city.

---

[1] Although he is associated with some of Labor Zionism's institutions, and the privileges that they afford secular, liberal intellectuals, Almagor was not a member of the ruling Mapai party, as evidenced by his writings in Uri Avnery's often-controversial weekly newspaper *This World* (*Ha-Olam Ha-Ze*), which subjected Mapai and its leaders to flamboyant forms of critique. NB: After running the newspaper, Avnery would transition to a career in politics. He was discussed in the previous chapter as the figure who tried to have "Jerusalem of Gold" chosen as the national anthem.

[2] This was Almagor's second pocket musical, after *Once There Was a Hasid* (*Ish Ḥasid Haya*, 1968), which was initially inspired by Martin Duberman's *In White America* (1963) and the growing phenomenon of off-Broadway rock musicals. As I write elsewhere, "By combining a desire for mass political mobilisation through music with the aesthetics of fringe theatre, such as distancing effects, visual minimalism and choreography highlighting the artificiality of the separation of actors and audience, Almagor attempted to tackle contemporary political issues through musical theatre" (Figueroa 2016: 266).

The building is depicted on the front cover of the LP released to showcase songs from the show (Figure 5.1).

Almagor was not a native Jerusalemite, so he wrote the musical as something of an outsider. Born in 1935 to parents who immigrated to Palestine from Poland, he was raised in Rehovot, a town southeast of Tel Aviv. Brought up by fiercely secular parents, and an atheist himself—he never even had a bar mitzvah—Almagor had limited experiences of Jerusalem as a child. For him, as for many others, it was a space whose distance was more cultural and ideological than geographical. He described his early memories of Jerusalem to me as "a very unpleasant place to be," owing to the presence of what he considered to be exilic culture: Orthodox Jews praying in their own "hot, stinking ghetto" (Almagor 2012). In his words, "It didn't move anything in us, didn't leave any impression." Here, Almagor seemed to echo a statement

Figure 5.1 Album cover, *My Jerusalem* (original cast recording, 1970).

by Ahad Ha'am, one of Zionism's early literary and political luminaries, who criticized the "atavistic righteousness" of late nineteenth-century Orthodox Judaism as practiced in Jerusalem:

> I went first to the Wailing Wall, of course, and there I found many of our brothers, residents of Jerusalem, standing and praying with raised voices— also with wan faces, strange movements, and weird clothing—everything befitting the appearance of that terrible wall. I stood and watched them, people and wall, and one thought filled the chambers of my heart: those stones are testaments to the destruction of our land. And those men? The destruction of our people. Which catastrophe is greater? (translated in Avishai 2017)

Almagor's own distaste for what he perceived as the city's overwhelming religiosity was compounded by his memories of wartime violence. The location of his hometown gave it strategic military value for the Jerusalem front. An abandoned British military camp there served as a waypoint for Jewish military mobilization and supply caravans during 1948. In our interviews, he recalled going there to interact with soldiers and drivers involved in the war, who would sit and talk to the neighborhood children on their way to fight, and in many cases die, for the cause of Jerusalem.

The establishment of Israeli sovereignty over West Jerusalem after the 1948 War did not lessen Almagor's view of the city as economically and culturally impoverished; he and many others of his generation often referred to it as a "second city"—second to the secular, cosmopolitan Tel Aviv on the Mediterranean coast (see Chapter 2). Almagor did eventually move to Jerusalem to study at the Hebrew University from 1958 to 1963. His experience of the city as a university student was markedly different from his childhood impressions. It was a secular city that, whereas it did not serve as the cultural center of Israel, was the intellectual capital of the Jewish world. It was the place where he met his spouse and where he formed lifelong relationships with other Israeli cultural elites.

As he worked on *My Jerusalem* from 1968 to 1969, Almagor drew on his student experiences and on sources in the city's libraries and archives. The show was a composite of multiple media, including songs, sketches, dialogue, poetry, and readings of other materials relating to Jerusalem's history. The show was intended to draw its expressive power from its documentary

Title	Lyrics	Music	Performer(s)
Mother, Shall We Go to Jerusalem	Dan Almagor, based on romanceros	Noam Sheriff	Danny Granott, ensemble
The Stones of Jerusalem	Dan Almagor	Sasha Argov	Danny Granott, Moti Fleischer, Hillel Tzadok, Yair Klinger
Cantata to Jerusalem's Chosen Sons	Dan Almagor	Noam Sheriff	Ensemble
The Jerusalem of Yesterday	Dan Almagor	Noam Sheriff	Moti Fleischer
Mother Sent Me to the Market	K.Y. Silman	Noam Sheriff	Geula Nuni, ensemble
Names of Jerusalem	Based on Heiman Hayerushalmi	Nurit Hirsch	Danny Granott
For Ever and Ever	Dan Almagor	Noam Sheriff, based on Hasidic song "Avenu Malkenu"	Ensemble
Twelve Gates to the Holy City	Traditional	Traditional	Ensemble
A City in Siege	Based on Heiman Hayerushalmi	Noam Sheriff	Hillel Tzadok
One Glass of Water	Dan Almagor	Danny Granott	Danny Granott, Moti Fleischer, Hillel Tzadok, Yair Klinger
Send the List	Dan Almagor	Yair Klinger	Yair Klinger, Danny Granott, Moti Fleischer, Hillel Tzadok
On the Roof of Notre Dame	Yitzhak Shalev	Noam Sheriff	Danny Granott, Hillel Tzadok
To Die in Jerusalem	Dan Almagor	Nurit Hirsch	Motti Fleischer
Song to the Landlady	Dan Almagor	Danny Granott	Danny Granott, Shosh Rosen
My Jerusalem	Dan Almagor	Nurit Hirsch	Ensemble

Figure 5.2 Running order of songs in *My Jerusalem*.

ethos. He composed lyrics for most of the songs, while others were set to poems by K. Y. Silman, Yitzhak Shalev, and Heiman Hayerushalmi. The musical components were composed by Noam Sheriff (b. 1935), Sasha Argov (1914–1995), Nurit Hirsch (b. 1942), and two cast members: Danny Granott (b. 1949) and Yair Klinger (b. 1944). Sheriff, serving as musical director, wrote the majority of the melodies and was also responsible for arrangement duties.

Figure 5.2 gives an approximate running order of the show, which sometimes fluctuated depending on the needs of each performance; this was especially true as the show traveled around the country.[3] Along with the actor-musicians on stage, some of whom played acoustic guitars, Yossi Mar-Haim and Dov Aharoni provided instrumental accompaniment on piano, drums, and various auxiliary percussion. Ada HaMei'rit designed the minimalist set, in keeping with the flexible, documentary style of American off-Broadway experimental theater on which Almagor modeled *My Jerusalem* (see Figueroa 2016: 7).

The accompanying ensemble for these musical representations consisted of rock-band instrumentation—piano, electric organ, bass guitar, and drums—with some of the actors on stage playing acoustic guitars throughout the show. Many of the songs had clear Anglo-American rock influences, while others seemed to stem from the straightforward, march-like rhythms of Israeli folksong. The same cast of actor-musicians performed in the original run of performances at the Khan Theatre and on the subsequently released LP recording.[4]

The first part of the show constructs a narrative of Jerusalem from antiquity to the establishment of the State of Israel in 1948. Songs appearing early in this act, such as "Stones of Jerusalem" and "Names of Jerusalem," describe Jerusalem as "the promised land" in terms of the exilic imagination. Almagor took the text for "Names of Jerusalem" from a fable by Heiman Hayerushalmi, the nom de plume of Abraham Meir Habermann (1901–1980), a Jerusalem-based literary scholar, librarian of medieval manuscripts, illustrator, and poet. The theme of longing for Zion through the generations is a common thread for "Mother, Should We Go to Jerusalem" and "For Ever and Ever." The timeline quickly proceeds to the Yishuv era, presenting a more recent nostalgia for the old settlements and rural life in "The Jerusalem of Yesterday," "Cantata to the Jerusalem Dignitary," and "Mother Sent Me to the Market." The content then turns toward more concrete historical phenomena, with the 1929 Palestine Riots and the murder of the Maklef family in Motza, the underground fight against British imperial forces, and the struggle for Jewish access to the Western Wall.[5] This includes dialogue taken

---

[3] Neither the printed program for the original run at Khan Theatre nor the commercial LP recording give the proper order—the program explicitly indicates this—probably due to the changing nature of the show. I have reconstructed the order of songs through conversations with Almagor and through several pieces of evidence, gathered from his papers, such as programs for reprisal shows given in schools and scripts for retrospective television programs.

[4] The LP omitted nonmusical components of the show, such as dialogue, sketches, and readings, as well as some of the original songs.

[5] For more on how the 1929 Palestine Riots transpired in Motza, see Cohen (2015: 166–87).

from Rabbi Abraham Isaac Kook's testimony before the British Enquiry Committee concerning places in the Old City that were sacred to Jews, Muslims, and Christians.

Together, the opening songs and readings prepare the heterotopian possibilities of the show by invoking the heterochronic character of the material city and its accumulations of time. In other words, this part of the show fulfills what Foucault describes as

> the will to enclose in one place all times, all epochs, all forms, all tastes, the idea of constituting a place of all times that is itself outside of time and inaccessible to its ravages, the project of organizing in this way a sort of perpetual and indefinite accumulation of time in an immobile place, this whole idea belongs to our modernity. (Foucault 1986: 26)

In so doing, Almagor constructs a prehistory of modern Jerusalem that casts the early statehood period (1948–1967) as the moment in which the city's modernity emerged, aligning with the dominant Zionist vision of Jerusalem that proliferated in the euphoric age during which the show appeared. As both nostalgia and history, this Jerusalem is heterotopian in the sense that it exists both within and outside of time.

National sacrifice during the 1948 War features centrally in the songs "A City in Siege," "Send the List," and "One Glass of Water." For these war-themed songs Almagor chose siege and sacrifice as conceptual frames. "A City in Siege" incorporates another fable by Heiman Hayerushalmi and focuses on an incident that resulted in the death of thirty-five Palmach fighters who were killed on their way to aid in the Central Command's defense of the Gush Etzion settlement block against its eventual Jordanian captors and hostage-takers. "Send the List" features a somber narrator imploring an unknown official authority to send a list of the names of people who died in the war. He does so through the naming of sites (and spoils) of important battles during the war— Jewish Quarter Road, Castel, Bab El-Wad, Ramat Rachel, Gush Etzion, Mount Hebron, and Latrun—most of which, save for Jewish Quarter Road (*Reḥov Ha-Yehudim*) and Ramat Rachel, are outside of Jerusalem. Yet verses play on the naturalistic imagery of Jerusalem song and, crucially, the refrain casts the city as an anthropomorphized mourner for its destroyed people and places.

Send them immediately, send the names
from the Jewish Quarter Road.
Send the names from Castel,
from Bab El-Wad and from Ramat Rachel.

Send them immediately, so we'll know who's been lost,
sacrificed on the comb and the radar,
the names of the nurses and the doctors,
who were in the burnt ambulances.

Immediately send the names of the boys
who will never again see the dawn in the mountains.
Immediately send the names of the girls
who did not arrive with the caravan.

[Refrain:]
This city has known many silences.
This city, whose eyes are red.
This city knows the meaning of names.

Send the names from Gush Etzion,
and disclose the names from Mount Hebron,
they stood alone until morning,
and then fell, stone in hand.

Send the names from the fields of Latrun,
they only came down from the deck last night,
pale faces in a strange sun,
they were cut down in front of the police.

[Refrain]

שִׁלְחוּ מִיָּד, שִׁלְחוּ אֶת הַשֵּׁמוֹת,
מֵרְחוֹב הַיְּהוּדִים בֵּין הַחוֹמוֹת,
שִׁלְחוּ אֶת הַשֵּׁמוֹת מִן הַקַּסְטֵל,
מִבָּאב אֶל וָאד וּמֵרָמַת רָחֵל.

שִׁלְחוּ מִיָּד, נֵדַע מִי נֶעֱדָר,
הַקְּרָב עַל הַמַּסְרֵק וְהָרְדָר,
אֶת שְׁמוֹת הָאֲחָיוֹת וְהָרוֹפְאִים,
אֲשֶׁר בְּאַמְבּוּלָנְסִים הַשְּׂרוּפִים.

שִׁלְחוּ מִיָּד אֶת שְׁמוֹת הַנְּעָרִים
שֶׁלֹּא יִרְאוּ עוֹד שַׁחַר בֶּהָרִים,
שִׁלְחוּ מִיָּד אֶת שְׁמוֹת הַנְּעָרוֹת
שֶׁלֹּא הִגִּיעוּ עִם הַשַּׁיָּרוֹת.

[פזמון:]
הָעִיר הַזֹּאת יָדְעָה הַרְבֵּה דְּמָמוֹת
הָעִיר הַזֹּאת עֵינֶיהָ אֲדֻמּוֹת
הָעִיר הַזֹּאת יוֹדַעַת פֵּשֶׁר הַשֵּׁמוֹת.

שִׁלְחוּ אֶת הָרְשִׁימָה מִגּוּשׁ עֶצְיוֹן,
וְלָמֵד-הֵא שְׁמוֹת מֵהַר חֶבְרוֹן,
עַד בֹּקֶר הֵם עָמְדוּ שָׁם לְבַדָּם,
וְאָז נָפְלוּ וְאֶבֶן בְּיָדָם.

שִׁלְחוּ אֶת הַשֵּׁמוֹת מִשְּׂדוֹת לַטְרוּן,
רַק אֶמֶשׁ הֵם יָרְדוּ מִן הַסִּפּוּן,
חִוְרֵי פָּנִים בְּשֶׁמֶשׁ הַזָּרָה,
הֵם נִקְצְרוּ לְמוּל הַמִּשְׁטָרָה.

[פזמון]

The lyrics combine classic representational strategies from Jerusalem song, including the invocation of place names, the stony imagery of Jerusalem's walls (*homot*, verse one), and the feminine personification of the city as a mourning woman (see Chapter 1). Combined with the contemporary practice of military mimesis in the song's instrumental accompaniment (see Chapter 3)—accents on the downbeats and subsequent quarter-notes as well as war-drumming patterns on the snare drum and crash cymbal—"Send the List" incorporates a high degree of symbolism and alliance with the Jerusalem song genre while simultaneously drawing attention to the public's outrage and sadness over the violence caused by the ideologies the songs helped inspire.

The song "One Glass of Water" is based on a darkly humorous, anonymous poem that Almagor found printed in a weekly soldiers' newspaper from the 1948 War. This poem employs the vehicle of a single glass of water, which had to be used and reused for various incompatible and unhygienic purposes, in order to draw attention to the scarcity of resources available in a besieged Jerusalem.

[Refrain:]
I had one glass,
one glass of water.
During the siege
of the city of Jerusalem.

I took a sip from the glass,
a drop or two.
Just like that, to wet
my lips a little.

I wet my lips!
I took the water
and with great caution
I brushed my teeth.

[Refrain]

I brushed my teeth
and with the rest of the water
I washed, forgive me,
a pair of pants.

I washed my pants
and slightly blackened the water.
So in that same glass
I washed a pair of socks.

[Refrain]

I washed my socks,
and then with the glass of water
I washed the floor,
which hadn't been cleaned for two months.

I wrung the damp rag
in my hands
and watered a potted lily,
maybe even two.

[Refrain]

I squeezed more,
and with God's help
dropped a little water
in the toilet, at last.

I went back to the glass.
One drop of water remained.
So with this drop
I washed my hands.

[Modified Refrain:]
I had one glass,
one glass of water.
A Hanukkah miracle
did not happen again
in the city of Jerusalem.

הָיְתָה לִי כּוֹס אַחַת,
כּוֹס אַחַת שֶׁל מַיִם.
הָיָה זֶה בַּמָּצוֹר
בָּעִיר יְרוּשָׁלַיִם.

לָגַמְתִּי מִן הַכּוֹס
טִפָּה אַחַת אוֹ שְׁתַּיִם.
רַק כָּכָה, לְהַרְטִיב
קְצָת אֶת הַשְּׂפָתַיִם.

הִרְטַבְתִּי אֶת שְׂפָתַי!
נָטַלְתִּי אֶת הַמַּיִם,
וּבִזְהִירוּת רַבָּה
צִחְצַחְתִּי תַּשִּׁנַיִם.

הָיְתָה לִי כּוֹס אַחַת,
כּוֹס אַחַת שֶׁל מַיִם.
הָיָה זֶה בַּמָּצוֹר
בָּעִיר יְרוּשָׁלַיִם.

צִחְצַחְתִּי אֶת שְׁנֵי
וּבִשְׁאֵרִית הַמַּיִם,
כִּבַּסְתִּי, בִּמְחִילָה,
זוּג שֶׁל מִכְנָסַיִם.

כִּבַּסְתִּי מִכְנָסַי,
הִשְׁחִירוּ קְצָת הַמַּיִם.
אָז בְּאוֹתָהּ הַכּוֹס
כִּבַּסְתִּי זוּג גַּרְבַּיִם.

הָיְתָה לִי כּוֹס אַחַת,
כּוֹס אַחַת שֶׁל מַיִם.
הָיָה זֶה בַּמָּצוֹר
בָּעִיר יְרוּשָׁלַיִם.

כִּבַּסְתִּי אֶת גַּרְבֵּי
וְאָז בְּכוֹס הַמַּיִם
שָׁטַפְתִּי תַּרִצְפָּה
שֶׁלֹּא רֻחֲצָה חֳדָשִׁים.

אֶת הַסְּמַרְטוּט הַלָּח
סָחַטְתִּי בַּיָּדַיִם,
הִשְׁקֵיתִי בְּעָצִיץ
שׁוּשָׁן אַפְלוּ שְׁנַיִם.

סָחַטְתִּי עוֹד יוֹתֵר,
וּבְעֶזְרַת שָׁמַיִם
בְּבֵית הַשִּׁמּוּשׁ
הוֹרַדְתִּי, סוֹף סוֹף, קְצָת מַיִם.

חָזַרְתִּי אֶל הַכּוֹס.
נוֹתְרָה טִפָּה שֶׁל מַיִם.
אָז בְּטִפָּה הַזֹּאת
רָחַצִי תַּ'יָּדַיִם.

הָיְתָה לִי כּוֹס אַחַת,
כּוֹס אַחַת שֶׁל מַיִם.
נֵס חֲנֻכָּה
שׁוּב לֹא קָרָה
בָּעִיר יְרוּשָׁלַיִם.

The concept from this song is taken from the story of Hanukkah, which marked the rededication of the Jewish Temple after the Maccabean Revolt in the second century BCE. At the end of the fighting, there remained only a single day's supply of untainted sacred oil, but according to traditional accounts it miraculously lasted eight full days, hence the modern holiday's eight-day observance. In "One Glass of Water," the ritual olive oil is replaced with water and the second-century siege is replaced with the one in 1948. The lyrics reinforce this parallel by taking the audience through a parallel eight-step miracle, narrated in eight stanzas that are bookended by an initial statement of the refrain and a concluding, modified version of the refrain.[6] In the conclusion, the soldier states plainly: "A Hanukkah miracle / did not happen again / in the city of Jerusalem." Thus, although his single glass of water, like the oil, lasted eight days, it did not mark a return of Jewish rule over the Holy City; instead, the site of the Jewish Temple in the Old City fell into Jordanian hands after the 1948 War.

Almagor included this song in the show for two main reasons. First, like any researcher, he wanted to share with his audiences the remarkable artifact he uncovered in the archives; this lost poem revealed intimate details about life in besieged Jerusalem. Second, he wanted to provide some comic relief to help transition into the show's second act, which deals mostly with death, violence, and displacement. The heavy symbolism of the lyrics meets with a light-rock musical arrangement that brings the comic intent of the song into relief. The guitar and piano provide a "bouncy" rhythmic figure; bass notes, plucked on a single low string on the guitar and struck on the piano

---

[6] The original cast recording does not contain the entire text but rather a truncated version that obfuscates the Hanukkah parallels. The version of the text I translate here is the version Almagor published in *Ma'ariv* (see Figure 5.3).

with the left hand, occur on downbeats and are followed by accented chords, strummed on upbeats. The tempo is fast, although it varies with the singer's rubato phrasing near the end of the song. In his vocal delivery, Danny Granott, who also composed the music for this song, exaggerates his pronunciation of each syllable in the verses, which signals a silly self-awareness; this is met in the final verse by the ensemble interjecting several whooping and yipping sounds before the whole song ends on a strong downbeat. Through this seemingly fraught music–text relationship, Almagor signals "a desire to distort tragic reality by making it laughable" (Nevo and Levine 1994: 126), in keeping with a long tradition of Jewish humor emanating from moments of crisis and in an attempt to rally Israelis around an intimate memory of bodily sacrifice.

At the time of rehearsals, this part of the show also included a reading from a famous poem by Uri Zvi Greenberg (1896–1981), called "Judea Today, Judea Tomorrow / A Burden of Sorrow and a Burden of Joy" (1937). Almagor told me he wanted to draw attention to the danger of extremist ideological attachments to Jerusalem by reminding people of the violent actions of the Irgun, a Jewish paramilitary group inspired by the teachings of Ze'ev Jabotinsky, who advocated political violence as a "means of achieving the goal of establishing a sovereign and democratic Jewish state" (Pedahzur and Perliger 2009). Irgun is sometimes referred to as "Etsel," an acronym for its full Hebrew name, *Ha-Irgun ha-Tsvai ha-Leumi [Be-Erets Israel]* (The National Military Organization in the Land of Israel). The other major Jewish terrorist organization of late Mandate-era Palestine was called Lehi, or "the Stern gang" after its leader Avraham "Yair" Stern. Greenberg himself was a member of this organization and eventually represented its interests as a member of the Knesset from 1949 to 1951 in the Herut party. The poem was originally published in 1937 as the closing piece of his *Book of Indictment and Faith*. The following is the excerpt Almagor chose to include:

> I see thick prisons, gallows, in Jerusalem, in Jaffa, in Acre—
> And the faces of Jewish Sicarii, condemned to the gallows.
> I see how they walk to the gallows,
> The dawn of Jerusalem reflected in the pallor of their faces.[7]

---

[7] Translation by Anita Shapira (1999: 245).

אֲנִי רוֹאֶה בָּתֵּי-כְּלֶא עָבִים.
תְּלִיּוֹת בִּירוּשָׁלַיִם, בְּיָפוֹ, בְּעַכּוֹ
וּפְנֵי סִיקְרִיקִין יְהוּדִים
נְדוֹנִים לִתְלִיָּה.

אֲנִי רוֹאֶה אֵיךְ הַלָּלוּ הוֹלְכִים לִתְלִיָּה
וְשַׁחֲרִית יְרוּשָׁלַיִם בְּשַׁעֲוַת פְּנֵיהֶם.

This is not the complete poem but rather a passage that became "a kind of cult text in right-wing circles in Palestine" (Shapira 1999: 245).[8] The passage concerns the so-called Gallows Martyrs, twelve Irgun and Lehi members who were executed by the British in 1938 for their insurgence against the British Mandate powers. It is still recited at right-wing ceremonies, such as an event held for the sixty-fifth anniversary of the Gallows Martyrdom at the Jabotinsky Institute in Israel during my fieldwork in December 2012.[9] According to Almagor, the poem's inclusion in *My Jerusalem* was meant to force audiences to confront the necessity of inflicting violence on others in pursuit of the Zionist dream envisioned by "fanatics," as Almagor referred to them, such as Jabotinsky, Greenberg, and their comrades.

As it turned out, this approach to ideological inclusion would end up backfiring on Almagor. On August 1, 1969, the daily newspaper *Ma'ariv* ran a two-page spread previewing *My Jerusalem* (Figure 5.3) that featured the lyrics of several songs from the show, including "One Glass of Water." That morning, Greenberg's wife Aliza Tur-Malka called the Khan Theatre and demanded that the poem be removed from the show. When asked for a motivation for this reversal—given that the Greenbergs had already granted advance written permission to perform the poem as a component of the show—she responded: "Because he doesn't want his poem to be read in a play which mentions 'Jerusalem' and 'toilet' together" (Almagor 2012). For a disappointed Almagor, it was a somewhat absurd idea that one of Jerusalem's most devoted poets, who wrote prolifically and panegyrically about the city's symbolic virtues in order to claim it for Jewish political theology, was

---

[8] The complete poem begins with a series of prophesies that, as Dan Miron muses, "today one cannot but read with a pencil in one's hand, jotting down the dates at which the many predictions the poem contained eventually became factual history" (2010: 229)—including war in Europe, the Holocaust, Indian independence, and, most relevant to the passage in question, the Gallows Martyrs.

[9] I did not attend this event but learned about the poem's recitation from a contact who did.

Figure 5.3 *My Jerusalem* preview in *Ma'ariv* (August 1, 1969).

unwilling to recognize that the city was inhabited by functioning bodies, even Jewish ones. The butchered bodies in Greenberg's poem were only present for their symbolic value, as martyrs to the cause of national liberation. In order to avoid the possibility of legal action, Almagor dropped the poem from the show.

Given his professed disagreement with Greenberg's politics, at least in retrospect during an interview more than four decades after the fact, it is curious why Almagor would have included this provocative poem in the show at all without subjecting it to explicit critique, and, if that were the intent, why Greenberg would have consented to such a thing in the first place. It is possible, however, that Almagor did not intend to criticize this branch of Zionism but rather was sympathetic to its adherents if not to some of their claims, even if he wished to bring them into the fold of his own liberal Zionist vision of a heterogenous Jerusalem that is as marked by opposing extremes as it is by the banalities of everyday life. In this sense, the poem engenders the contradictory visions of Jerusalem involved in its heterotopian rendering throughout the show when viewed as a whole.

The second act of *My Jerusalem* aimed to depict daily life in "divided" Jerusalem between 1948 and 1967 and in the "united" city following the

Six-Day War of 1967. "On the Rooftop of Notre Dame" was set to a 1953 poem by Yitzhak Shalev (1919–1992). The poem was written about the experience of looking into the Old City from the rooftop of the Notre Dame monastery—the best vantage point available for viewing the Jewish Quarter, Western Wall, and Hurva Synagogue ruins since the city was divided. Dan Almagor experienced the rite of passage of climbing to the top of the Notre Dame monastery as a boy on a school trip:

> When I was thirteen . . . they took us from Rehovot on a tour to see Jerusalem for the first time. And we were there at the Notre Dame monastery, which was mostly ruined [from the war], and we had to climb to the top, to the roof. You had to climb, because everything was ruined—I remember some broken pieces from the windows, from the walls. And we walked, and walked. I was a child, it was quite traumatic to walk all the way, seven floors or so, to the top. And we got to the top of Notre Dame, and they showed us, they said: "See there, there is the Kotel. And there is the Hurva [Synagogue]." (Almagor 2012)

During our conversations, Almagor remembered the scene with a mixture of nostalgia and concerned bemusement—concern at the futility of viewing these relics of an antiquated form of worship from a vantage point set atop remnants of violence and destruction. He placed the song in the show to elicit a similar reaction in his audiences. This shared memory is made expedient by Almagor's manipulation of the "gazing" trope that characterized the miniscule body of Jerusalem literature developed in the Yishuv (consider the song "From the Top of Mt. Scopus," discussed in Chapter 1 and the examination of Jerusalem's spatial ethos across sonic and visual domains in Chapter 2), producing a sense of ambivalent nostalgia for a shared experience of longing.

One of Almagor's main reasons for writing *My Jerusalem* was to demonstrate how this shared longing was in many ways a narrative construction that did not represent his and others' authentic experiences in divided Jerusalem. Almagor drew on his own memories of divided Jerusalem, in order to provide a counternarrative to the idea that Israel's conquest of Jerusalem in 1967 represented the realization of a widespread desire to return to the city. In other words, he argued that prior to 1967 very few Israeli Jews actually longed for a return to Old Jerusalem. Referring to his luminary Hebrew University classmates Haim Gouri, Dan Pagis, Dan Miron, Gershon Shaked, and others, Almagor told me:

> Listen, we the intelligentsia of Israel, the top poets, writers, teachers, professors—today, Israel Award winners—[we] never said "Let's go and liberate Jerusalem!" . . . We were very happy. We had a little wall there in Mamilla [a central Jerusalem neighborhood], down from Terra Sancta [old Hebrew University campus]. There was a Bulgarian restaurant; the wall was there . . . we knew that behind the wall was [Old] Jerusalem. We didn't care much about the Temple, about the *Kotel* [Western Wall], about anything. And the amazing thing is that—this is true, and it's very important that you know it—with this "trauma" of the Old City falling in the hands of the Jordanians, evacuated of Jews, nineteen years had passed between '48 and the Six-Day War . . . but nobody cared, nobody said a word! (Almagor 2012)

These statements depart significantly from the statements that Jews with pre-1948 roots in the Old City were making around 1967, such as Rivka Michaeli's exhortations about her father longing for a return to his old neighborhood, discussed in the previous chapter as context for Naomi Shemer's revisions to "Jerusalem of Gold." The idea of Jewish "return" to an undivided Jerusalem was not merely fabricated to fit a narrative of territorial conquest; it was part of a longer, though still modern, history of nostalgic attachment to the terrestrial city, as opposed to the metaphorical city I described in Chapter 1.

In his poetic representations of Jerusalem, Almagor attempted to write against the idea of the pre-1967 city being a divided territory waiting to be conquered and unified by the Jewish state; he instead wanted to promote the memory of Israeli West Jerusalem as a center for secular social life that produced the country's intellectual elite. In order to do this, he supplanted fantastical representations of a heavenly city that proliferated in the euphoria following 1967 with realistic representations that would "authentically" capture the student culture that flourished within the earthly city, as he put it during an interview (Almagor 2013).

His strategy is well illustrated by "Song to the Landlady," a song from the second act that depicts West Jerusalem as a secular university town. The lyrics describe a common experience for the many students who lived in rented rooms with strict curfews and visitor regulations. The lyrics detail a conversation between people making plans about sneaking in after visiting hours. The refrain contains a humorous exchange between two characters who are terrified of their landlady. Actors Danny Granott and Shosh Rosen alternate vocal lines in a dialogical manner: "You'll see how to have a good time in a college town— / Are you nuts? You'll wake the landlady!" In her part, Rosen implores Granott's character to be quiet. This exchange highlights the gendered nature of this phenomenon, with female students housed in private rooms and male students trying to figure out how to sneak their way in to see them; the comedic effect stems from their shared fear of the landlady. Rather than having some broader allegorical meaning, as in other songs from the show, these lyrics index a common memory of courtship and anxiety, which are part of the nostalgic patterning of other representations of interwar Jerusalem, such as in the novel *My Michael* by Almagor's Hebrew University classmate Amos Oz ([1968] 1972):

> We strolled down Isaiah Street towards Geula Street. Sharp stars glittered in the Jerusalem sky. Many of the street lamps of the British Mandate period were destroyed by the shell-fire during the War of Independence. In 1950 most of them were still shattered. Shadowy hills showed in the distance at the ends of the streets.
>
> "This isn't a city," I said, "it's an illusion. We're crowded in on all sides by the hills—Castel, Mount Scopus, Augusta Victoria, Nebi Samwil, Miss Carey. All of a sudden the city seems very insubstantial."
>
> Michael said:
>
> "When it's been raining Jerusalem makes one feel sad. Actually, Jerusalem always makes one feel sad, but it's a different sadness at every moment of the day and at every time of the year." (Oz [1968]1972: 19–20)

These works employ mimetic representations of the city's everyday sights and sounds in order to evoke shared memories of a lost city— Jerusalem as a small, secular university town whose importance lay in personal narratives rather than in political or religious motivations. By foregrounding the city's nonsymbolic, everyday state as a divided, secular space for the living, Almagor uses collective memory to combat collective forgetting.

Perhaps the purest distillation of this premise, the contradictory play of Zionisms within the play, and the clearest critique of the exclusionary, utopian politics of Naomi Shemer's "Jerusalem of Gold," is the show's title song,

"My Jerusalem." Appearing late in the running order, here Almagor relies on multivocality, humor, and markers of Jerusalem's peculiarity that were familiar to audience members through the proliferation of Jerusalem songs that served as immediate context for the play. The song serves as a kind of bridge from prewar to postwar Jerusalem and demonstrates how cultural difference was always present there, even when the city was divided into ostensibly homogeneous parts along cultural and religious (and therefore national) lines.

> Said the peddler from Mazkeret Moshe:
> "My Jerusalem
> is Mahane Yehuda on holiday eves,
> hummus from Rachmo and the stench of fish.
> Shabbat with pepitas, drivers swearing.
> Laundry on the sidewalk and a shower from a bucket—
> My Jerusalem . . ."

> Said the cobbler from the neighborhood of Katamon:
> "My Jerusalem
> is seven years of rains on the balcony,
> a neighborhood without a store, a free ride on the bus.
> Shabbat—a matinee at the Orion.
> Katamon Gimmel is also for me
> My Jerusalem . . ."

> Said the bath attendant from Me'a She'arim:
> "My Jerusalem
> is a black streimel, grey books,
> and 'A daughter of Israel does not walk in shorts.'
> It is whispered prayers for other days.
> Not here, because up above she winks to me
> My Jerusalem . . ."[10]

[10] The third verse was not included on the recorded version but was performed in the original show, according to the program. The verse is also attested and corroborated across a variety of resources, including Beit La-Zemer Ha-Ivri, a song database run by the National Library of Israel (see http://zemer.nli.org.il/song/Bait_Lazemer003753994).

Said the young guy, next to Damascus Gate:
"My Jerusalem
is a cross on a store and police at midnight.
A bomb in a cellar, a sister informant.
An Independence Day parade and clenched hands,"
—"Yes sir, what would you like: kebab or shishlik?"
"My Jerusalem . . ."

Said the soldier from Ashdot Ya'akov:
"My Jerusalem
I was there once on a morning of bereavement.
An alley and a sniper in a tower on the left.
Since then I haven't returned, I simply can't.
Avner and Gadi, for me they are
My Jerusalem . . ."

Jerusalem, Jerusalem,
My Jerusalem . . .

אָמַר הָרוֹכֵל מִמַּזְכֶּרֶת מֹשֶׁה:
יְרוּשָׁלַיִם שֶׁלִּי
הִיא מַחֲנֶה יְהוּדָה בְּעֶרֶב חַגִּים
וְחוּמוּס שֶׁל רַחֲמוֹ וְרֵיחַ דָּגִים,
שַׁבָּת שֶׁל "פֵּפִּיטָס", קְלָלוֹת נֶהָגִים
כְּבִיסָה עַל הַכְּבִישׁ וּמִקְלַחַת מִדְּלִי
יְרוּשָׁלַיִם שֶׁלִּי...

אָמַר הַסַּנְדְּלָר מִשְּׁכוּנַת קַטָמוֹן:
יְרוּשָׁלַיִם שֶׁלִּי
הוּא שֶׁבַע שָׁנִים שֶׁל גֻּשְׁמִים בַּבַּלְקוֹן
שִׁכּוּן בְּלִי חָנוּת, אוֹטוֹבּוּס בְּלִי חֶשְׁבּוֹן,
שַׁבָּת- הַצְּנָה רִאשׁוֹנָה בְּאוֹרְיוֹן
גַּם קַטָמוֹן ג' הִיא בִּשְׁבִילִי
יְרוּשָׁלַיִם שֶׁלִּי...

אָמַר הַבַּלָּן מִמֵּאָה שְׁעָרִים:
יְרוּשָׁלַיִם שֶׁלִּי
הִיא שְׁטְרַיְמְל שָׁחֹר וּסְפָרִים אָפֹרִים
וּ"בַת יִשְׂרָאֵל לֹא תֵּלֵךְ בִּקְצָרִים"

הִיא לַחַשׁ תְּפִלָּה לְיָמִים אֲחֵרִים
לֹא כָּאן, כִּי לְמַעְלָה קוֹרֶצֶת הִיא לִי
יְרוּשָׁלַיִם שֶׁלִּי...

אָמַר הַצָּעִיר שָׁם לְיַד שַׁעַר שְׁכֶם:
יְרוּשָׁלַיִם שֶׁלִּי
הִיא צְלָב עַל חֲנוּת, וְשׁוֹטְרִים בַּחֲצוֹת
אָחוֹת שֶׁהִלְשִׁינָה וּבוֹר עִם פְּצָצוֹת,
מִצְעַד עַצְמָאוּת, וְיָדַיִם קְפוּצוֹת,
"Yes sir, what would you like: kebab or shishlik?"
יְרוּשָׁלַיִם שֶׁלִּי...

אָמַר הַחַיָּל מֵאַשְׁדּוֹת יַעֲקֹב:
יְרוּשָׁלַיִם שֶׁלִּי
הָיִיתִי בָּהּ פַּעַם בַּבֹּקֶר שֶׁל שְׁכוֹל
סִמְטָה וְצָלַף בַּצְּרִיחַ מִשְּׂמֹאל
מֵאָז לֹא חָזַרְתִּי פָּשׁוּט לֹא יָכוֹל
אַבְנֵר וְגַדִּי—שְׁנֵיהֶם בִּשְׁבִילִי
יְרוּשָׁלַיִם שֶׁלִּי...

Eschewing the metaphor and hyperbole of other popular Six-Day War songs, "My Jerusalem" employs various kinds of mimesis in an attempt to show "life as lived" in the city—that is, life as lived from several different subject positions. Almagor accomplishes this through the vehicle of emic stereotypes that Jerusalemites and other Israelis recognized as representing different social groups. The first stanza features a peddler from a West Jerusalem neighborhood located just south of Shuk Mahane Yehuda, the Jewish open-air market. He gives sensory details of Jerusalem's dirty, profane side: the taste and smell of cheap street foods, simple pleasures enjoyed on special occasions, the crude language of taxi drivers and people washing their laundry out on the street. The next stanza's character is a cobbler who lives a boring working-class existence in the West Jerusalem neighborhood of Katamon. This is followed by a description of a man who runs a ritual bath in the Orthodox neighborhood of Me'a She'arim. His character presents well-known images from that neighborhood: black, wide-brimmed hats, old religious tomes being pored over in *yeshivot* (religious study institutions), and street signs demanding modest attire ("A daughter of Israel does not walk in shorts").

The final two stanzas signal the new reality of a postexilic Jerusalem after 1967. The first of these characters is marked as Palestinian by his presence at the Damascus Gate, an area that previously had been under Jordanian control and that is now, as it was at the time of the show, a bustling center for Palestinian commerce and western tourism. It is also the location of an ancient open-air market, which today serves as the Palestinian counterpart to the aforementioned Shuk Mahane Yehuda. This character's account gives the impression of a noisy, chaotic life, full of people working at cross-purposes, such as his sister, who is an informant for the Israeli authorities.[11] Daily life is interrupted by police raids in the middle of the night and the humiliation of having to witness expressions of Israeli nationalism on holidays. Of course, he is not innocent either, because he is hiding bombs in his cellar for one of the underground militant groups. Then, we learn that he works at one of the neighborhood's many food stands, as he asks a tourist in heavily accented English for his food order. The choice offered— "*kebab* or *shishlik*?"—is the song's true punch line, because both options are in fact the same food (grilled skewered meat) rendered into respective Arabic and Hebrew terms. It is as false a choice as would be answering the question of who may exclusively claim such a complicated and diverse city to be "my" Jerusalem.

The final character is a soldier coping with trauma resulting from combat during the 1967 War. To him, Jerusalem is associated with violence and snipers hiding along the walls—which he would rather avoid by sticking to his safe, rural kibbuts in northern Israel, Ashdot Ya'akov. Greater Israel is his Jerusalem—that is, his redemptive space. This representation also suggests a view of Jerusalem held by some Israelis living outside the city, including Almagor himself prior to his university days: it is a violent place best avoided.

Each of the sensory and spatial details offered is synechdochic for a certain vision of the city. Their framing by the first-person possessive "my" does not signal possession in the territorial sense but rather in terms of identification; that is, people belong to Jerusalem, not vice versa. By bringing together familiar, sometimes humorous, images with the very real fear of violence, Almagor sought to capture the ambiguity and multiple valences that the city

---

[11] This has been a common, but highly controversial, phenomenon since the Yishuv era; see Cohen (2004).

took on for social groups with differing levels of agency and sovereignty in Jerusalem.

The evidence presented in the song, and in the show, undermines the singular political significance attributed to Jerusalem by the official political Zionism promoted by the state and its then-contemporary soundtrack voiced by Shuly Nathan and Naomi Shemer in "Jerusalem of Gold." Compositionally speaking, the song's strophic form nevertheless unifies Jerusalem's peoples into a heterotopian community of difference, idealized here according to Almagor's liberal Zionist sensibility and opposition to his country's fresh military occupation. Each strophe is voiced by a different character and is punctuated by a final line: "My Jerusalem." Although in each case these words form complete thoughts with the lines preceding them— that is, they have a local semantic purpose—they collectively serve as a kind of refrain throughout the song. Each utterance of the phrase occurs through an alternating perfect-fourth motif, which at the end of the song is repeated over and over by the whole ensemble with a cadence on a C# minor thirteenth chord. The development of this multivocality, which coalesces into a strangely sweet extended harmony at the end of the song, suggests that the contemporary idea of unified Jerusalem is a myth complicated by a high degree of cultural difference and multiple, conflicting agendas. These formal elements together lend musical continuity to the lyrical indications of heterotopian difference that give the song its intended political message.

At the same time, the tone of the lyrics and gentle ribbing of Jerusalemite stereotypes clearly align with the collectivist ethos of Jerusalem song and Zionist music-making more generally. Therefore, the question must be raised about what power rests in the authority of representation. As a Zionist Israeli Jew of European descent who enjoys the full benefits of citizenship and a successful career in the cultural sphere, Dan Almagor was a member of the region's dominant—in his own words, "hegemonic" (Almagor 2013)— cultural group during the 1960s and 1970s. As such, the first-person singular possessive pronoun in the musical's title *My Jerusalem* is a pragmatic and correct one. Since the 1967 War, when all of once-divided Jerusalem fell under Israeli sovereignty, the city and its inhabitants were in Almagor's possession to be represented in song for an Israeli audience. To be sure, unlike many Israeli stage works during the 1960s, in *My Jerusalem* Palestinians are presented as sympathetic characters with lines; but it is with Almagor's voice that they speak. My interviews with Almagor corroborate this claim. During our conversations, Almagor referred to the characters in the sketch and to Palestinians in general as "Arabs" and not as "Palestinians," a choice of ethnonym that at once signaled his desire to accept them as fully developed characters alongside their Jewish Israeli counterparts, while simultaneously—perhaps unwittingly—denying their identification with the cause of Palestinian national self-determination. Much like the various cultural tensions at work here, this gesture runs the risk of contradicting the very political aims of the music itself.

My Jerusalem was the first Hebrew show that dealt with life in "unified" Jerusalem after the 1967 War and represents an early example of Israeli stage performance that acknowledges the presence of Palestinians in the city. The show was quite successful and played more than 200 times in theaters and schools all over Israel. In 1969, the title song "My Jerusalem" was played in the hit parades for both of Israel's major radio stations, Kol Israel and Galei Tzahal. During one of our interviews, Almagor summarized his concept for the show by saying, "All of them [are about] authentic things about authentic people who live in Jerusalem" (Almagor 2012). This statement makes one wonder whether Almagor positioned himself as the authentic voice of Jerusalem's various things and people or whether he simply wished to present what he believed to be "real life" in Jerusalem, in contradistinction to the utopianism of other musical and poetic tributes to the city. The former position creates an ethical problem, in which a singular vision of the city attempts to conquer other singular visions—a familiar strategy in both domestic and international political rhetoric about Jerusalem. The latter indicates a programmatic attempt to embrace the city's cultural diversity and to represent the possibility of coexistence in spite of the violent crisis that served as the musical's original context.

Dan Almagor's version of Jerusalem is peculiarly cosmopolitan; it is small, familiar, and yet capable of being claimed as "mine" by many culturally distinctive groups, who encounter each other in uncharacteristically (perhaps unrealistically) peaceful ways through the course of the show. Almagor's cultural authority and privilege furthermore raise the question of whether his musicals were, or could have been, truly subversive. Can a critique of power really come from the powerful? In our interviews, Almagor expressed a felt responsibility to foreground his ambivalence toward the cultural lexicon of his own dominant social group in order to inscribe the topics of his shows, particularly issues of cultural pluralism, onto Israeli discourse. Ultimately, however, the intended critique is limited by its reliance on a set of source materials and symbolic resources drawn exclusively from that cultural lexicon, even if somewhat agonistically, and on a Zionist mode of narration, here rendered through heterochronic but selective accumulations of time that mark Jerusalem as heterotopian in a way that managed to frustrate the utopian thinking of Almagor's ideological rivals while simultaneously remaining within the conventional bounds of Zionist musical discourse on Jerusalem chronicled throughout this book.

From this perspective, *My Jerusalem* represents a well-intentioned musical intervention into Jerusalemite politics in the immediate aftermath of 1967, and yet in retrospect it also symbolizes the toothlessness of Labor Zionist politics in the ensuing decade and beyond. Following 1967, after all, what material advantage would political actors realize in presenting something other than a utopian Jerusalem—a space set aside for Jews alone—that would serve as the spatial-teleological conclusion of the political-theological narrative towards which Israeli nationalism would increasingly turn? The fate of the city and of the state itself became by the end of the 1970s fully entwined, to the point where the small, divided town that Almagor nostalgically memorialized in his compositional activities became a distant memory.

Epilogue

Wounded by the hymns of glory,
that were carved with daggers
in the flesh of its shoulders, crowned by the halo
of sacred fire, all the legions
stormed to search for their redeemer
in her arms, and made her the heart of the world
for all the seekers of miracles, and they bound her,
and crucified her in order to extol her name—
and never stopped and never wondered why
she hides, a wall within a wall.

The eternal city, like a dark brown fist
clenched in stone, still waiting
in its fenced, enclosed obstinacy,
to be calm, fingers joined.
But within her all the invokers of miracles
and the necromancers are praying for the sign
that would come down on her from heaven
turn her face upside down, and lay her soul
in a handful of dust, and sanctify her
at their feet, as a graveyard.

פְּצוּעָה בְּמִזְמוֹרֵי הַתְּהִלָּה
שֶׁנֶּחְרְתוּ בִּפְגִיּוֹנוֹת
עַל דַּל כְּתֵפֶיהָ, מְעֻטֶּרֶת בְּהִלָּה
שֶׁל אֵשׁ הַקֹּדֶשׁ, כָּל הַלְּגִיוֹנוֹת
עָטוּ לְבַקֵּשׁ אֶת גּוֹאֲלָם
בֵּין זְרוֹעוֹתֶיהָ, וְשָׂמוּהָ לֵב עוֹלָם
לְכָל דּוֹרְשֵׁי הַנֵּס, וַעֲקָדוּהָ,
וּצְלָבוּהָ לְפָאֵר אֶת שְׁמָהּ—

City of Song. Michael A. Figueroa, Oxford University Press. © Oxford University Press 2022.
DOI: 10.1093/oso/9780197546475.003.0007

וְלֹא עָצְרוּ וְלֹא תָּמְהוּ מַדּוּעַ
הִיא מִתְחַבֵּאת חוֹמָה בְּתוֹךְ חוֹמָה.

עִיר הַתָּמִיד, כְּמוֹ אֶגְרוֹף שָׁחוּם
קְפוּצָה בָּאֶבֶן, וּמְצֻפָּה עָדַיִן
בְּקַשְׁיֵי עָרְפָּה הַמְגֻדָּר וְהַתָּחוּם
לִחְיוֹת שְׁלֵוָה וּשְׁלוּבַת אֶצְבָּעוֹת.
אַךְ בְּתוֹכָהּ כָּל מַשְׁבִּיעֵי הַפֶּלֶא,
קוֹסְמֵי הָאוֹב, מְפַלְלִים לְאוֹת
אֲשֶׁר יֵרֵד עָלֶיהָ מִשָּׁמַיִם
וְיַהֲפֹךְ פָּנֶיהָ, וְיַטְמִין
אֶת נִשְׁמָתָהּ בִּצְרוֹר עָפָר, וִיקַדְּשֶׁנָּה
לְעַד לְרַגְלֵיהֶם, כְּבֵית-עָלְמִין.
—Dan Pagis, "The Eternal City" (1959)[1]

On its surface, this 1959 poem by Dan Pagis may seem to bear some of the attributes of modern Jerusalem song, the emergent genre of Israeli music that assembled "across a range of discourses and institutions" (Brackett 2016: 6) during the long-twentieth century in Zionist and Israeli national culture. In the text, the city is imbued with human attributes, and feminine ones at that, intermingled with iconic renderings of the city's materiality—its walls and dust—and interspersed with a sacred lexicon, here repurposed in service of a biting critique. The poem, like other texts introduced in the preceding exposition, presents a metacommentary on the role of poetic expression in the evolution of the city's status vis-à-vis Israeli national culture.

The poet's outlook on this matter is, of course, a great deal bleaker than the majority of the songs and poems discussed in this book. Aminadav A. Dykman characterizes "The Eternal City" as "a daring challenge to the conventional image of Jerusalem." He continues, "But the opening line, with the key word *mizmorim* ('hymns,' 'chants'), clearly points in the direction of a sentiment of *textual* overloadedness" (Dykman 1994: 48; emphasis in original). But as has become clear over the preceding five chapters, the overload-edness that dominates Jerusalem sentiment within Israeli national culture is not merely textual but *musical* in profound ways. The function of lyrical texts is important, but they cannot be fully grasped without accounting for how music has served as a medium for germinating sentiment, as an

---

[1] Original poem in Pagis (1959: 40–41); translation by Aminadav A. Dykman (1994: 48).

intermediary transformation of meaning that heightens or modifies emotional content, and as a vehicle for creating conditions for literary Jerusalem's *presence* through performances of collectivity at auspicious and ordinary moments alike. Pagis's poetic intervention was plainly a critical one, meant as a rejoinder to other poets—or "invokers of miracles" (*mashbi'ey ha-pele*)— whose hymns of glory have, in his opinion, wounded Jerusalem, a real city with smaller histories that resist the totalizing narrative tendencies of musical, poetic, and political discourse.[2]

Is there a more poignant testament to the power of poets and musicians to shape a place, or a discourse? By employing a genealogical approach to the study of music, in this book I have embraced the messiness of historical process and worked to show how people use music to continually produce the present in alignment with their social needs or political goals. The past presents that I have examined over these five chapters were succeeded by many historical developments occurring within, because of, or adjacent to Jerusalem, which rapidly became the political center of the country as the late twentieth and early twenty-first centuries unfolded.

Within broader Israeli society, all aspects would soon become bigger and more diverse: population, politics, music, media institutions, and more. The Ashkenazi Labor Zionist camp would lose grip on its ethnic and political hegemony after its defeat in the 1977 election at the hands of the Likud Party, which has retained most of its legislative power to this day, with few interruptions. The First Lebanon War (1982–2000) would mark for many commentators a breakdown in national consensus, which, as I have shown, had always been full of contingencies if not outright conflict, especially on the issue of Jerusalem. Israeli peace movements would ebb and flow with the tides of two Palestinian Intifadas (1987–1991, 2000–2005). Benjamin Netanyahu would become Israel's longest-serving prime minister (1996–1999, 2009–2021), a leader whose policies on Jerusalem were morally reckless, revealed by his own pronouncements, such as "Jerusalem had been the capital of Israel for 3,000 years and had never been the capital of any other people" (BBC News 2017), and his references to the building of illegal settlements in East Jerusalem as "our natural right" (Newman 2015).

Meanwhile, Israelis' thirst for global musics would grow, and Israeli musicians' aesthetic innovations would displace at many points the national song

---

[2] Dan Miron interprets a direct criticism of Uri Zvi Greenberg; see his analysis for elaboration on the gendered nature of Jerusalem's representation in Miron (2010: 383–84).

tradition, which had previously represented its own kind of cosmopolitanism with melodies and lyrics drawn from east central Europe and neighboring regions, for the sounds of rock, tropicalia, world beat, hip hop, and many other global sounds. The state would lose its tight grip over broadcasting, with the proliferation and privatization of more radio stations, the introduction of television, satellite television, and the world wide web, all intensifying during the 1990s and 2000s and allowing Israelis unprecedented access to music from elsewhere, not to mention granting musicians access to audiences elsewhere. (Do you see how such a sweeping summary flattens the past, fitting it to a framework that I myself have created?)

This book has been my attempt to capture a moment—a series of moments, really—when the future represented by our present was not a given, when things were open to challenge, even the fate of a city that is today presumed by the majority to be the eternal capital of the Jewish people, while also being home to so many others, including Palestinians who consider the city to be their capital, too. During the moments under investigation, the future was full of possibilities that are now forgotten. My purpose has not been merely to render those futures unforgotten, but rather to analyze the emergence of multiple visions of modern Jerusalem within the field of popular song, the most privileged domain of political discourse among the arts in Israeli society.

I have written this history during a time when the political status quo is total Israeli sovereignty over Jerusalem's western and eastern portions, the latter of which is assumed by most of the international community to be the capital of a future Palestinian state, but where the majority Palestinian population lives under the domination of an oppressive police state and a settler regime that expropriates Palestinian-owned land. Life on the other side of the city is quite different. West Jerusalem and parts of the Old City are home to thriving Jewish Israeli civil life. But as I wrote in the Introduction, Jerusalem is greater than any national concept that would count the city among its physical territories; in an ethical sense, I believe that the sooner that people realize this, the closer they will be to moving past the crisis. As Shlay and Rosen write about Jerusalem,

It is a place filled with ideas, ideas about who should rule, what is wrong, what is right, who belongs and who does not—ideas with no absolute truth, only points of view held by the powerful and the subaltern. How do some ideas about Jerusalem prevail while others do not? How do the ideas about the prevailing Jerusalem manage to dominate over others? (Shlay and Rosen 2015: 31)

The conceptual frameworks that I have introduced in the book have been designed to address these questions from a musicological standpoint. More study—much more study—of how Jerusalem's multiple communities grapple with the question of the city's importance to their political and spiritual histories is needed. In the meantime, it is my hope that this musicological accounting for the making of modern Jerusalem within the development of the Zionist territorial imaginary, in all its remarkable diversity and dynamism, will aid in the treatment of the city's wounds.

References

Abowd, Thomas. 2000. "The Moroccan Quarter: A History of the Present." *Journal of Palestine Studies* 7: 6–16.

Abu El Haj, Nadia. 2001. *Facts on the Ground: Archaeological Practice and Territorial Self-Fashioning in Israeli Society*. Chicago: University of Chicago Press.

Ackerman, Maya. 2015. "Jerusalem of Gold" (voice and remix). [https://youtu.be/BV2PiZaarqs]

Adler, Larry, and Hedva & David. 1967. *Jerusalem the Golden City*. RCA Victor ISL-0011, LP disc.

Alajaji, Sylvia Angelique. 2020. "Music and the Mediation of Remembrance: Reflections on the Commemoration of the Centennial of the Armenian Genocide." In *Performing Commemoration: Musical Reenactment and the Politics of Trauma*, edited by Annegret Fauser and Michael A. Figueroa, 219–39. Ann Arbor: University of Michigan Press.

Alcalay, Ammiel. 1993. *After Jews and Arabs: Remaking Levantine Culture*. Minneapolis: University of Minnesota Press.

Alexander, David. 1998. "Political Satire in the Israeli Theatre: Another Outlook on Zionism." In *Jewish Humor*, edited by Avner Ziv, 165–74. New Brunswick, NJ: Transaction Publishers.

Almagor, Dan. 2012. Interview with the author, June 17. Tel Aviv.

Almagor, Dan. 2013. Interview with the author, September 6. London.

Almog, Oz. 2000. *The Sabra: The Creation of the New Jew*. Berkeley: University of California Press.

Alter, Robert. 1987. "Jewish Humor and the Domestication of Myth." In *Jewish Wry: Essays on Jewish Humor*, edited by Sarah Blacher Cohen, 25–36. Detroit: Wayne State University Press.

Alter, Robert, ed. 2015. *The Poetry of Yehuda Amichai*. New York: Farrar, Straus & Giroux.

Alterman, Nathan. 1957. *City of the Dove [Ir Ha-Yona]*. Kinneret: Machbarot Lesifrut. [Hebrew]

Alterman, Nathan. 1976. *Tunes and Songs [Pizmonim ve-Shirey Zemer]*. Tel Aviv: Hakibbutz Hameuchad. [Hebrew]

Amichai, Yehuda. 1968. *Now, Noisily: Poems, 1963–1968 [Akhshav Be-Ra'ash: Shirim, 1963–1968]*. Tel Aviv: Schocken. [Hebrew]

Anderson, Benedict. (1983) 2006. *Imagined Communities: Reflections on the Origin and Spread of Nationalism*. London: Verso.

Ankri, Etti. 2009. *Rabbi Yehuda Halevy Sung*. The Eighth Note 9996075, compact disc.

Appert, Catherine M. 2017. "Engendering Musical Ethnography." *Ethnomusicology* 61(3): 446–67.

Ariel, Meir. 1967. *Jerusalem of Iron*. Hed-Artzi BMN 564, EP disc.

Ariel, Meir. 1988. *Yerukot*. CBS 460077-1, LP disc.

Assaf, Roy. 2017. Interview with the author, October 6. Washington, DC.

Assi, Seraj. 2018. "In Palestine, World War I Has Never Really Ended." *Haaretz*, November 14. [https://www.haaretz.com/middle-east-news/.premium-in-palestine-the-first-world-war-has-never-really-ended-1.6653807]

Associated Press. 2008. "Jerusalem's Bridge of Chords—a New Addition to City of Ancient Symbols." *Haaretz*, June 25. [https://www.haaretz.com/israel-news/travel/1.4995783]

Avishai, Bernard. 2017. "The Battle over Jerusalem: A New Year's Story." *New Yorker*, September 20. [https://www.newyorker.com/news/daily-comment/the-battle-over-jerusalem-a-new-years-story]

Avnery, Uri. 2012. Interview with the author, June 5. By telephone.

Azaryahu, Maoz. 2007. *Tel Aviv: Mythography of a City*. Syracuse, NY: Syracuse University Press.

Azoulay, Ariella 2001. *Death's Showcase: The Power of Image in Contemporary Democracy*. Cambridge, MA: MIT Press.

Balfour, Alan. 2015. *Solomon's Temple: Myth, Conflict, and Faith*. Chichester, West Sussex, UK: Wiley-Blackwell.

BBC News. 2017. "Netanyahu: Palestinians Must Face Reality over Jerusalem." *BBC News*, December 10. [https://www.bbc.com/news/world-middle-east-42301004]

Beckles Willson, Rachel. 2013. *Orientalism and Musical Mission: Palestine and the West*. Cambridge: Cambridge University Press.

Belkind, Nili. 2021. *Music in Conflict: Palestine, Israel and the Politics of Aesthetic Production*. London: Routledge.

Ben, Zehava. 2003. *My Father's House*. NMC 20835-2, compact disc.

Ben-Porat, Ziva. 1987. "History in Representations of Jerusalem in Modern Hebrew Poetry." *Neohelicon* 14(2): 353–58.

Benjamin, Mara. 2007. "Building a Zion in German(y): Franz Rosenzweig on Yehuda Halevi." *Jewish Social Studies* 13(2): 127–54.

Benvenisti, Meron. 1998. *City of Stone: The Hidden History of Jerusalem*. Berkeley: University of California Press.

Benvenisti, Meron. 2008. "The Bridge and the Wall." *Haaretz*, 27 June. [https://www.haaretz.com/1.4996744]

Billboard. 1967. "'Jerusalem of Gold': Israel Song Festival, Strikes Gold." *Billboard*, October 21.

Black, Ian. 2017. *Enemies and Neighbours: Arabs and Jews in Palestine and Israel, 1917–2017*. New York: Atlantic Monthly Press.

Blum, Ruthie. 2014. "Recalling the Nazi Parallel." *Jerusalem Post*, April 27. [http://www.jpost.com/Opinion/Op-Ed-Contributors/Recalling-the-Nazi-parallel-350584]

Bohlman, Andrea F. 2020. *Musical Solidarities: Political Action and Music in Late Twentieth-Century Poland*. New York: Oxford University Press.

Bohlman, Philip V. 1989. "The Land Where Two Streams Flow": Music in the German-Jewish Community of Israel*. Urbana: University of Illinois Press.

Bohlman, Philip V. 1992. *The World Centre for Jewish Music in Palestine, 1936–1940: Jewish Musical Life on the Eve of World War II*. New York: Oxford University Press.

Bohlman, Philip V. 1994a. "Afterword." In *Israeli Folk Music: Songs of the Early Pioneers*, edited by Hans Nathan, 39–55. Madison, WI: A-R Editions.

Bohlman, Philip V. 1994b. "Foreword." In *Israeli Folk Music: Songs of the Early Pioneers*, edited by Hans Nathan, ix–x. Madison, WI: A-R Editions.

Bohlman, Philip V. 1999. "Ontologies of Music." In *Rethinking Music*, edited by Nicholas Cook and Mark Everist, 17–34. Oxford: Oxford University Press.

Bohlman, Philip V. 2008. *Jewish Music and Modernity*. Oxford and New York: Oxford University Press.

Bohlman, Philip V. 2018. "Dynamic Diasporas: 'The Song of Zion' in South Asia." In *Sounding Cities: Auditory Transformations in Berlin, Chicago, and Kolkata*, edited by Sebastian Klotz, Philip V. Bohlman, and Lars-Christian Koch, 157–80. Berlin: LIT Verlag.

Brackett, David. 2016. *Categorizing Sound: Genre and Twentieth-Century Popular Music*. Oakland: University of California Press.

Brinner, Benjamin. 2009. *Playing across a Divide: Israeli-Palestinian Musical Encounters*. New York: Oxford University Press.

Buzaglo Meir. 2003. "Salim, Haim, and David: Variations of Forgetfulness" [*Salim, Haim ve-David: Vari'atsiyot shel Shikhha*]. *Teoria U'Bikoret* 22: 171–84. [Hebrew]

Cahan, Leonard, ed. 1998. *Siddur Sim Shalom for Shabbat and Festivals*. New York: United Synagogue of Conservative Judaism.

Calderon, Nissim. 2009. *The Second Day: On Poetry and Rock in Israel after Yona Wallach* [*Yom Sheni: Al Shira ve-Rok be-Israel Aharey Yona Wallach*]. Kinneret, Israel: Dvir Publishing House Ltd. [Hebrew]

Calderon, Nissim. 2016. *An Erol: Meir Ariel, a Biography* [*Erol Ehad: Meir Ariel, Biyografia*]. Hevel Modi'in: Devir. [Hebrew]

Certeau, Michel de. 1984. *The Practice of Everyday Life*. Translated by Steven Rendall. University of California Press.

Ching, Leo T.S. 2000. "Globalizing the Regional, Regionalizing the Global: Mass Culture and Asianism in the Age of Late Capitalism." *Public Culture* 12(1): 233–57.

Choshen, Maya, ed. 2008. *Statistical Yearbook of Jerusalem*. 2008 edition. Jerusalem: Institute for Jerusalem Studies. [http://en.jerusaleminstitute.org.il/?cmd=statistic.30]

Choshen, Maya, ed. 2018. *Statistical Yearbook of Jerusalem*. 2018 edition. Jerusalem: Institute for Jerusalem Studies. [http://en.jerusaleminstitute.org.il/?cmd=statistic.582]

Cidor, Peggy. 2014. "The Sephardi Singing Rabbi." *Jerusalem Post*, October 2. [https://www.jpost.com/Not-Just-News/The-Sephardi-singing-rabbi-377876]

Cohen, Beth B. 2007. *Case Closed: Holocaust Survivors in Postwar America*. Piscataway, NJ: Rutgers University Press.

Cohen, Brigid. 2012. *Stefan Wolpe and the Avant-Garde Diaspora*. Cambridge, UK: Cambridge University Press.

Cohen, Hillel. 2004. *Army of Shadows: Palestinian Collaboration with Zionism, 1917–1948*. Berkeley: University of California Press.

Cohen, Hillel. 2015. *Year Zero of the Arab-Israeli Conflict: 1929*. Lebanon, NH: Brandeis University Press.

Cohen, Hillel. 2017. "The Temple Mount/al-Aqsa in Zionist and Palestinian National Consciousness: A Comparative View." *Israel Studies Review* 32(1): 1–19.

Cohen, Leonard. 1984. *Various Positions*. Columbia PCC 90728, LP disc.

Cohen, Mark. 1995. *Under Crescent and Cross: The Jews in the Middle Ages*. Princeton: Princeton University Press.

Cohen, Uri. 2003. "The Zionist Animal" [*Ha-Haya Ha-Tsiyonit*]. *Jerusalem Studies in Hebrew Literature* 19: 167–217.

Collins, Karen. 2008. "Grand Theft Audio? Popular Music and Intellectual Property Rights in Video Games." *Music and the Moving Image* 1(1): 35–48.

Colton, Miriam. 2004. "A Nation Mourns Naomi Shemer, Iconic Songstress." *Forward.com*, July 2. [http://forward.com/articles/4929/a-nation-mourns-naomi-shemer-iconic-songstress/]

Daliot, Yisrael. 2009. "Nechama Hendel." *Jewish Women: A Comprehensive Historical Encyclopedia*, February 27. Jewish Women's Archive. [https://jwa.org/encyclopedia/article/hendel-nechama]

Dardashti, Galeet. 2007. "The Piyyut Craze: Popularization of Mizrahi Religious Songs in the Israeli Public Sphere." *Journal of Synagogue Music* 32: 142–63.

Davis, Rochelle, and Dan Walsh. 2015. "'Visit Palestine': A Brief Study of Palestine Posters." *Jerusalem Quarterly* 61: 42–54.

Davis, Ruth F., ed. 2015. *Musical Exodus: Al-Andalus and Its Jewish Diasporas*. Lanham, MD: Rowman & Littlefield.

Dinnerstein, Leonard. 1982. *America and the Survivors of the Holocaust*. New York: Columbia University Press.

Dolev, Diana. 2016. *The Planning and Building of the Hebrew University, 1919–1948*. Lanham, MD: Lexington Books.

Dupree, Nancy Hatch. 2001. "Afghan Women under the Taliban." In *Fundamentalism Reborn? Afghanistan and the Taliban*, edited by William Maley, 145–66. London: Hurst and Company.

Dykman, Aminadav A. 1994. "A Poet in the Eternal City: The Case of Dan Pagis." *Compar(a)ison: An International Journal of Comparative Literature* 2: 41–56.

Eisenstein Baker, Paula. 2019. "Jewish Folk Songs: Exile and Return." In *Next Year in Jerusalem: Exile and Return in Jewish History*, edited by Leonard J. Greenspoon, 111–26. West Lafayette, IN: Purdue University Press.

Eliram, Talila. 2008/9. "From Poland to Mt. Scopus: The Metamorphosis of a Tune." *Min-Ad: Israel Studies in Musicology Online* 7(1): 1–15. [https://www.biu.ac.il/hu/mu/min-ad/8-9/Talila-03-09.pdf] [Hebrew]

Eliran, Ron. 1973. *Ten Lashir*. Hed-Arzi BAN 14396, LP disc.

Epley, Nicholas, Adam Waytz, and John T. Cacioppo. 2007. "On Seeing Human: A Three-Factor Theory of Anthropomorphism." *Psychological Review* 114(4): 864–86.

Erez, Oded. 2015. "The Practice of Everyday Quotation: Quotation as a Political Act in the Songs of the Band Habiluim" [*Ha-Praktika shel Tsitut Ha-Yomyom: Ha-Tsitut Ke-Ma'ase Politi Be-Shirim shel Lehakat Habiluim*]. *Teoria U'Bikoret* 45: 169–95. [Hebrew]

Erez, Oded. 2016. "Becoming Mediterranean: Greek Popular Music and Ethno-Class Politics in Israel, 1952–1982." PhD thesis, University of California, Los Angeles.

Eric B., and Rakim. 1987. *Paid in Full—The Coldcut Remix*. Island BRWX 78, EP disc.

Ezrahi, Sidra Dekoven. 2007. "'To What Shall I Compare You?': Jerusalem as Ground Zero of the Hebrew Imagination." *PMLA* 122(1): 220–34.

Feld, Steven, Aaron A. Fox, Thomas Porcello, and David Samuels. 2004. "Vocal Anthropology: From the Music of Language to the Language of Song." In *A Companion to Linguistic Anthropology*, edited by Alessandro Duranti, 321–45. Malden, MA: Blackwell.

Figueroa, Michael A. 2016. "Aesthetics of Ambivalence: Dan Almagor and Rock Ideology in Israeli Musical Theatre." *Ethnomusicology Forum* 25(3): 261–82.

Figueroa, Michael A. 2020. "Musical Memory, Animated Amnesia: The Soundtrack of Exoneration in *Waltz with Bashir*." In *Performing Commemoration: Musical Reenactment and the Politics of Trauma*, edited by Annegret Fauser and Michael A. Figueroa, 121–41. Ann Arbor: University of Michigan Press.

Fink, Bernarda, and Gerold Huber, piano. 2008. *Schubert: Lieder*. Harmonia Mundi HMC 901991, compact disc.

Fischer, Michael M.J. 2018. *Anthropology in the Meantime: Experimental Ethnography, Theory, and Method for the Twenty-First Century*. Durham, NC: Duke University Press.

Fleischer, Ezra. 1996. "'The Essence of Our Land and Its Meaning'—Towards a Portrait of Judah Halevi on the Basis of Geniza Documents." *Pe'amim* 68: 4–15. [Hebrew]

Fleischer, Tsippi. 2005. *Harmonization of Songs*. Haifa: Levinsky College of Education. [Hebrew]

Foucault, Michel. 1977. *Discipline and Punish: The Birth of the Prison*. New York: Pantheon.

Foucault, Michel. 1986. "Of Other Spaces." Translated by Jay Miskowiec. *Diacritics* 16(1): 22–27.

Frishman, Elyse C., ed. 2007. *Mishkan T'filah: A Reform Siddur*. New York: CCAR Press.

Frith, Simon, and Lee Marshall. 2004. *Music and Copyright*. Second edition. New York: Routledge.

Gaon, Yehoram. 1971. *I Was Born in Jerusalem [Ani Yerushalmi]*. CBS S 70093, LP disc.

Garland, David. 2014. "What Is a 'History of the Present'? On Foucault's Genealogies and Their Critical Preconditions." *Punishment and Society* 16(4): 365–84.

Gavriely-Nuri, Dalia. 2007. "The Social Construction of 'Jerusalem of Gold' as Israel's Unofficial National Anthem." *Israel Studies* 12(2): 104–20.

George, Alan. 1979. "'Making the Desert Bloom': A Myth Examined." *Journal of Palestine Studies* 8(2): 88–100.

Gill, Geula. 1967. *Songs after the 6-Day War*. CBS 63123, LP disc.

Ginsburg, Shai. 2014. "The City and the Body: Jerusalem in Uri Tsvi Greenberg's *Vision of One of the Legions*." In *Jerusalem: Conflict and Cooperation in a Contested City*, edited by Madelaine Adelman and Miriam Fendius Elman, 143–71. Syracuse, NY: Syracuse University Press.

Glasser, Jonathan. 2016. *The Lost Paradise: Andalusi Music in Urban North Africa*. Chicago: University of Chicago Press.

Goitein, S. D. 1954/55. "The Last Phase of Rabbi Yehuda Halevi's Life in the Light of the Geniza Papers." *Tarbiz* 24: 21–47. [Hebrew]

Goitein, S. D. 1959. "The Biography of Rabbi Juda Ha-Levi in the Light of the Cairo Geniza Documents." *Proceedings of the American Academy for Jewish Research* 28: 41–56.

Goitein, S. D. 1977. "Did R. Judah Halevi Reach the Land of Israel?" *Tarbiz* 46: 245–50. [Hebrew]

Golden Poets: Spanish Romances and the Poetry of Sephardic Jewry [Meshorerey Zahav: Romansot Sfardiot u-me-Shirat Yehudat Sfarad]. 1993. Hataklit 191, compact disc.

Goldhill, Simon. 2008. *Jerusalem: City of Longing*. Cambridge, MA: The Belknap Press of Harvard University Press.

Goldsmith, Martin. 2014. *Alex's Wake: A Voyage of Betrayal and a Journey of Remembrance*. Boston: Da Capo Press.

Gorenberg, Gershom. 2011. "Political Memory in the Mideast." *The American Prospect*, May 19. [http://prospect.org/cs/articles?article=political_memory_in_the_mideast]

Goswami, Manu. 2002. "Rethinking the Modular Nation Form: Toward a Sociohistorical Conception of Nationalism." *Comparative Studies in Society and History* 44(4): 770–99.

Gottlieb, Linda. 1967. "The Song That Took a City." *Reader's Digest*, December: 112–15.

Gouri, Haim. 1949. *Flowers of Fire [Pirhey Esh]*. Bnei Brak: Sifriat-Poalim. [Hebrew]

Gracyk, Theodore. 1996. *Rhythm and Noise: An Aesthetics of Rock*. Durham, NC: Duke University Press.

Gradenwitz, Peter. 1996. *The Music of Israel: From the Biblical Era to Modern Times*. Portland, OR: Amadeus Press.

Greenberg, Uri Zvi. 1937. *The Book of Indictment and Faith* [*Sefer Ha-Kitrug Ve-Ha-Emuna*]. Tel Aviv: Sadan. [Hebrew]

Gregory, Derek. 1997. "Lacan and Geography: The Production of Space Revisited." In *Space and Social Theory: Interpreting Modernity and Postmodernity*, edited by Georges Benko and Ulf Strohmayer, 203–31. Oxford: Blackwell.

Haaretz. 2012. "Legendary Israeli singer Yafa Yarkoni dies at 86." *Haaretz*, January 1. [http://www.haaretz.com/misc/article-print-page/legendary-israeli-singer-yafa-yarkoni-dies-at-86-1.404925]

Habiluim. 2007. *Bereavement and Failure* [*Shikkul ve-Kishalon*]. NMC 20821-2, compact disc.

Hacohen, Eliyahu. 2018. *Jerusalem in Hebrew Song during the Yishuv Era* [*Yerushalayim Ba-Zemer Ha-Ivri Bi-Tekufat Ha-Yishuv*]. Jerusalem: Ariel. [Hebrew]

Hadass, Rakhel. 1966. *Songs of Israel*. Monitor MFS 364, LP disc.

Halkin, Hillel. 2010. *Yehuda Halevi*. New York: Schocken.

Hammer, Reuven. 1995. *The Jerusalem Anthology: A Literary Guide*. Philadelphia: The Jewish Publication Society.

Handelman, Don, and Lea Shamgar-Handelman. 1997. "The Presence of Absence: The Memorialism of National Death in Israel." In *Grasping Land: Space and Place in Contemporary Israeli Discourse and Experience*, edited by Eyal Ben-Ari and Yoram Bilu, 85–128. Albany: State University of New York Press.

Handelman, Don, and Lea Shamgar-Handelman. 1999. "The Presence of Absence: The Memorialism of National Death in Israel." *International Journal of Politics, Culture and Society* 7(3): 441–59.

Hankins, Sarah E. 2015. "Black Musics, African Lives, and the National Imagination in Modern Israel." PhD thesis, Harvard University.

Harvey, David. 2006. *Spaces of Global Capitalism: Towards a Theory of Uneven Geographical Development*. London: Verso.

Hastrup, Kirsten. 1995. *A Passage to Anthropology: Between Experience and Theory*. London: Routledge.

Haza, Ofra. 1984. *Yemenite Songs*. Hed Artzi ANP 15110, LP disc.

Helman, Anat. 2010. *Young Tel Aviv: A Tale of Two Cities*. Translated by Haim Watzmann. Waltham, MA: Brandeis University Press.

Hendel, Nechama. 1967. *And Maybe . . . .* Hed Arzi BAN 49-55, LP disc.

Hendel, Nechama. 1997. *Outside the Storm*. Hed Arzi, compact disc.

Hess, Carol. 2001. *Manuel de Falla and Modernism in Spain, 1898–1936*. Chicago: University of Chicago Press.

Hess, Christin. 2008. "What Are 'Reverse Diasporas' and How Are We to Understand Them?" *Diaspora: A Journal of Transnational Studies* 17(3): 288–315.

Hever, Hannan. 2002. *Producing the Modern Hebrew Canon: Nation Building and Minority Discourse*. New York: NYU Press.

Hirshberg, Jehoash. 1996. *Music in the Jewish Community of Palestine, 1880–1948: A Social History*. Oxford and New York: Clarendon Press.

Hoffman, Adina, and Peter Cole. 2011. *Sacred Trash: The Lost and Found World of the Cairo Geniza*. New York: Schocken.

Holtzman, Avner. 1994. "Close and Forbidden to Us There: Divided Jerusalem in the Mirror of Hebrew Literature" [*Karov Ve-Asur Lanu Sham: Yerushalayim Ha-Hatsuya Bi-R'i Ha-Sifrut Ha-Ivrit*]. In *Divided Jerusalem, 1948–67: Sources, Summaries, Selected*

Chapters and Reference Material [Yerushalayim Ha-Ḥatsuya, 1948–1967: Mekorot, Sikumim, Parshiyot Nivḥarot Ve-Ḥomer Ezer], edited by Avi Bar'eli, 202–23. Jerusalem: Yad Yitzhak Ben-Zvi. [Hebrew]

Holtzman, Avner. 2003. "Mandatory Jerusalem in Hebrew Literature" [*Yerushalayim Ha-Mandatorit Ba-Sifrut Ha-Ivrit*]. In *Jerusalem in the Mandate Period: The Achievement and the Legacy [Yerushalayim Bi-Tkufat Ha-Mandat: Ha-Asiya Ve-Ha-Moreshet]*, edited by Yehoshua Ben-Arieh, 98–115. Jerusalem: Yad Yitzhak Ben-Zvi. [Hebrew]

Holtzman, Avner. 2010. "Hame'iri, Avigdor." *YIVO Encyclopedia of Jews in Eastern Europe*. [https://yivoencyclopedia.org/article.aspx/Hameiri_Avigdor]

Horowitz, Amy. 2005. "Dueling Nativities: Zehava Ben Sings Umm Kulthum." In *Palestine, Israel, and the Politics of Popular Culture*, edited by Rebecca L. Stein and Ted Swedenburg, 202–30. Durham, NC: Duke University Press.

Horowitz, Amy. 2010. *Mediterranean Israeli Music and the Politics of the Aesthetic*. Detroit: Wayne State University Press.

Ibáñez, Paco and Imanol. 1999. *Oroitzen*. Universal 77949, compact disc.

Idelsohn, Avraham Zvi. 1914–1932. *Hebräisch-orientalischer Melodienschatz*. 10 vols. Leipzig: Breitkopf & Härtel.

Ish Hasid Haya [Once There Was a Hasid]. 1968. Tel Aviv: Israphone AP 332. LP disc.

Israel Song Festival 1967. 1967. With Kol Israel Symphony Orchestra, conducted by Moshe Wilensky. CBS 63046, LP disc.

Jalal, Nader, Issa Boulos, and Heather Bursheh. 2013. "A Musical Catastrophe: The Direct Impact of the Nakba on Palestinian Musicians and Musical Life." In *Palestinian Music and Song: Expression and Resistance since 1900*, edited by Moslih Kanaaneh, Stig-Magnus Thorsen, Heather Bursheh, and David A. McDonald, 37–52. Bloomington: Indiana University Press.

Jameson, Frederic. 1991. *Postmodernism, or, the Cultural Logic of Late Capitalism*. Durham, NC: Duke University Press.

Jawhariyyeh, Wasif. 2014. *The Storyteller of Jerusalem: The Life and Times of Wasif Jawhariyyeh, 1904–1948*, edited by Salim Tamari and Issam Nassar. Northampton, MA: Olive Branch Press.

Jerusalem of Gold: Songs of the Six Day War. Hed-Artzi BAN 49-52, LP disc.

Jerusalem of Steel: More Songs of the Six Day War. 1967 Hed-Artzi BAN 49-66, LP disc.

Kanaaneh, Moslih. 2013. "Do Palestinian Musicians Play Music or Politics?" In *Palestinian Music and Song: Expression and Resistance since 1900*, edited by Moslih Kanaaneh, Stig-Magnus Thorsén, Heather Bursheh, and David A. McDonald, 1–14. Bloomington: Indiana University Press.

Kaplan, Danny. 2006. *The Men We Loved: Male Friendship and Nationalism in Israeli Culture*. New York: Berghahn Books.

Kaplan, Danny. 2009. "The Songs of the Siren: Engineering National Time on Israeli Radio." *Cultural Anthropology* 24(2): 313–45.

Kaufman, David. 2007. "Striking Chords in Jerusalem." *Time*, July 16. [http://content.time.com/time/specials/2007/article/0,28804,1642444_1849541_1849538,00.html#ixzz0iWuABfDF]

Keidar, Noga. 2018. "Making Jerusalem 'Cooler': Creative Script, Youth Flight, and Diversity." *City & Community* 17(4): 1209–30.

Klein, Menachem. 2001. *Jerusalem: The Contested City*. Translated by Haim Watzman. New York: New York University Press.

Klein Halevi, Yossi. 2013. *Like Dreamers: The Story of the Israeli Paratroopers Who Reunited Jerusalem and Divided a Nation*. New York: HarperCollins.

Krims, Adam. 2007. *Music and Urban Geography*. New York: Routledge.

Kritzman Lawrence D., ed. 1988. *Michel Foucault: Politics, Philosophy, Culture: Interviews and Other Writings, 1977–1984*. New York: Routledge.

LA Times. 2012. "Yaffa Yarkoni Dies at 86; Israeli Singer." *LA Times*, January 2. [http://articles.latimes.com/2012/jan/02/local/la-me-yaffa-yarkoni-20120102]

Labajo, Joaquina. 2003. "Body and Voice: The Construction of Gender in Flamenco." In *Music and Gender: Perspectives from the Mediterranean*, edited by Tullia Magrini, 67–86. Chicago: University of Chicago Press.

Lakoff, George and Mark Johnson. 1980. *Metaphors We Live By*. Chicago: University of Chicago Press.

Lakoff, George and Mark Johnson. 1999. *Philosophy in the Flesh: the Embodied Mind & its Challenge to Western Thought*. New York: Basic Books.

Landler, Mark, and Steven Lee Myers. 2011. "Obama Sees '67 Borders as Starting Point for Peace Deal." *New York Times*, May 19. [http://www.nytimes.com/2011/05/20/world/middleeast/20speech.html]

Laor, Dan. 1999. "The Last Chapter: Nathan Alterman and the Six-Day War." *Israel Studies* 4(2): 178–94.

Larkin, Craig. 2014. "Jerusalem's Separation Wall and Global Message Board: Graffiti, Murals, and the Art of *Sumud*." *Arab Studies Journal* 22(1): 134–69.

Lefebvre, Henri. (1974) 1991. *The Production of Space*. Translated by Donald Nicholson-Smith. Malden, MA: Blackwell Publishers.

Lefebvre, Henri. 2004. *Rhythmanalysis: Space, Time and Everyday Life*. Translated by Stuart Eldon and Gerald Moore. New York: Continuum.

Lefkovits, Etgar. 2008. "J'lem parents slam 'Taliban' dress code for dance troupe." *The Jerusalem Post*, June 26. [https://www.jpost.com/srael/jlem-parents-slam-taliban-dress-code-for-dance-troupe]

Levine Katz, Yael. n.d. *Jerusalem of Gold*. Website. [http://www.jerusalemofgold.co.il/]

Levy, Lital. 2014. *Poetic Trespass: Writing between Hebrew and Arabic in Israel/Palestine*. Princeton: Princeton University Press.

Lis, Jonathan. 2008. "Discord at Opening of Chords Bridge." *Haaretz*, June 26. [https://www.haaretz.com/1.4996212]

Llano, Samuel. 2011. "Hispanic Traditions in a Cross-Cultural Perspective: Raoul Laparra's 'La habanera' (1908) and French Critics." *Journal of the Royal Music Association* 136(1): 97–140.

Lysloff, René T. A. 2016. "Worlding Music in Jogjakarta: Tales of the Global Postmodern." *Ethnomusicology* 60(3): 484–507.

Mack, Merav, and Benjamin Balint. 2019. *Jerusalem: City of the Book*. New Haven, CT: Yale University Press.

Magonet, Jonathan, ed. 2008. *Forms of Prayer*. London: The Movement for Reform Judaism.

Maier, Christl. 2008. *Daughter Zion, Mother Zion: Gender, Space, and the Sacred in Ancient Israel*. Minneapolis: Fortress Press.

Makdisi, Saree. 2010. "The Architecture of Erasure." *Critical Inquiry* 36(3): 519–59.

Malkiel, David J. 2010. "Three Perspectives on Judah Halevi's Voyage to Palestine." *Mediterranean Historical Review* 25(1) 1–15.

Mann, Barbara E. 2001. "The Vicarious Landscape of Memory in Tel Aviv Poetry." *Prooftexts* 21(3): 350–78.

Mann, Barbara E. 2006. *A Place in History: Modernism, Tel Aviv, and the Creation of Jewish Urban Space*. Stanford, CA: Stanford University Press.

Mann, Barbara E. 2012. *Space and Place in Jewish Studies*. Piscataway, NJ: Rutgers University Press.

Manuel, Peter. 2009. "From Contradanza to Son: New Perspectives on the Prehistory of Cuban Popular Music." *Latin American Music Review / Revista de Música Latinoamericana* 30(2): 184–212.

Marcus, George E. 1999. "What Is at Stake—and Is Not—in the Idea and Practice of Multi-Sited Ethnography." *Canberra Anthropology* 22(2): 6–14.

Mazor, Yair. 1996. "The Sexual Sound and the Flowery Fury: The Role of Yona Wollach in Contemporary Hebrew Poetry." *Modern Judaism* 16(3): 263–90.

Mbembe, Achilles. 2001. "At the Edge of the World: Boundaries, Territoriality, and Sovereignty in Africa," in *Globalization*, edited by Arjun Appadurai, 22–51. Durham, NC: Duke University Press.

McCann, Anthony. 2001. "All That Is Not Given Is Lost: Irish Traditional Music, Copyright, and Common Property." *Ethnomusicology* 45(1): 89–106.

McDonald, Christopher. 1996. "Judah ha-Levi's *Kuzari*: Proto-Zionism, the Paradox of Post-Colonial Prosody, and the Ridiculous Rabbi." *Bulletin of Hispanic Studies* 73(4): 339–50.

McDonald, David A. 2013. *My Voice Is My Weapon: Music, Nationalism, and the Poetics of Palestinian Resistance*. Durham, NC: Duke University Press.

Meltzer, Françoise. 2012. "Writing the Words to the Music." In *Intertextuality in Literature and Culture: A Festschrift in Honor of Ziva Ben-Porat*, edited by Michael Gluzman and Orly Lubin, 59–74. Tel Aviv: Hakibbutz Hameuchad. [Hebrew]

Menocal, María Rosa. 2002. *The Ornament of the World: How Muslims, Jews and Christians Created a Culture of Tolerance in Medieval Spain*. Boston: Little, Brown and Company.

Miron, Dan. 1987. Miron, "Songs from It-Never-Happened Land." *Jerusalem Quarterly* 42: 119–44.

Miron, Dan. 2010. *The Prophetic Mode in Modern Hebrew Poetry*. New Milford, CT: Toby Press.

Monk, Daniel Bertrand. 2005. "Diskotel 1967: Israel and the Western Wall in the Aftermath of the Six Day War." *RES: Anthropology and Aesthetics* 48: 166–78.

More, Thomas. (1516) 1965. *Utopia*. London: Penguin.

Morris, Benny. 2008. *1948: The First Arab-Israeli War*. New Haven: Yale University Press.

Moughalian, Sato. 2019. *Feast of Ashes: The Life and Art of David Ohannessian*. Stanford: Stanford University Press.

Mualem, Mazal. 2011. "After Obama Speech, Netanyahu Rejects Withdrawal to 'Indefensible' 1967 Borders." *Haaretz*, May 19.

Naor, Arye. 2011. "Jabotinsky's New Jew: Concept and Models." *Journal of Israeli History: Politics, Society, Culture* 30(2): 141–59.

Nathan, Hans, ed. 1938. *Folk Songs of the New Palestine*. New York: Nigun.

Nathan, Hans, ed. 1994. *Israeli Folk Music: Songs of the Early Pioneers*. Completed by Philip V. Bohlman. Madison, WI: A-R Editions.

Nathan, Shuly. 2012. Interview with the author, June 6. Jerusalem.

Nelson, Kristina. 1985. *The Art of Reciting the Qur'an*. Austin: University of Texas Press.

Nettl, Bruno. 2005. *The Study of Ethnomusicology: Thirty-One Issues and Concepts*. Champaign: University of Illinois Press.

Neustadt, Robert. 2002. "Buena Vista Social Club versus La Charanga Habanera: The Politics of Cuban Rhythm." *Journal of Poplar Music Studies* 14(2): 139–62.

Nevo, Ofra, and Jacob Levine. 1994. "Jewish Humor Strikes Again: The Outburst of Humor in Israel during the Gulf War." *Western Folklore* 53(2): 125–45.

Newman, Marissa. 2015. "Netanyahu: Jerusalem won't be divided again." *The Times of Israel*, May 18. [https://www.timesofisrael.com/netanyahu-jerusalem-construction-our-natural-right/]

Nissim, Ofer. 2005. *The Remixes*. IMP 2124, compact disc.

Nitzan-Shiftan, Alona. 2007. "The Walled City and the White City: The Construction of the Tel Aviv/ Jerusalem Dichotomy." *Perspecta* 39: 92–104.

Nitzan-Shiftan, Alona. 2017. *Selling Jerusalem: The Architectures of Unilateral Unification*. Minneapolis: University of Minnesota Press.

Olmert, Dana. 2013. "Mothers of Soldiers in Israeli Literature: The Return of the Politically Repressed." *Prooftexts* 33(3): 333–64.

Omer, Morchechai. 1999. "The Theme of Jerusalem in the Works of the Israeli Fathers of Conceptual Arts." In *In Search of Identity: Jewish Aspects in Israeli Culture*, edited by Dan Urian and Efraim Karsh, 200–18. London: Frank Cass.

Omer-Sherman, Ranen. 2006. "Yehuda Amichai's Exilic Jerusalem." *Prooftexts* 26(1–2): 212–39.

Oz, Amos. (1968) 1972. *My Michael*. Translated by Nicholas de Lange. London: Chatto and Windus.

Pagis, Dan. 1959. *She'on hatsel*. Tel Aviv: Sfiriat hapo'alim. [Hebrew]

Pedahzur, Ami, and Arie Perliger. 2009. *Jewish Terrorism in Israel*. New York: Columbia University Press.

Penslar, Derek. 2020. *Theodor Herzl: The Charismatic Leader*. New Haven, CT: Yale University Press.

Rabikovitch, Dalia. 2008. "Around Jerusalem." Translated by Chana Bloch and Chana Kronfeld. *Tikkun* 23(3): 31. Originally published in Rabivokitch, Dalia. 1959. *Ahavat Tapu'ach Ha-Zahav* [Hebrew]

Ram, Uri. 2005. *The Globalization of Israel: McWorld in Tel Aviv, Jihad in Jerusalem*. New York and London: Routledge.

Raz, Carmel. 2015. "Tafillat's 'Soulmate' and the Israeli *Piyyut* Revival." In *Musical Exodus: Al-Andalus and Its Jewish Diasporas*, edited by Ruth F. Davis, 165–80. Lanham, MD: Rowman & Littlefield.

Rechnitzer, Haim O. 2008. "Haim Guri and Rabbi David Buzaglo: A Theo-Political Meeting Place of Zionist Sabra Poetry and Jewish Liturgy." *Journal for the Study of Sephardic and Mizrahi Jewry* 2(1): 37–62.

Regev, Motti, and Edwin Seroussi. 2004. *Popular Music and National Culture in Israel*. Berkeley: University of California Press.

Regev, Motti, and Edwin Seroussi. 2013. *Popular Music and National Culture in Israel* [*Musika Popularit ve-Tarbut Isra'elit*]. Ra'anana: The Open University of Israel. [Hebrew]

Reshef, Yael. 2001. "The Use of Biblical Verbal Forms in the Hebrew Folksong." *Leshonenu* 63: 107–29. [Hebrew]

Reshef, Yael. 2004. *The Early Hebrew Folksong: A Chapter in the History of Modern Hebrew*. Jerusalem: Bialik Institute. [Hebrew]

Reshef, Yael. 2012. "From Hebrew Folksong to Israeli Song: Language and Style in Naomi Shemer's Lyrics." *Israel Studies* 17(1): 157–87.

Reynolds, Dwight F. 2015. "Jews, Muslims, and Christians and the Formation of Medieval Andalusian Music." In *Musical Exodus: Al-Andalus and Its Jewish Diasporas*, edited by Ruth F. Davis, 1–24. Lanham, MD: Rowman & Littlefield.

Riley, Robert B. 1997. "The Visible, the Visual and the Vicarious: Questions about Vision, Landscape and Experience." In *Understanding Ordinary Landscapes*, edited by Paul Groth and Todd W. Bressi, 200–10. New Haven, CT: Yale University Press.

Ricoeur, Paul D. 2004. *Memory, History, Forgetting*. Translated by Kathleen Blamey and David Pellauer. Chicago: University of Chicago Press.

Rolling Stone. 2012. "50 Greatest Hip-Hop Songs of All Time." *Rolling Stone*, December 5. [http://www.rollingstone.com/music/lists/the-50-greatest-hip-hop-songs-of-all-time-20121205]

Saada-Ophir, Galit. 2006. "Borderland Pop: Arab Jewish Musicians and the Politics of Performance." *Cultural Anthropology* 21(2): 205–33.

Sabra, Mahmoud M., Abdel Hakeem, Ahmad Eltalla, and Abdel Rahman Alfar. 2015. "The Shadow Economy in Palestine: Size and Causes." *International Journal of Economics and Finance* 7(3): 98–108.

Sarfatti, Tami. 2012. Interview with the author, February 16. Tel Aviv.

Scheindlin, Raymond P. 2008. *The Song of the Distant Dove: Judah Halevi's Pilgrimage*. Oxford: Oxford University Press.

Schindler, Colin. 2008. *A History of Modern Israel*. Cambridge, UK: Cambridge University Press.

Schmemann, Serge. 1998. "A 50th Jubliee For Israel." *New York Times*, April 26.

Sebba-Elran, Tsafi, and Haya Milo. 2016. "The Struggle over Locality in Israeli Humoristic Memes from the 2014 Military Conflict in Gaza." *Narrative Culture* 3(2): 206–30.

Segev, Tom. 2005. *1967: Israel, the War, and the Year That Transformed the Middle East*. Translated by Jessica Cohen. New York: Metropolitan Books.

Sermer, Tanya. 2015. "The Battle for the Soul of Jerusalem: Musical Language, Public Performance, and Competing Discourses of the Israeli Nation-State." PhD thesis, University of Rochester.

Seroussi, Edwin. 2006. "Jewish Musicians in the Lands of Islam." *Tapasam: A Quarterly Journal of Kerala Studies* 1(3): 596–609.

Seroussi, Edwin. 2013. "Judeo-Islamic Sacred Soundscapes: The Maqamization of the Eastern Sephardic Liturgy." In *Jews and Muslims in the Islamic World*, edited by Bernard Dov Cooperman and Zvi Zohar, 279–302. Bethesda, MD: University of Maryland Press.

Seroussi, Edwin. 2014. "Nostalgic Soundscapes: The Future of Israel's Sonic Past." *Israel Studies* 19(2): 35–50.

Seroussi, Edwin. 2015. "Hatikva: Conceptions, Receptions and Reflections." *Yuval Online* 9. [http://www.jewish-music.huji.ac.il/sites/default/files/Seroussi%20Hatikvah%20for%20Website%20Final.pdf]

Shalom from Jerusalem: Songs from Jerusalem. 1968. Galyon C-5883, LP disc.

Shannon, Jonathan Holt. 2015. *Performing Al-Andalus: Music and Nostalgia across the Mediterranean*. Bloomington: Indiana University Press.

Shapira, Anita. 1999. *Land and Power: The Zionist Resort to Force, 1881–1948*. Stanford, CA: Stanford University Press.

Shapiro, Moshe. 2017. Interview with the author, May 26. Jerusalem.

Shapiro, Matan, and Nurit Bird-David. 2017. "Routinergency: Domestic Securitization in Contemporary Israel." *Environment and Planning D: Society and Space* 35(4): 637–55.

Shemesh, Moshe. 2008. *Arab Politics, Palestinian Nationalism and the Six Day War: The Crystallization of Arab Strategy and Nasir's Descent to War, 1957–1967*. Brighton and Portland: Sussex Academic Press.

Shelleg, Assaf. 2014. *Jewish Contiguities and the Soundtrack of Israeli History*. New York: Oxford University Press.

Shelleg, Assaf. 2019. "Imploding Signifiers: Exilic Jewish Cultures in Art Music in Israel, 1966–1970." *Hebrew Studies* 60: 255–91.

Shemer, Naomi. 1968. *Naomi Shemer Sings Her Famous Jerusalem of Gold*. Israel SI 31018, LP disc.

Shemer, Naomi. 1987. "How a Song Was Born" [*Eikh Nolad Shir*]. *Yediot Aḥronot*, May 22.

Shemer, Naomi. 2004. Letter to Gil Aldema, June 12. Series D, Naomi Shemer Archive. National Library of Israel.

Shlay, Anne B., and Gillad Rosen. 2010. "Making Place: The Shifting Green Line and the Development of 'Greater' Metropolitan Jerusalem." *City & Community* 9(4): 358–89.

Shlay, Anne B., and Gillad Rosen. 2015. *Jerusalem: The Spatial Politics of a Divided Metropolis*. Cambridge, UK: Polity Press.

Sigalov, Haddasah. 196?. *Nashir Lakh Yerushalayim*. Makoliy 54119, EP disc.

Six Days in June. 1967. HaTaklit 30 300, LP disc.

Songs of Jerusalem. 1968. CBS S 63576, LP disc.

Songs of the War and Victory. 1967. CBS S 63124, LP disc.

Songs of Yerushalayim. 1968. Hed-Arzi, LP disc.

Spielberg, Steven, dir. 1993. *Schindler's List*. Universal Pictures, video cassette.

Sprigge, Martha Anne. 2013. "Abilities to Mourn: Musical Commemoration in the German Democratic Republic (1945–1989)." PhD thesis, University of Chicago.

Sprigge, Martha Anne. 2021. *Socialist Laments: Musical Mourning in the German Democratic Republic*. New York: Oxford University Press.

Stanton, Andrea L. 2013. *This Is Jerusalem Calling: State Radio in Mandate Palestine*. Austin: University of Texas Press.

Stokes, Martin. 2010. *The Republic of Love: Cultural Intimacy in Turkish Popular Music*. Chicago: University of Chicago Press.

Stowe, David W. 2016. *Song of Exile: The Enduring Mystery of Psalm 137*. New York: Oxford University Press.

Tamari, Salim. 2005. "Wasif Jawhariyyeh, Popular Music, and Early Modernity in Jerusalem." In *Palestine, Israel, and the Politics of Popular Culture*, edited by Rebecca L. Stein and Ted Swedenburg, 27–50. Durham, NC: Duke University Press.

Tamari, Salim. 2017. *The Great War and the Remaking of Palestine*. Berkeley: University of California Press.

Taylor, Timothy D. 2016. *Music and Capitalism: A History of the Present*. Chicago: University of Chicago Press.

Tilley, Christopher, and Kate Cameron-Daum. 2017. "The Anthropology of Landscape: Materiality, Embodiment, Contestation and Emotion." In *Anthropology of Landscape: The Extraordinary in the Ordinary*, edited by Christopher Tilley and Kate Cameron-Daum, 1–21. London: University College London Press.

Tsamir, Hamutal. 2008. "Jewish-Israeli Poetry, Dahlia Ravikovitch, and the Gender of Representation." *Jewish Social Studies* 14(3): 85–125.

Turino, Thomas. 2008. *Music as Social Life: The Politics of Participation*. Chicago: University of Chicago Press.

Waltke, Bruce K., and Michael Patrick O'Connor. 1990. *An Introduction to Biblical Hebrew Syntax*. Warsaw, IN: Eisenbrauns.

We Grew Up Together [*Gadalnu Yaḥad*]. 1998. Hed Arzi, compact disc.

Wharton, Annabel Jane. 2006. *Selling Jerusalem: Relics, Replicas, Theme Parks*. Chicago: University of Chicago Press.

Webster-Kogen, Ilana. 2018. *Citizen Azmari: Making Ethiopian Music in Tel Aviv*. Middletown, CT: Wesleyan University Press.

Wolfe, Patrick. 2006. "Settler Colonialism and the Elimination of the Native." *Journal of Genocide Research* 8(4): 387–409.

Wood, Abigail. 2013a. "Performative Languages I: Sound, Music, and Migration in Jerusalem's Old City." In *Rescripting Religion in the City: Migration and Religious Identity in the Modern Metropolis*, edited by Jane Garnett and Alana Harris, 51–61. London: Ashgate.

Wood, Abigail. 2013b. "Sound, Narrative and the Spaces in Between: Disruptive Listening in Jerusalem's Old City." *Middle East Journal of Culture and Communication* 6: 286–307.

Wood, Abigail. 2014. "Urban Soundscapes: Hearing and Seeing Jerusalem." In *The Routledge Companion to Music and Visual Culture*, edited by Tim Shephard and Anne Leonard, 286–93. New York and London: Routledge.

Yahalom, Joseph. 1995. "Diwan and Odyssey: Judah Halevi and the Secular Poetry of Medieval Spain in the Light of the New Discoveries from Petersburg." *Miscelanea de Estudios Arabes y Hebraicos: II. Filologia Hebrea, Biblia y Judaismo* 44: 23–45.

Yarkoni, Yaffa. 1949. *Bab El-Wad*. Hed Arzi 680, 78 RPM disc.

Yarkoni, Yaffa. 1966. *Bab El-Wad: The Gate to Jerusalem*. CBS S 63534, LP disc.

Yerushalayim Sheli [My Jerusalem]. 1970. Tel Aviv: CBS S 63790. LP disc.

Zbikowski, Lawrence M. 2002. *Conceptualizing Music: Cognitive Structure, Theory, and Analysis*. New York: Oxford University Press.

Zerubavel, Yael. 1995. *Recovered Roots: Collective Memory and the Making of Israeli National Tradition*. Chicago: University of Chicago Press.

Zerubavel, Yael. 2019. *Desert in the Promised Land*. Stanford, CA: Stanford University Press.

Zipperstein, Steven. 2018. *Pogrom: Kishinev and the Tilt of History*. New York: Liveright.

Žižek, Slavoj. 2008. *Violence: Six Sideways Reflections*. New York: Picador.

Zwiep, Irene E. 1998. "To Remember and to Forget—Jerusalem in Jewish Poetical Memory." *European Judaism* 31 (2): 54–66.

Index